Early Childhood Adventures in Peacemaking

Second Edition

DISCARD

This project was made possible by the generous support of The William and Flora Hewlett Foundation, the Lippincott Foundation of the Peace Development Fund, and individual contributors.

Early Childhood Adventures in Peacemaking by William J. Kreidler and Sandy Tsubokawa Whittall with Nan Doty, Rebecca Johns, Claudia Logan, Laura Parker Roerden, Cheryl Raner, and Carol Wintle.

Editors: Jeffrey Perkins, Caroline Chauncey

Production Editor: Jeffrey Perkins

Editorial Assistants: Sarah Warren, Stephanie Spellers

Designers: Chris McGee, Linda Lecomte

Illustrators: Liza Donnelly, Lynn Laur

Early Childhood Adventures in Peacemaking was developed by Educators for Social Responsibility in conjunction with Work/Family Directions. The project was funded by the AT&T Family Care Development Fund, a joint project of AT&T/Lucent Technologies, the Communications Workers of America, and the International Brotherhood of Electrical Workers.

EDUCATORS
for
SOCIAL
RESPONSIBILITY

23 Garden Street
Cambridge, MA 02138
(617) 492-1764

wfD

Work/Family Directions
930 Commonwealth Avenue West
Boston, MA 02215

Thanks to Nan Doty, Rebecca Johns, Claudia Logan, Cheryl Raner, and Carol Wintle, along with Sarah Pirtle, Abby Gedstad, and Chris Gerzon, for their expertise, research, and activities that have made this project such a success.

Special thanks also to Diane Levin for her contributions in the area of building a Peaceable Classroom and to Diane Levin and Nancy Carlsson-Paige for their expert review of the manuscript. Articles by Diane Levin and Nancy Carlsson-Paige addressing issues of media violence have been reprinted with permission in this activity guide.

Many thanks to the reviewers who provided key feedback during the development of the guide: Edward Knopping, Gail Desmarais, Abby Gedstad, Chris Gerzon, Emily White, Mary Ellis Schreiber, Lisa Furlong, and Lisa M. Cureton.

Several staff people from Work/Family Directions provided vital project management and content expertise in the development of this guide: Ronnie Mae Weiss, Janette Roman, Patricia Simmons, Jane Meagher, and Mary Ann Duddy.

Thanks also to the staff of Project Adventure, who collaborated with ESR on the school-age edition of Adventures in Peacemaking, which laid the groundwork for this guide.

The overall administrative and editorial work on the second edition of Early Childhood Adventures in Peacemaking involved key staff from ESR, including Larry Dieringer, Carol Miller Lieber, Laura Parker Roerden, Jeffrey Perkins, Caroline Chauncey, Sonali Gulati and Kim Jones. Thanks also to Jeremy Rehwaldt-Alexander and Eden Steinberg.

We are grateful for Liza Donnelly's talents in illustrating the discussion pictures, feeling cube model, and several other illustrations in the guide.

Sandy Whittall would like to thank her husband, Jimmy Whittall, for his time, support, and love.

Early Childhood
Adventures
in Peacemaking

by William J. Kreidler and
Sandy Tsubokawa Whittall

with Nan Doty,
Rebecca Johns,
Claudia Logan,
Laura Parker Roerden,
Cheryl Raner,
and Carol Wintle

Project funded by the
AT&T
Family Care
Development Fund
a joint project of AT&T,
the communications Workers
of America, and the
International Brotherhood
of Electrical Workers.

About the Authors

William J. Kreidler is a former teacher with more than twenty years of experience. He works with educators internationally on issues of conflict resolution, violence prevention, and appreciation of diversity. Mr. Kreidler is the author of the following highly-praised guides for teachers: *Creative Conflict Resolution, Elementary Perspectives: Teaching Concepts of Peace and Conflict, Teaching Conflict Resolution Through Children's Literature,* and *Conflict Resolution in the Middle School.* He is currently senior conflict resolution specialist at ESR.

Sandy Tsubokawa Whittall has more than 24 years of experience teaching at the preschool, elementary, middle, and college levels. She was the founder/director of a large, NAEYC-accredited child care center. She is currently a national early childhood trainer/consultant for ESR.

Nan Doty has 28 years of experience teaching at the preschool, elementary, middle, and graduate levels. She has extensive experience integrating conflict resolution and mediation with special needs and project-based learning. She is an experienced family and community mediator and has also trained and directed school peer mediation programs for grades 3-8.

Rebecca Johns has been a classroom teacher for 25 years. She began her teaching career as a special education teacher in Reno, Nevada, teaching children with multiple handicaps from the ages of 3 to 21. She has taught in a variety of settings with children of all ages in public schools in several western states. Rebecca is currently a consultant for Head Start in Region VIII providing training technical assistance for both regular and special educators. She also teaches conflict resolution for young children, and school-age children, and does staff development for school personnel on conflict resolution.

Claudia Logan is a former teacher and the author of a forthcoming nonfiction children's book. She is currently a consultant in the education department of the Museum of Fine Arts in Boston, Massachusetts.

Laura Parker Roerden is a teacher, writer, and curriculum developer. As the director of publications for Educators for Social Responsibility, she has worked for several years developing materials that help teachers empower their students. She has consulted and written on many different topics including environmental education and the use of the internet in education. She is the author of *Net Lessons: Web-based Projects for Your Classroom.*

Cheryl Raner became interested in education in 1972 when her children began attending a cooperative nursery school. She currently teaches in the lab preschool at Mendocino College in Ukiah, Calif., working with three- and four-year-olds and college students.

Carol Wintle is a clinical therapist in the Boston Public Schools, a consultant, and a visiting lecturer at Fitchburg State College. She served for several years as the coordinator of conflict resolution programs for Boston Area ESR. She is the author of several curricula including *Stopping Bullying at School.* Ms. Wintle is also a storyteller, teacher of storytelling, and author of two books of children's spontaneously created tales, *Chelsea Children Story Talk* and *Spontaneous Storytelling.*

Table of Contents

Introduction

The goal of this guide is to help you, the early childhood educator, teach young children effective, nonviolent ways to resolve conflicts and promote healthy social and emotional development. Adults working with young children spend many hours every day helping children work out differences and difficulties as they play and study together. There is a growing need for developmentally appropriate, hands-on activities for teaching young children the skills to resolve conflicts peacefully. Though many teachers and caregivers have been creative in adapting materials designed for school programs to their own settings, this guide was developed to meet the unique needs of early childhood programs. The work of an early childhood teacher combines the work of caring and educating children in a nurturing environment. This guide will assist you in four areas:

- ❖ Creating an approach to conflict resolution that meets the developmental needs of the children in your program

- ❖ Implementing direct instruction in key conflict resolution skills and concepts

- ❖ Incorporating social and emotional learning into your daily routines

- ❖ Further developing children's skills through games, music, art, drama, storytelling, and other activities

The Peaceable Program*

Early Childhood Adventures in Peacemaking is designed to help you implement a comprehensive conflict resolution curriculum in your early childhood program. It is based on an approach to teaching conflict resolution skills called the Peaceable Program model. The Peaceable Program envisions the early childhood setting as a caring, respectful community that fosters:

- ❖ Cooperation
- ❖ Communication
- ❖ Emotional expression
- ❖ Appreciation of diversity
- ❖ Conflict resolution

The reason for emphasizing these themes is simple. Conflict resolution is most effectively taught not in isolation but in the context of a caring and respect-filled community. Establishing a Peaceable Program is one of the best ways you can manage conflict. By establishing a Peaceable Program, you can address some of the

---

* The Peaceable Program model is based on the Peaceable Classroom model, which is discussed more thoroughly in William J. Kreidler, *Creative Conflict Resolution* (Glenview, Ill.: Scott Foresman and Co., 1984) and William J. Kreidler, *Elementary Perspectives: Teaching Concepts of Peace and Conflict* (Cambridge, MA: Educators for Social Responsibility, 1991).

root causes of conflict, such as poor cooperation and communication skills, difficulty expressing feelings, intolerance of difference, and lack of conflict resolution techniques. Ultimately, being part of a caring community motivates children to resolve conflicts nonviolently. It also prepares a foundation for social and emotional learning which will help children go beyond resolving conflicts to create a meaningful and responsible life.

A Three-Minute Introduction to Conflict Resolution

Conflicts are a normal and natural part of everyone's life. Conflicts are simply the disputes and disagreements that occur between people. While we tend to think of conflict only in terms of its negative effects, the fact is that conflict can also be positive. Conflict can lead to learning and growth. One could argue that without conflict there is no growth or progress, only stagnation. It is the constructive use of conflict that allows society to move forward.

Conflict can, of course, be destructive. The goal of conflict resolution education is not to eliminate conflict. That is neither possible nor desirable. Instead, its aim is to help children learn from conflict and use it for its constructive potential. Conflict resolution education seeks to help children avoid the destructive aspects of conflict.

Many children—and more than a few adults—look at conflict as if it were a contest in which one person must win and the other must lose. This guide promotes striving toward "win-win" conflict resolution—conflict resolution where all parties get what they need and feel good about the solution.

There is no one right way to handle all conflicts. Different conflict resolution approaches are appropriate for different situations. Conflict resolution is an umbrella term that covers every approach from a punch in the nose, to sitting down and talking it out, to running away and hiding. The activities in this guide will help children recognize the options they have in conflict situations and encourage them to choose options that are nonviolent, that meet the needs of the people involved, and that improve relationships.

A Developmental Approach

The Peaceable Program reflects a developmental approach[*] to conflict resolution. It is based on the understanding that children's development follows a fairly predictable sequence. At each level of social and emotional development, they need adult intervention and guidance to help them progress to the next level. Appreciating their needs, concerns, and limitations at each developmental level helps you become more effective as a teacher and caregiver. The key ingredients in a developmental approach to conflict resolution are to:

1. Honor each child's own understanding and experience.

2. Listen and observe carefully to find out what developmental issues children are grappling with and how you can help them move forward.

3. Use daily routines and teachable moments as well as direct instruction to help children master the developmental skills they need to resolve conflicts peacefully.

4. Model prosocial values and conflict resolution skills in your daily interactions with children.

5. Have fun!

This Revised Second Edition

This completely revised second edition of *Early Childhood Adventures in Peacemaking* includes many new features to help you create a Peaceable Program:

❖ An introduction to developmentally appropriate practice, with sections on stages of child development in each skill-based chapter

❖ Tips on setting up your classroom space and materials to minimize conflict and make the most of opportunities for social and emotional learning

❖ Step-by-step instructions for incorporating core social and emotional skills into your daily routines

---

[*] For more information about developmentally appropriate early childhood practice see Sue Bredekamp ed., *Developmentally Appropriate Practice*. (Washington D.C.: NAEYC, 1986.)

❖ Strategies and suggestions for troubleshooting when things don't go exactly as planned

❖ Additional activities and materials for parents that help them reinforce the themes, skills, and concepts of the Peaceable Program at home

In addition, the entire guide has been reorganized to make it even easier to use in the classroom. Chapters are organized first by theme and then by types of activities (music, storytelling, etc.)

How to Use This Guide

There are many ways to introduce *Early Childhood Adventures in Peacemaking* into your program. The guide is organized to help you choose among a variety of options:

❖ Chapter 2 gives you the tools to step back and assess the needs of your program. It also provides tips from other teachers on successful strategies for implementing the Peaceable Program. You can read this section first if you'd like to get an overview of the philosophy and methods of the program.

❖ Chapters 3 through 8 focus on the five key themes of the Peaceable Program: communication, cooperation, expressing emotions and managing anger, appreciating diversity, and conflict resolution. Each chapter provides an introduction to one of the five themes and a brief review of the developmental issues involved. It contains sections that help you set goals for children in this area, identify the skills they need to master, and assess their progress. Each chapter also includes tips and troubleshooting strategies for incorporating these themes into your program. It's not necessary to read the chapters in order since the activities in them are not sequenced. If you've already identified a particular area in which you'd like to strengthen children's skills, you might want to focus on that chapter first.

❖ Chapters 10 through 16 contain a wealth of activities in a variety of media, using music, puppets, storytelling, even parachute play. If you're looking for a story for circle time, a new song, or an exciting way to get kids moving around, this is the place to start. Feel free to leaf through and choose any activity that you think will appeal to your children. You can also turn to the index at the end to choose from the full range of activities in the book, including those incorporated into the theme-based chapters.

❖ Chapter 16 includes ways to involve parents as partners in building a Peaceable Program. You'll find letters you can copy and send home to parents to share resources and ideas that you are using in your program. There are also 12 tip sheets you can reproduce and send home to parents that give them ideas for things they can do at home with their children to support the skills and concepts you are introducing to their children during the day.

The Kit of Manipulatives

This symbol 💼 appears after many of the materials listed in the activities. It indicates that the item is included in the Early Childhood Adventures in Peacemaking Kit of Manipulatives. The kit contains all the essential and hard-to-find materials needed for the activities, packaged in a large toy chest. The kit includes a Lending Library designed to link the classroom with the home. The Lending Library includes children's books, parenting resources, and tapes for parents to check out from the center to use with their children at home. See Chapter 16 for more information on the Lending Library and how to extend Adventures in Peacemaking into the home. For more information about the kit see the information at the end of this book or call ESR at 1-800-370-2515.

Let's Get Started!

Because conflict plays a large part in children's lives, it's one of the most motivating topics you can teach. It's also a lot of fun. Conflict resolution skills, like reading skills, are something that children can use every day for the rest of their lives. By starting now, when children are young, we can get a head start on helping children acquire skills that will not only make a difference in their lives today, but will also lead to a more peaceful world in the future.

Practices for a Peaceable Program

A Peaceable Program is a caring community that emphasizes five themes: cooperation, communication, the expression of feelings, the valuing of diversity, and conflict resolution. In working with early childhood programs around the country, we have found that the most successful programs have certain practices in common. This chapter describes those practices, many of which you may already have in place.

This chapter includes tips and strategies about:

❖ Planning for a Peaceable Room

❖ Setting up a Peace Place

❖ Welcoming all children

❖ Building community

❖ Listening to children and observing their behavior

❖ Group meetings

❖ Using charts effectively

❖ Children's play

❖ Planning for anti-bias work

❖ Encouraging courtesy and manners

Planning for the Peaceable Room

In order for any program to address the kinds of issues and conflicts that arise daily in children's lives, it is important to establish a peaceable environment, built on the following key elements:

- ❖ A sense of trust and safety
- ❖ A regard for the physical and emotional well-being of others
- ❖ An atmosphere of mutual respect
- ❖ The use of problem-solving discussions to resolve conflicts
- ❖ An appreciation of diversity

The topics covered in this section include:

- ❖ An overview of developmental characteristics of young children
- ❖ Some easy ways to set up the Peaceable Room
- ❖ Assessing your program's needs and evaluating progress
- ❖ Transition charts
- ❖ Tips and teachable moments

A Developmental Overview

Whether you are working with children in a child care setting, an afterschool program, a kindergarten, or a preschool, the conflicts and problems that arise give you an opportunity to help children learn effective ways to handle their relationships with others and peaceful ways to solve problems. Research shows that young children learn more readily during the first three or four years of their lives than at any other time. The kinds of experiences young children have with each other every day provide an ideal opportunity for them to learn important skills for handling emotions and solving problems.

Social competence is one of the main underlying goals of early childhood education in any forum. By "social competence" we mean those skills necessary to make and maintain new and diverse relationships with others. In these relationships children create new avenues for their own and others' growth.

Before planning a program, it's helpful to understand the general developmental characteristics of preschool children. Depending on your program, it is also useful to recognize the types of transitions children experience before they arrive each day. Incorporating this information will be helpful not only for planning and scheduling activities, but will also provide realistic expectations as you help children learn how to manage conflicts.

Some benchmarks in development*

Recognizing the following general characteristics of preschool children will provide insight into the way children approach problems and conflicts.

Egocentric: Young children tend to look at things from their own point of view and have a difficult time recognizing how others might interpret a situation. Young children are concerned primarily with how they might be affected by the actions of others. Although young children are naturally egocentric, they are also capable of great empathy and will independently try to comfort or help a peer. Adults can build on this quality by helping children recognize different points of view and encouraging them to support others.

---

* Adapted from Diane E. Levin, *Teaching Young Children in Violent Times: Building a Peaceable Classroom* (Cambridge, Mass.: Educators for Social Responsibility, 1994). See this book for more information on applying these benchmarks to classroom practice.

Single-Minded: Young children are most able to focus on one thing at a time. When children are engaged in a fight, they are likely to be concerned with one aspect of the problem rather than considering the many aspects of the situation. A four-year-old might react to someone grabbing a toy from him, rather than being able to see that he took the toy first. An adult can help widen a child's perspective on a situation through discussion.

All or Nothing: Children tend to see situations and people in strict categories that are all or nothing, good or bad. Someone is a friend or an enemy, but there is rarely a middle ground. Discussions and guidance can help a child consider the possibility of situations or people being more than one thing at a time.

What You See (or Literal Thinkers): Young children deal with the world in fairly concrete terms. They respond more often to actions or words that they have actually witnessed than to abstract ideas and intangible feelings. Because of this, it is hard for a young child to understand how someone can feel sad or hurt when there is no way to see these feelings. Using children's own experiences and pointing out facial clues can begin to make abstract thinking less difficult for children.

Cause and Effect: Children have a hard time understanding the relationship between causes and effects. Consequently, it is difficult for them to plan their actions and foresee what might happen as a result. When looking back on how a problem started, children need help reconstructing how one event might have led to another. Using activities that help children preview and predict certain situations can help them build this skill.

Static vs. Dynamic: Children have a hard time seeing beyond the moment. When they are angry or upset it is hard for them to imagine feeling differently about a person or a situation. They may also have difficulty understanding that they can change a particular scenario. Through discussion and problem solving, children have an opportunity to play a role in making changes. It can also be helpful to remind children of other experiences and situations where they have successfully worked through an issue or made a positive change.

Some Easy Ideas for Setting Up a Peaceable Room

Whether your space is a permanent location or one that requires daily setup, here are some quick ideas that will promote a peaceable environment. You may want to include children in planning the space. This may seem difficult, but it can help them respect and maintain some of the structures and routines that will be part of the program. Involving children in some decisions also gives them a feeling of ownership about their environment. Here is a quick checklist for your space.

☐ Containers

Use clearly marked plastic containers or baskets for materials that are child-friendly. Containers should be clear so that children can see what belongs where and so they know where to find things when they need them. If containers are not clear, they should have pictures on the outside representing what is inside. Consider the height and accessibility of materials so that children can participate in some of the setup and cleanup. Invite children to help decorate signs for materials and locations. Remember to keep materials at eye-level for children. One way to see if your room is child-friendly is to walk around on your knees or at the height of the children in your group to see how things look from their perspective.

☐ Clearly Designated Areas

Be sure to have clearly designated areas for different activities and to provide appropriate materials for sharing. Try to make each area suggest the kinds of activities that are done there—use chairs and tables for an art center, pillows for a reading corner, and an empty space for building blocks.

Encourage children to help make some of the decisions about each area themselves. Invite children to take a tour of each area and ask them some simple questions about how each space could work.

* Should the reading corner be quiet? Why?

* Should the art table be a talking space? What kinds of voices should be used there?

* Where should the blocks be kept so that everyone can use them?

* If some children are doing a particular project, how can they politely remind others to respect their space?

Another approach might be to help children make these choices as they begin to use the different materials and areas. Keep the focus simple and directed by limiting decisions to noise level, materials, and what children need from each other in order to do an activity. Use the block area as an example: What noise level is appropriate? Where should blocks be kept? How much room will we need for building towers?

Depending on your group, you may want to focus on a different area each day instead of dealing with the whole room at once. Keep the decisions simple and be sure to summarize the group's decisions after looking at each space.

☐ On the Walls

Ideally, some displays should be created by the children. They should reflect both the diversity of the group and its similarities. Children need to feel some ownership of their space by seeing their own work and creativity displayed. That doesn't mean provider-designed displays are inappropriate. You can bring unique perspectives, or fill in the gaps in displays children create. For example, one of your roles might be to make sure that the walls and other display spaces have pictures of children from many different cultures. (See p. 7-5 for tips on how your space can reflect diversity.)

☐ Meeting Space

Designate a spot to use consistently for group meetings. A Peace Place is another important area. See "Setting Up a Peace Place" on p. 2-13 for a description.

Assessing Your Program Needs and Evaluating Progress

Depending on whether your program is a preschool, a day-care center, or an afterschool program, the children in your care will have different needs. Kindergarten children who make the transition to an afterschool program must cope with two different environments as well as the physical effort of going from one place to another. The child who attends day care or preschool may be experiencing some anxiety about leaving home for the first time. Recognizing what might be demanding for the children in your program will help you set reasonable expectations and discover which activities and skills will best serve their needs.

When looking at the needs of your program, consider the following issues and questions:

❖ What are the issues that might be stressful or challenging for the children in your group? Some examples are: too much choice in activities; lack of balance between quiet activities and very active, noisy activities; lack of direction during transition periods; etc.

❖ What physical or emotional demands might be difficult for the children in your program? For example, some children might have a crowded, noisy bus ride to your program and may be out of sorts when they arrive.

❖ How do these stresses affect the behavior of the children?

❖ List the types of conflicts and problems that are most common in your group. Over a week-long period note any patterns or trends. For example, do certain problems occur around the same times in the day, over the same materials, or with a particular group of children?

❖ List five skills you would like the children in your group to learn. Make sure that these are developmentally appropriate. Examples of such skills are: beginning to listen to others, sharing materials, working out problems independently, and waiting for a turn.

Use the following chart to help evaluate the types of activities and routines you are doing to meet these goals. The first step is to identify the type of behavior you would like to see in your children, such as "Children share toys and materials" or "Children take turns listening and talking." In the "Skill" column, list the skills you want to work on. In the "Daily Routine" column, list the daily routines that will help children develop the particular skill. In the "Activities" column, note the activities that you will use to practice the skill. Finally, use this chart to record the progress your group is making in the identified skill areas.

Skill	Daily Routine	Activities	Observable Changes in Behavior
Waiting for a turn to talk	Use a talking stick during circle time	Ring, Ring! (p. 3-17)	Less noise of children talking simultaneously

Put yourself in the role of observer and watch to see what behaviors are occurring. Try to write it all down. If you feel that the group is not progressing in a particular area, it doesn't mean you're not doing a good job, it means you want to look at what they *are* doing and record what you are seeing. This might help you focus on one specific skill and make it a goal for your group to work on. Consider using outside resources: you may want to invite a colleague to observe the group or read some of the books included in this kit that are related to the skills you want to develop.

As you consider the skills you want to develop in the children in your program, and as you observe them to assess progress, be aware of your own behavior and expectation as well. Are you:

❖ Grounding your day in what is developmentally appropriate? Expecting behavior that is beyond a child's developmental level will lead to frustration and stress and from there to conflict, irritability, and disorder. That doesn't mean that you should never do activities that are a little above a child's developmental level—you do want children to stretch occasionally. Make sure that *most* of your activities are within the bounds of what your children will be able to accomplish.

❖ Modeling the behavior you want? Children learn social skills in part by watching the adults around them.

❖ Providing opportunities for children to learn the skills you want them to master? Modeling alone isn't enough. Through daily routines and activities, you can help children develop and practice core conflict resolution skills.

❖ Providing appropriate structure to prevent conflicts where children don't have the necessary skills? When children are not developmentally able to accomplish a particular task, such as walking down the sidewalk in an orderly fashion, they will need structure to help them do so, such as holding a partner's hand.

❖ Observing and commenting positively on children's mastery of new skills? As children incorporate new skills into their play and conversation, you can reflect back to them a sense of pride in this accomplishment.

Transition Charts

Many of the conflicts in early childhood programs come from the stress of making transitions from one activity to another or from one place to another. Use the following questions to gather information about the transitions children in your group are dealing with. Then use the information to create a "transition chart" for each child (see example p. 2-10).

❖ Where do children come from before entering your program? (Home, school, etc.)

❖ What types of transitions might they have dealt with before arriving? (A busy household, difficulty in saying good-bye to a parent, a carpool or bus.)

❖ What types of physical behavior might you see when they arrive? (Tired, energetic.)

❖ What kinds of emotional behavior might you see? (Anxious from being rushed, overwhelmed, excited.)

❖ Is there a rhythm or a particular order of activities that works best with these needs?

You can create two versions of this chart. One you can fill in yourself; the other can be filled in by the children at the beginning of the program. Children can color in faces for their moods, draw something that happened before they arrived, or use stickers or crayons to describe how they feel.

Transition Chart

Provider's version

Name of child	Comes from	Transitions	Physical	Emotional
Gus F.	home	comes from hectic a.m. carpool	tired or jumpy	has a hard time saying good-bye to Mom

Child's version

Name	I just came from...	This morning (afternoon) I...	I feel...
Gus	home	ran to the car	happy

Tips and Teachable Moments

Children learn a great deal from observing the adults around them. Many teachable moments will occur as you model language and respond to children. Opportunities will crop up throughout the day to help children anticipate a situation, make appropriate decisions, and brainstorm solutions. When children can depend on an adult to respond calmly and with nonconfrontational language, they are more likely to learn.

❖ Appreciate children when they "do good." Offer positive reinforcement throughout the day when you see children treating each other in respectful and compassionate ways. Sharing specific observations, such as the way children are sharing materials, helping each other, solving a problem, cleaning up, or using calm voices, helps children keep in mind the kinds of behaviors that are valued in a Peaceable Program.

❖ Anticipate problems and predict ways to solve them. Certain activities lend themselves well to modeling problem-solving skills for children. For example, a cooking activity allows you to invite children to think about how to divide up the tasks. Outline the activity with the children first, and then ask them for suggestions on a specific aspect, such as how to give everyone a turn mixing. Even simple routines such as cleaning up or setting up materials give children an opportunity to practice previewing situations and solving problems before they occur.

❖ When children are engaged in a conflict you will need to determine how to respond. Recognize that there is a problem, help children identify it, tell them what you see, and then help them to brainstorm solutions. This method of responding to conflicts need not take a lot of time and will foster an understanding that there is a consistent, effective approach to conflicts that is nonconfrontational and nonviolent. For more information about responding to conflicts, see chapter 8.

❖ Set an example of courteous behavior through daily greetings and interactions. Courteous behavior by adults provides a valuable model for children. Children will imitate the language and expressions they hear around them and will often take their cues from adults. It is important for children to see you using simple manners, such as saying "please" on a consistent basis. You can also point out examples of courteous behavior on the part of children. Rude or discourteous behavior can provide a learning opportunity: you may say, for example, "Can you think of a way to ask for the markers that uses some of our 'magic words'? That's a better way to get what you want."

Setting Up a Peace Place

A Peace Place is a corner or area of your room that is set aside for children to use when they are solving their conflicts. In our experience, it is an essential component of establishing a Peaceable Program. It's best to use an area that has room for a small table and wall space for posting charts, but any area will do. One program we know of had an old bathroom rug they unrolled whenever there was a conflict. It was called the "Conflict Carpet." Similarly, your Peace Place can be called whatever you want. Some of the names we've heard are: Talk It Out Table, Conflict Corner, Problem Place.

The goals of a Peace Place are to:

- ❖ Help children learn to solve conflicts independently
- ❖ Provide a focal point for peacemaking activities in a program
- ❖ Provide a space for children to calm down after a conflict

❖ Acknowledge that conflicts are important and that they can be solved

To introduce the Peace Place you will need to:

1. **Establish a corner or area as the Peace Place.**

   Post a copy of the "Talk It Out Together Process" on p. 8-16 and put out a kitchen timer.

2. **Introduce the Peace Place during a group meeting.**

   Explain that the Peace Place is a place where children can go and try to solve conflicts. Explain that there is a timer they can set. Children should work at problem solving for seven minutes before asking an adult for help. (You may want to make the time shorter for younger children.) Introduce the "Talk It Out Together Process" on p. 8-16 and discuss how it might be used to solve conflicts. This a great time to demonstrate the Talk About It method using the Peace Puppets.

3. **Demonstrate how to use the Peace Place.**

   With another staff person, role-play two children going to the Peace Place and working out their problem. Set the timer for seven minutes and explain that you will try to solve the problem in that time. Begin the role-play by walking through the steps on the Talk It Out Together Chart. If your group has made a conflict resolution chart, refer to it when it comes time to brainstorm solutions. Suggest some solutions based on what's listed there. Try to come up with a solution within the seven-minute limit. When the role-play is finished, shake hands.

4. **Encourage children to use the Peace Place.**

   It's very helpful for young children to have a place they can go to solve conflicts. It helps them learn and internalize some of the peacemaking skills we are trying to teach. So when children bring you conflicts, ask them if they want to try going to the Peace Place on their own first. Even when you need to be involved, say, "Let's go to the Peace Place to work this out." Before long you will hear children say to each other, "We need to go to the Peace Place."

Welcoming All Children

Every child is born capable of loving, celebrating, and contributing to the world and the people in it. Parents and caregivers in an early childhood program can work together to nurture this zest for life in all children. By affirming that each child is unique and special, parents and caregivers can act as a mirror to help children develop a healthy sense of well-being. A child who feels loved and appreciated is more able to love and appreciate others.

Building a sense of self-esteem is an essential first step toward creative conflict resolution. Through greetings, affirmations, and circle time activities, adults and children signal that each child is a valued and respected member of the group. That climate of trust lays the foundation for communication, emotional expression, and cooperation, and gives children the motivation to resolve conflicts peacefully. By demonstrating caring and cooperation, caregivers can say to each child, "You're okay, and it's good that you are here with us today." The goals of building self-esteem are:

❖ To affirm that each child is a unique, lovable human being

❖ To help children feel accepted and valued by the group

❖ To build children's confidence in their abilities and skills

❖ To develop trusting relationships as the basis for cooperation

Some daily practices for welcoming each child into the program are:

1. **Establish ground rules about how staff and children treat each other.** This is a good topic for a staff meeting, parent meeting, or group meeting with the children. Some guidelines to consider are:

   ❖ The Golden Rule: Treat each other as you would like to be treated.

   ❖ Greet each other by name. Be sure to learn what each person likes to be called.

   ❖ Encourage teachers to describe children's behavior without labeling the child ("Don't push!" rather than "Don't be mean!")

2. **Introduce the concept of positive affirmations.** Explain how words and actions can help us feel good about ourselves or make us feel bad. Use puppet role-plays or stories to help children learn the difference between "put-ups" and "put-downs."

3. **Demonstrate kind acts and words.** Address each child by name. Model ways to help others join a conversation or enter a group. Look for opportunities to compliment or praise a child. Be as specific as possible in praising a child's work or actions ("The way you mix the blue and red is really exciting!" or "You were very helpful in showing Elijah where the crayons are.")

4. **Make sure each child receives individual attention from the group.** You can use circle time or class meeting to give the group a chance to show respect and caring for each member. For instance, you can use the song "Come Join the Circle" from *Linking Up!* as a way to call the group together. Each child can bring something special to the group and have a chance to explain why it is important. You can also post pictures of each child on the bulletin board, write about things children do or say in a class newsletter, or make up songs that include something about each child.

Building Community

A new group of young children can become a community by creating a shared history and shared experiences. For this to happen young children need consistent, repeated rituals that bring them together, such as a daily "circle time." It is by being part of a community that children learn to respect each other, value diversity, and treat each other in caring ways. In this section you will find:

- ❖ Strategies for building a community
- ❖ Tips and teachable moments
- ❖ Activities and routines that promote community

Strategies for Building a Community*

Young children need to see how their needs are similar to the needs of others. It is also important to establish individual boundaries within the group. For example, though circle time is a shared group time, children need to know where they can sit without interfering with each other's physical space.

Early on, it is important to establish that everyone in the program needs to feel safe. In this context, "safe" means feeling part of the group (not left out) and feeling that you won't be hurt either physically or with words. One of the first group meetings can focus on what each child needs to feel safe. Each child can say what he or she needs while you draw a corresponding picture on a chart. Children can learn the symbol for "no" (a red circle with a slash through it), which can be used to represent some of their safety rules. This chart can be used for reference when a child breaks a safety rule.

As situations arise, children need to learn skills and behaviors that help them act in caring ways towards each other. Caring behavior is most meaningful when it comes from direct experiences that guide children to consider the needs of others.

At various points throughout the day, it is helpful for children to evaluate whether their behavior towards others is or is not caring. After a group activity you can ask what each child did that was helpful to the others in their group. Reinforcing caring behavior and helping children to see that what they do has an impact on others fosters a feeling of community.

Create traditions and rituals around shared experiences such as birthdays, the end of a month, or beginning and ending times in the day. These traditions or rituals need to be consistently enacted or they will have little effect on children. Use activities such as making books about the group (see chapter 12, "Bookmaking") and celebrating birthdays to help children see themselves as individuals who share commonalties.

When problems occur, reinforce the idea that this is a room where people care for one another and need to feel safe. Work through problems using conflict-

---

* Adapted from Diane E. Levin, *Teaching Young Children in Violent Times: Building a Peaceable Classroom* (Cambridge, Mass.: Educators for Social Responsibility, 1994)

resolution or problem-solving techniques rather than smoothing things over or ignoring issues and differences. (See chapter 8 "Resolving Conflict.") Remind children that they can learn ways to help each other solve problems or work through mistakes.

Tips and Teachable Moments: Building Community

Community building often takes place when children are in situations where they must assume some responsibility for each other. The following situations illustrate times when community building can take place.

❖ A child named Jerome has hit a child named Carlos. Carlos is holding his eye and crying and Jerome is upset. The provider intervenes to find out what happened and to act as a mediator. Instead of demanding an apology, the provider uses the following dialogue with the children.

Provider:	Carlos seems really hurt. Ask him if he's okay.
Jerome:	Are you okay?
Carlos:	No.
Provider:	Jerome, Carlos is not okay. Ask him what he needs from you to feel better right now.
Jerome:	What do you need?
Carlos:	Ice.

[Jerome goes and gets ice for Carlos. Other typical requests could be to go away, get a cold cloth, or some other tangible item.]

Provider:	Is there anything else you need? Does your eye still hurt?
Carlos:	It's feeling better.
Jerome:	Is there anything else I can do?
Carlos:	No. I guess I'm okay.

A variation of this dialogue enables both the child who has been hurt and the child who has caused the hurt to go through a process of reparation. When the "hurter" has to confront the injury or emotional upset of the other person and take action, he or she assumes a caring position that is also calming to the other child. A quick "I'm sorry" cannot provide this kind of exchange or sense of genuine responsibility and is not as effective in preventing a recurrence.

❖ A child named Kindra has spilled a basket of crayons that are now rolling all over the floor. Another child points to the accident and tells the provider that Kindra has knocked the basket on the floor. The provider can ask the child what he could do to help Kindra get the crayons back in the basket. Turning accidents, mistakes, and "tattle-tale" situations into opportunities to be helpful or problems to be solved reinforces the idea that your community is a place where people can make mistakes and be supported.

Activities and Routines that Promote Community*

Fabric Patterns

Get fabric swatches of various patterns and assign each child a different pattern. (Select patterns that have one color contrasting with white.) At the beginning of the program fabric swatches can be used to identify each of the children on a job chart or sharing schedule or to locate each child's seat in the circle. Swatches can also be used for job chart name tags, name tags on card stock, and pillows for sitting. You can take attendance by having children lay out their patterns and figure out who is absent. Young children very quickly become familiar with each other's patterns, which gives them another way of thinking about the other children in a group.

> **note** While fabric pieces are the most versatile for these activities, other materials can be substituted. Wallpaper stores will often give away old books of wallpaper samples. Wrapping paper is another possible substitute.

Birthday Wishes

When a child celebrates a birthday he or she can be invited to sit in a special chair and hold a cup filled with water. The other children in the group are each given one kidney bean to drop in the cup, one at a time, along with a special wish for the birthday child. After all the wishes have been made, the birthday child can plant

---

* ESR wishes to thank Abby Gedstad and Chris Gerzon for contributing many of these ideas.

his or her kidney beans and watch the "wishes" grow. (Allow the beans to soak in the water overnight before planting.) The planters should be set up in a special section of the room so that, by the end of the year, a small garden has been planted.

Take-Home Friend

Each weekend a member of the group may take a turn bringing home the class puppet or stuffed animal. (The children can help to choose a name for the animal.) A stuffed frog, a tote bag, a story book, and a journal are included in the kit for this purpose. The child must take care of the animal and, with the help of a parent, record some of the activities he or she did with the stuffed animal during the weekend in drawings, photos, or writing. Children can share their journal entry with the rest of the group on Monday. (See "Take the Frog Home" on p. 11-4 for more information about this activity.)

Calendar

At the end of each day, with the input of the group, write or draw on an index card one important event or experience the group had that day. At the end of the month attach these cards to a large wall calendar to create a "What Happened in [name of month]" display. The cards can be made into a group book at the end of the year or photocopied into memory books for each child. (See chapter 12, "Bookmaking," for other bookmaking activities.)

Listening to Children and Observing Their Behavior

Children need to feel that the adults in their lives are listening to them and are interested in them. This happens when an adult greets children in a friendly way and asks about their pets or what they did over the weekend. Children feel recognized when they are engaged in an activity and an adult makes a specific observation about what they are doing, such as, "Wow, that is a big block tower you built." When you notice and remark that a child feels tired or is having a hard time, the child feels that he or she has an opportunity to share what is going on with someone who cares.

Listening to children and observing them carefully provides important information about them and helps build real relationships between you and the children.

Children cannot learn how to manage conflict or become part of a caring community if they do not feel that they have a real connection to the adult in charge. By listening carefully and knowing the children in the group, you provide the foundation for a peaceful room where children feel safe and supported. While time constraints and the demands of an active and busy group can make this challenging, there are specific strategies that you can use.

This section includes:

❖ A checklist of listening and observation skills

❖ Strategies for careful observing

❖ Strategies for attentive listening

❖ Guidelines for active listening

Checklist for Observing and Listening

This checklist is intended to provide a starting point for observing and listening to children. There are many variations on the way you can effectively make connections with children. This checklist highlights some key places where children need to feel recognized.

When children arrive do you

- ❑ greet them by name?
- ❑ notice their physical demeanor?
- ❑ notice their general mood?
- ❑ observe whether their emotional and physical state is unusual?
- ❑ make a positive comment about something personal, such as a new haircut, recent event, or a child's remembering to bring a particular item?

When children are engaged in a particular activity do you

- ❑ observe carefully what they are doing and saying?
- ❑ notice a particular effort they are making?
- ❑ notice if they are having difficulty with the task or with a peer?
- ❑ offer encouragement for a particular effort or accomplishment?
- ❑ recognize what the child is trying to do (build a bridge, make a collage, learn a new game)?
- ❑ ask questions about what the child is doing?

When a child is having difficulty do you

- ❑ share your observation in a one-on-one conversation?
- ❑ ask the child what he or she has noticed about the situation?
- ❑ describe patterns to help the child see the situation more clearly (e.g., "After lunch you seem to have a hard time sharing . . . ")?
- ❑ use the child's comments to help figure out a next step?

Strategies for Observing and Listening

When you observe and listen to children, you don't always have to stay in the role of "silent observer." In fact, it helps if you to talk about your observations so that children know that you are aware of what they are doing and how they are feeling. For example, "I noticed how you and Heather cooperated on the block tower. You looked like you were having fun. How did you do it?" One way to think about this is to consider your observations as feedback. Since children tend to internalize what they hear about themselves, it is important that you use caring and nonthreatening language to give this feedback.

Observing Positive Actions

Children feel valued when adults notice the positive things they do. When you compliment a child for helping a friend clean up, for saying something kind, or for working hard on a project, a child feels that his or her efforts have been recognized and appreciated. While children like and need to be noticed on an individual basis, there is a lot to be gained from praising a whole group for accomplishments like going from one place to another quietly or gathering in a circle without any problems.

The important thing to remember about any kind of praise is that it needs to be specific. Global praise like "What a nice drawing" or "You're doing a good job" may cause competition among children or confuse them with its lack of specificity. How is the drawing nice? Good job at what? Again, it helps to think in terms of providing feedback and encouragement for children.

Observing Things That Don't Work

Individual conferences are a good way to talk with a child who is having a problem. Children can handle hearing about their own behavior if it is described in caring terms and presented as a problem to be worked out with the help of the adult. These talks provide a good place for children to hear some real feedback from you. Simply stating a problem may not provide the child with enough information to figure out what is going on. Describing this situation clearly can make a child feel much more understood and can even clarify a difficult situation.

For example, you might say, "I've noticed that you are having a hard time in the sandbox."

This acknowledges the problem but may not help the child see what he or she is doing that is making others upset. What's a "hard time"? What kind of difficulty is the child having at the sandbox? This statement doesn't make clear what the problem is.

Here's another way to say this:

> "I've noticed that when you are building things in the sandbox you don't seem to want other kids to join you. Some of the other children are upset when you take all the shovels and tell them to leave. Have you noticed that happening?"

Providing a child with this kind of feedback gives them a broader perspective on the problem and allows room for further discussion. The adult could then ask if the child feels like he or she needs a lot of space for building or worries that his or her castle could get knocked down. Children can really benefit from your insight and observations and might become more able to explore some of the reasons for their behavior and work towards a solution.

With some situations it may not be possible to provide this kind of detailed observation. Another approach might be to ask children questions so that they can help create a fuller picture. Asking a child what he or she is building or doing in the sandbox and how he or she feels when other children want to join in the activity can provide similar information while also modeling self-reflection.

Listening to Learn

Much of what you can do as a caregiver is listen. As you move around the room listening to interactions among children, you can gather information about the group and individual children. This helps you discover the issues they are dealing with and gives you the information needed to understand any problems arising in the room.

When listening to children ages three to six, keep in mind that they are looking at the world from an egocentric point of view. They do not think and perceive in the same way that adults do. As you listen to young children, you can gently question or correct any misinformation or misunderstandings, while affirming perceptions that are accurate.

Active Listening to Defuse Anger

You can also use listening for a very specific purpose: to defuse anger and hostility. Conflicts evoke strong feelings, and usually one of the feelings is anger. When young children know that their feelings have been heard and acknowledged, their anger usually subsides and they can move on to problem-solving.

Guidelines for Active Listening

Active listening encourages children to speak by showing that you care about what they are trying to say. Here are some guidelines for active listening:

❖ You can show understanding and acceptance through nonverbal behaviors such as nodding; tone of voice; gestures; facial expressions; kneeling down to be at child's eye level.

❖ You can restate children's important thoughts and feelings. For example: "You sound upset that Eliza has the ball right now and you want it."

❖ You can empathize with children and put yourself in their place by saying something like, "Sometimes it's frustrating, isn't it? Learning to take turns and wait patiently takes a lot of practice." Or for younger children: "Waiting is hard, isn't it?"

By modeling these communicative behaviors for children, you can acknowledge the difficulty of various situations and help them learn how to deal with obstacles through perseverance and practice.

Guided Listening

Guided listening is an approach that invites the child to come up with more information through questions and clarification. When children are trying to explain their own behavior, a number of things can be going on inside them, primarily fear that they are going to get into trouble. In spite of reassurances, children can still worry that there will be punishment or some unknown consequence for what they have done.

Often children experience confusion and uncertainty about what has happened or can only see part of the problem, or they may be genuinely stuck in trying to figure out what to do next. Their responses to questions about a situation might be "I don't know," or they may focus on one small event in the situation. These are perfectly appropriate responses for this age group.

It helps to summarize what the child has said and invite further responses by asking questions that might help the child take a broader view of the situation.

For example, "Do you think that it would help you sit quietly at circle time if we had a signal? Do you think that you might be excited when you first arrive and that's why you don't notice what the other kids are doing?"

Even when a child is unable to offer any comment, it is possible to use guided listening to help them.

"It seems like you feel sad about this fight," or
"You don't look like you feel very good about this problem."

Rephrasing what a child has said and summarizing her ideas is a time-tested method that can clarify a child's thinking and point her in a fruitful direction, while also bringing closure to a conversation.

Some key phrases for sharing observations

- ❖ I've noticed . . .
- ❖ I see that you are . . .
- ❖ What have you noticed about . . .
- ❖ Do you think . . .
- ❖ It looks / sounds like you feel . . .
- ❖ It sounds like what you want to do is . . .
- ❖ It sounds like . . . happens when . . .

Group Meetings*

Group meetings provide an opportunity for children to share ideas and help each other find ways to resolve problems through discussion. Though group meetings are often times for focusing on problems, they can also provide a time for shared decision making. Regular group meetings are a good way to begin the program time, and they provide children a time to share, sing, or play group games.

In this section you will find information on:

- ❖ Structuring group meetings
- ❖ Tips and teachable moments for using group meetings
- ❖ Description of a sample group meeting

---

* Material in this chapter is based in part on Diane E. Levin's, *Teaching Young Children in Violent Times:Building a Peaceable Classroom* (Cambridge, Mass.: Educators for Social Responsibility, 1994). See this book for more information on group meetings and group discussions.

Structuring Group Meetings

Group meetings allow young children a consistent place to practice the speaking and listening skills that provide the building blocks for solving problems. Your role is to establish certain basic expectations for group meetings and to help children learn some of the basic skills they need. A useful strategy is to use role-playing activities and games during group meetings as well as focused discussions that teach children directly how to communicate in a group.

Keep in mind that young children have a limited attention span and will probably only be able to participate effectively in a group meeting for fifteen minutes. Even when a discussion is still going strong, a good plan is to summarize the discussion and give children a clear goal that can be discussed at the next meeting. Children will need to have problem-solving meetings scheduled close together in order to keep the momentum going.

Research shows that it is appropriate for young children to try to learn the following skills:*

- ❖ Describe a problem without accusing another peer or using put-downs
- ❖ Share an opinion in the group
- ❖ Use the "I" voice to express a particular view
- ❖ Make eye contact
- ❖ Wait instead of interrupting
- ❖ Listen to someone else's ideas or comments
- ❖ Say something positive to support another child's idea
- ❖ Consider more than one possible solution
- ❖ Choose to try out a workable solution and stick to it

Again, group meetings provide one forum for helping children learn about and practice these skills.

---

* See Ruth Charney, *Teaching Children to Care* (Greenfield, Mass.: Northeast Foundation for Children, 1992) for more information about young children's development.

Some ground rules to establish with children:

❖ Try to have your group meetings in the same physical space every time. Children should sit in a circle on the floor or on chairs where they can all see each other and be comfortable.

❖ Group meetings can have different purposes. Regular group meetings that begin in the morning or at other regularly scheduled times can be used for sharing, singing, or group games. Other group meetings can be used for discussing problems and trying to find different solutions. Regular meetings should be held at the same time of day so that it is easier for children to distinguish these discussions from problem-solving meetings.

❖ At all group meetings children need to agree not to use any put-downs. This will require that you label put-downs when they occur and suggest positive alternatives.

❖ The most important skills for the children to learn so that they can effectively participate in meetings are taking turns talking and listening without interrupting. Using a "talking stick" ▪ or some special object that is held by the child who is speaking will help minimize interrupting and talking out of turn.

❖ The group needs to choose a signal to use when someone wants to say something. The signal can only be used when someone has stopped speaking.

Tips and Teachable Moments: Group Meetings

❖ Deciding to call a group meeting for problem solving requires some judgment. Certain problems are best handled through discussion with the children directly involved. Other problems lend themselves well to group discussion and give children an opportunity to think through important issues that relate to their own experiences. Problems with sharing materials, fighting on a playground, or teasing, because they are situations most children face, lend themselves to group discussions.

❖ Early group meetings can focus on issues that are easy for the children to solve, boosting their confidence and helping them become familiar with the speaking and listening rules. You may wish to keep an ongoing list of issues that you observe or hear about from children to use for group meetings, but topics must be relevant, real, and solvable.

❖ Meetings should take place when children feel calm and can handle the expectations of listening to others and speaking without using put-downs. A calming-down period after an incident will help the meeting work more smoothly, though children may be anxious to address a topic while it is still "hot" in their minds.

❖ Your role is to act as a facilitator by presenting the problem, summarizing the different opinions, and bringing the meeting to a close with a clear goal for what the next step will be. During the discussion you can help children to express their views in nonconfrontational ways and you can point out examples of good listening, sharing ideas, and decision making.

❖ Problem-solving meetings should begin with you describing the problem in neutral terms. Don't use the names of any children so that the problem becomes a general one that requires everyone's involvement. Children need to feel safe and comfortable during these meetings and it may be reassuring for them to hear you remind the group that no one will be singled out and that there will not be any punishments.

Description of a Sample Group Meeting

Here is an example of how a problem-solving group meeting could proceed:

The adult makes sure everyone is sitting comfortably and is ready to focus.

"I've noticed that there are some problems at the art table. A lot of kids want to use the materials and I see some pushing, name calling, and kids feeling upset because they don't get a chance to paint or draw. That doesn't make our room feel like a good place to be. Can we all try to listen to each other to solve this problem?"

Make sure everyone understands the expectations of the group meeting, then ask a question to get everyone involved. The question should help children begin to think about the kinds of feelings and actions that take place in a conflict situation.

"What made it hard for some of you to share the art table this week? Some of you may want to think about how you felt and what you did when you didn't get a chance to use the art table."

Throughout the discussion, summarize some of the general comments to help provide information that children can use to find a solution.

"It sounds like a lot of kids wanted to do some painting this week and there wasn't enough room for everyone. Since some kids didn't know if they would get a turn, they felt mad and started name calling."

The heart of the discussion should focus on what children need to do to solve this kind of problem.

"What are some things we need to do when we have to share materials or a space?"

After children offer their different thoughts, the group can work towards concrete solutions. After each suggestion, you can repeat it to the group without commenting on whether it is feasible or not. Try to choose a solution during the same session in which you brainstorm solutions.

Using Charts Effectively

Charts can provide an effective way to support the routines and rules that are part of a room. Charts can do more than simply display a message or a schedule. Not only can they serve as visual reminders, but they can often be used to initiate an activity or to focus on a particular task or issue.

Young children respond best to words accompanied with pictures. They also enjoy charts they can use themselves. Velcro name-tags, charts that spin, or pockets with pull-out features all provide children with a tactile experience that help make charts more meaningful.

In this section you will find:

- ❖ Tips and teachable moments about charts
- ❖ Ideas for charts
- ❖ Resources for learning more about using charts

Tips and Teachable Moments: When To Use Charts

❖ Charts can be helpful at the beginning of the program year or when new children join the group. Early in the year, you can use charts to familiarize the group with basic routines such as the daily schedule or cleanup and for community building. Listing the names of the children in the group along with photographs or words that describe something about them can help children get to know each other. Class contracts that list the rules children feel they need in order to make their room safe and fun can help set the tone for a peaceable room. Often, creating a chart can be a group-building experience and can help children feel comfortable participating in the group.

❖ Charts can initiate an activity or a task, but children may still need support. A sign-up sheet for a choice activity does not guarantee that the activity will go smoothly or that a child will know what to do for a clean-up job. Charts provide a certain amount of structure, but it is important to recognize that young children can only use them to a certain extent.

❖ When a group has worked together to solve a particular problem, a chart can help bring closure to the discussion and provide a reminder of the hard work that was done, as well as function as a way to handle the problem if it recurs. For example, if sharing materials has been a problem, a chart can list some specific ways to take turns.

❖ In general, charts for young children should be brief and stated in positive terms. It is much more helpful for children to know what they should do than what they should not. Charts that are in the form of a list should be limited to a few items so that they are manageable. Use as many pictures and symbols as you can.

❖ Introduce new charts over time, not all at once. Let charts emerge to fill a need in the classroom, and, as much as possible, involve children in creating them. For example, while you might develop the overall design of a job chart, the children can draw the necessary illustrations and make the name tags needed.

❖ Vary the types of charts that are used in the classroom. This not only makes them a less predictable device for children, but also shows different types of thinking and uses. For instance, a schedule, a job chart, and a list of playground rules should not look the same.

❖ Involve parents in making charts to use at home. Start by helping parents become familiar with the charts you use in your program. You can do this through letters home, through a newsletter if your program has one, or when chatting with parents who come to pick up their children at the end of the day. (In this case, have the child show and explain the chart to the parent.) Encourage parents to use charts at home for such things as keeping track of chores and monitoring TV time.

Ideas for Charts*

Names and Faces

This chart is best used early in the year or when new children join your program. Using library card pockets, write a child's name on each pocket. Next, take a photograph of each child in your program. Attach the photograph to a 3" x 5" index card. Do this in a way that allows the card to fit in the pocket without the photo getting hidden. Place this chart in an area where children will see it often to help them become familiar with each other. A Names and Faces Chart can go next to a coat rack or outside a room so that parents can also get to know the other children in the group.

The Names and Faces Charts can also be used to take attendance. As children arrive, have them take their picture card out of a box and place them in the appropriate pocket. Then you'll know at a glance who's present and who's not present on any given day. Children also enjoy using the chart for a simple game. Take all the pictures out of the pockets and have children match the pictures to the names.

Calendar

Create a calendar that chronicles one special event from each day of the year. At the end of the day, write or draw a picture of a significant event on a card. Attach it to a calendar. At the end of the year it can be photocopied and given to each

---

* ESR wishes to thank Abby Gedstad and Chris Gerzon for contributing many of these ideas.

member of the group. Events such as birthdays, classroom activities, and trips can be recorded.

A Safe Place

At the beginning of the year ask each child what she needs to feel safe and happy in this program. Write each child's name and let her dictate her idea. Keep this up early on to initiate discussions about what is important to each person and how it can be put into practice.

Daily Schedule

This chart should have words and pictures to show what will happen during each day. It can be introduced when the group arrives so that children can anticipate the day.

Job Chart

You can design a Job Chart using library card pockets for the names of jobs, then inserting cards with children's names into them. Or you can make a Job Chart using two concentric, rotating circles; one with the names of the children, one with the names of jobs. In both cases, jobs can be symbolized with pictures, and children, after completing their jobs, can move their name to the next job on the chart.

Problem Solvers

Problem-Solver Charts are best used for problems that affect the whole group. They don't need to be a permanent part of your room, but can be made as a great follow up to a group problem-solving discussion. The chart should show the steps used to solve the problem, both in picture and words, so that children can refer to it if the problem recurs. This is a situation where you, not the children, should make the illustrations for the chart. Simple stick figures are fine. The important thing is that the illustrations be clear.

Sharing, a common concern for young children, works well as a Problem-Solver Chart. During a group discussion have the children identify ways to share, then create a chart that lists the strategies. Some possibilities for this chart are:

❖ Ask before you take something away.

❖ Flip a coin or "flipper" to decide who gets it first.

❖ Sign up for something if a lot of kids want to use it.

- ❖ Help the other person find something to use while they wait.

- ❖ Find a way to use it together.

- ❖ Use it for ten minutes, then give someone else a turn.

Helper Chart*

This chart lists every child in the group
along with a picture of something each child can help others with.

---

* Adapted from Diane Levin, *Teaching Young Children in Violent Times: Building a Peaceable Classroom* (Cambridge, Mass.: Educators for Social Responsibility, 1994) See this book for more information on using class charts and class graphs to build a Peaceable Classroom.

Children's Play*

Play is children's work. Through play, children make meaning of their world and develop important social, physical, emotional, and cognitive skills.

> *"The maxim that play is the work of the young child is valid when children define their own play."*
>
> —*Vivian Paley*

Two young children scooping and pouring sand into containers are not only developing readiness for early math concepts such as volume and conservation. They are also practicing motor skills, exploring the properties of sand, and working out social issues. Given ample time and rich resources, children's healthy play will take the unique shape of the child, following the themes and issues that the child is most ready to work through.

* ESR gratefully acknowledges the contribution of Diane E. Levin, Ph.D., in the area of children's play and violence and thanks her and ESR's Early Childhood Peaceable Classroom group, who, under Diane's direction and based on her book published by ESR, *Teaching Young Children in Violent Times,* have contributed greatly to this area. Teachers Abby Gedstad, Chris Gerzon, and Cheryl Raner are also thanked for their important contributions to this section.

Conflict is a natural part of children's play. Young children have a strong need to feel safe. Children often process this issue in their dramatic play by exploring themes related to power and safety. In the secure haven of a peaceable program, children can be chased by monsters and be rescued by hiding in the castle. They can process with a playmate a conflict that happened that morning with a parent— "Now, I'll be the mommy, and you be the baby." Children can save the world from evil space invaders by inventing a special, magical shield from nothing more than paper. In healthy dramatic play, conflict can serve children's developmental needs.

But what about when play is not healthy? When children are hitting or biting? When one child is reduced to tears because another's play does not make him or her feel safe? Or when a child's play is stuck in imitating a television superhero?

This section includes tips and ideas about

❖ Planning for peaceable play

❖ Facilitating play

❖ Six strategies for intervening in children's play

❖ Confronting violent play

❖ Resources for learning more about children's play

Planning for Peaceable Play

Careful planning will help prevent pointless conflict and help young children's play better serve their needs. (For more information about planning for peaceable play see *Teaching Young Children in Violent Times*: *Building a Peaceable Classroom* 💼 by Diane E. Levin, Ph.D., and *Who's Calling the Shots? How to Respond Effectively to Children's Fascination with War Play, War Toys and Violent TV* 💼 by Nancy Carlsson-Paige, Ed.D. and Levin.)

Providing a Structure for Productive Play

In planning for peaceable play it is important that you:

❖ **Provide adequate time for play.** Research shows that children need long stretches of uninterrupted time for quality play. Forty-to fifty-minute time blocks are best.

❖ **Provide sufficient, organized space for play.** Organizing your space into partitioned play areas such as a dress-up/house corner, block area, art table, reading area, etc., will encourage children to participate in more dramatic, rich play.

❖ **Provide interesting props with which children can identify.** Since play imitates real life, it's important that children have props for their play that relate to their lives. Simple household items like milk cartons, egg trays, brooms, dress-up clothes, etc., will provide rich hours of play. Props that stimulate the imagination, such as dinosaurs, magic wands, puppets, etc., are also important.

❖ **Be sure that your resources are sufficient and are in good working order.** Dried-out markers or insufficient quantities of play items like favorite colored paper or play dough can lead to many conflicts during play. Be sure that you have enough of what's needed before you offer it to the children.

❖ **Add variety and unusual materials to play areas.** Provide shoe boxes in the block area to encourage creative play. Children can make modular apartments, space ships, doll-houses, etc. Include brightly colored fabric in your dress-up area. Also link this to the curriculum by discussing dress in different cultures. Provide pictures of people from all walks of life in different types of dress.

Facilitating Play*

Free play is the time we allow children to follow the wanderings of their own imaginations. The play is child-directed rather than provider-directed. However, there is a great deal that you can do to facilitate such play to serve young children's healthy development. This section includes guidelines for facilitating play as well as techniques to avoid.

Facilitation Guidelines

❖ **When facilitating play, move beyond the role of supervisor and manager of children to become an active observer.** Look for moments to join children in play as another player and to encourage a child to try on a new role. Suggest variations on their play to enrich it and move children to new levels in their development. This is particularly important for a child who appears stuck in repetitive play. As children try on new roles, they begin to imagine what might be instead of what is.

❖ **Carefully observe children's play before you join it,** being careful to pick a moment that will not disrupt child-directed play.

❖ **Guide children through the day in a planned and thoughtful manner,** alternating quiet activities with active games and structured activities with free play.

❖ **Use play as an opportunity to reinforce children's pro-social behaviors.** For children who have difficulty sharing, give them an opportunity to work this out in their play. You could enter into their play as a player rather than as an adult authority figure and, for example, highlight a scenario where everyone becomes friends because they share. Also, when children are the stars in their own stories, they feel less need to defend themselves and are more eager to try out new roles.

❖ **Enrich children's play by providing an array of interesting and changing props.** Choose props that link directly to children's experience such as props related to house play. As you enrich their experiences through your curriculum, expand your repertoire of props to link to the curriculum. For example, dinosaurs can be added to the block

---

* For more information on facilitating children's play see Diane E. Levin, *Teaching Your Children in Violent Times: Building a Peaceable Classroom* (Cambridge, MA: Educators for Social Responsibility, 1994). 💼

and manipulatives areas for a few weeks when you are studying dinosaurs, then switched with farm animals when creating a farm. Offer suggestions as you help facilitate the change in children's play with the new props.

❖ **Support and extend play opportunities as they arise.** For example, when you notice a child spanking a baby too hard in the housekeeping area, suggest a more positive response: "Maybe if we can get baby interested in something else, baby will stop crying. What could we try?" Model positive nonverbal behavior by stroking the baby's head or bouncing the baby gently on your knee as you talk.

Roadblocks to Facilitation

Using the following techniques is counterproductive to the process of facilitating play:

❖ Trying to force your idea on unwilling children by disrupting child-directed play instead of joining it

❖ Using directed teaching instead of facilitation to change the activity so it is no longer play at all

Six Strategies for Intervening in Children's Play*

1. **Parallel Play**—Model appropriate play strategies without interacting with the child. Think out loud by talking to yourself as a way to offer suggestions without directing the child. For example, a child is building towers with clay but is growing frustrated because they keep falling over. Sit down and ask if you can borrow some clay to build something. Begin building towers that soon fall over once they get to a certain height. Think aloud and comment, "I wonder how I can keep these towers from falling over?" "Maybe I can build some bridges and connect them." Then build a bridge between two towers. This encourages the child to see what you are doing and begin to build something similar.

---

* ESR thanks Jay Altman for his research on play intervention strategies.

2. **Spectator**—Make comments as a visitor to the dramatic play. For example, a group of children are playing farm, each acting out a different farm animal or pretending to work on the farm. Become a visitor to the farm, commenting on the characteristics of the different animals or on the work of the farmers. Ask the farmers questions such as, "What do you feed the cows?" or "What vegetables are you growing this year?"

3. **Thematic Fantasy**—Engage the children in reenacting favorite fairy tales, folk tales, and stories with predictable and repetitive plots. Children take on and swap roles, re-enact the story in various ways, and use simple props. For example: Ask children if they know the story of Little Red Riding Hood. Ask children to retell the story, with each child telling a part or adding something that has been left out. Ask children what roles they would like to play. Bring out props if they are available. As the children act out the story, develop the play by asking questions from the side, such as, "What did the Wolf do next?"

4. **Play Training**—Make suggestions and encourage children to reenact stories and fairy tales in their play. For example, read a short story together with a group of children. Discuss the different characters and ask children to choose a character they would like to play. Choose a character for yourself. During the enactment of the story, follow the cues from the children most of the time, but also ask questions and make suggestions when needed to move the story along.

5. **Matchmaker**—Encourage interaction among children. For example, several children are separately making vehicles and buildings from Lego®. Join them and make a helicopter. Ask a child if you can land the helicopter at his/her building to drop off a passenger. Ask two other children if they would use their vehicle to help transport people from one building to another.

6. **Co-Play**—Join a child-directed play scenario and respond to the actions and comments of the children. Specific strategies for doing this include: asking for information, adding new elements, responding to children's initiative, facilitating play-related language exchanges, asking higher level questions to extend the play, and including other children in the play. For example, a group of children are playing "restaurant." One child is playing the waiter, while another is playing cook, and several others are playing customers. Ask a child who is looking on, not participating, if he would like

to go to lunch. Walk into the play area with the child and sit down at a table. When the waiter comes over to take your order, ask what is being served. Ask questions and respond to the pretend play throughout.

Confronting Violent Play

Speaking of Superheroes*

by Diane E. Levin

Many children receive large daily doses of pretend danger, fighting, and war from children's superhero television programs. A full line of toys and licensed products ranging from bedsheets to lunch boxes extends the influence of cartoon characters. When young children (often boys) adopt the fighting behaviors of their favorite superheroes during play in the program, conflicts often occur. One way to deal with the effect of such play is to make sure that your program is democratic and peaceful, and that it offers children nonviolent ways of resolving conflicts and solving problems that come up. Group dialogues can be an effective tool for helping you create a Peaceable Program.

Creating a Peaceable Program is a dynamic process. What it looks like and how it works will depend on the unique constellation of needs, interests, abilities, and experiences of each provider and group of children. In fact, there are probably as many ways to create peaceable environments for young children as there are programs, providers, and groups of children.

Any effort to create such an environment involves helping young children work together to make and abide by decisions about how to act and treat one another. One effective way to do this is through give-and-take dialogues about issues that are meaningful to children. In the following example, a teacher helps kindergarten children to problem solve a way to keep rough superhero play from upsetting other children. This give-and-take dialogue helps the children learn to participate in class discussions and to share responsibility with their teacher for how their classroom functions. It also suggests a way for you to respond whenever violent play-themes enter your program. Use it to think about how you could adapt this

---

* This section is adapted from D. E. Levin, *Teaching Young Children in Violent Times: Building a Peaceable Classroom* (Cambridge, MA: Educators for Social Responsibility, 1994). Adaptation by Scholastic Early Childhood Today.

strategy to your own needs and situations, and to the ages and developmental stages of your children.

Talking It Over Together: Teachable Moments

Imagine a scenario in which several kindergarten children are playing in a large appliance carton covered in aluminum foil. Suddenly, three boys race over and begin to karate chop and kick the box. When a provider comes over to investigate the commotion, a child in the box sticks out a fist and hits an "attacker," who bursts into tears, crying "But, I'm a Power Ranger!"

Now imagine that this is the third time that this teacher has confronted a crisis created by the presence of various superheroes among her children. This time, in addition to dealing with the immediate problem, she decides to bring the issue to a group meeting where all the children can work on a solution together. Here is the discussion that ensues:

1 Identifying the problem:

Teacher:	I've noticed a problem and I need your help to solve it. You know how a lot of children have been playing superheroes like the Power Rangers lately? [Several children nod.] Well, it seems to often end up with someone getting upset or hurt and even crying. What ideas do you have about it?
Jenna:	I hate those guys. I never play.
Henry:	I do. It's fun. Anyway, we need to kill the bad guys.
Raymond:	I hit them if they bother me. That stops them.
Jenna:	I go to a teacher if they bother me.

What's happening: Without casting blame, the teacher states the problem by referring to children's recent direct experience. She then brings the children into the discussion and acknowledges both sides of the problem.

2 Analyzing the problem:

Teacher:	Running to a teacher and hitting are usually things you do when you don't feel safe. What do the Power Rangers do that doesn't make you feel safe?

Raymond: They messed up the spaceship today.

Lai Ling: They're too mean. They yell in your face and they try to kick and punch. I hate them!

Teacher: So you really don't like their noise and their kicking.

Pete: But that's what they're supposed to do. They need to fight the bad guys.

Teacher: So it sounds like that's the problem. That some children like to play-fight, but other don't like it when they come near them or interrupt their games. It makes it hard to feel safe.

What's happening: In this part of the dialogue, the teacher elicits from children the concrete ways in which they are affected. She highlights for everyone what it is about the behavior that creates the problem, acknowledges both sides, and refers again to the issue of safety.

3   Finding solutions:

Teacher: We need to find something to do about superhero play so everyone feels safe. Does anyone have any ideas?

Lai Ling: Play somewhere else.

Teacher: You mean, if you want to play superheroes, you could play in an area away from other children? [Lai Ling nods.]

Riannan: Use your words.

Mark: Say, "Go away."

Gilda: Say, "Don't hit" or "Be quiet."

Raymond: Say, "No play-fighting at school."

Pete: Oh, brother. [Groans.]

Teacher: Pete, it sounds like you don't like that idea. Tell us more.

Pete: Superheroes need to fight. That's what they do to get the bad guys.

Teacher: I wonder if there are other things they could do besides fight.

Henry: Some of them go to high school.

Jenna: Some like to eat pizza.

Darcy: Hey! They could eat at our restaurant [set up in the dramatic play area].

What's happening: Once the problem is clarified, the teacher quickly moves on to brainstorming possible solutions. Playing the part of a translator, she helps children see how their ideas could be put into action and reminds them that feeling safe is the most important requirement of any solution. When she picks up on Pete's groan, she demonstrates that differing viewpoints will be respected, and Pete is comfortable saying what he thinks, rather then what he thinks the teacher wants to hear.

4 Reviewing the problem and solution:

Teacher: You've come up with a lot of good ideas. What if we try some of them tomorrow to see how they work? What if we choose a special place outside away from the others where you can play superheroes? Do you think you could try that? [Several children nod.] And children in the restaurant, do you think you can make a meal for the superheroes? They must get really hungry! [More nods.] Okay, I like that the children who like to play superheroes will have something to do when they play in the classroom besides fighting. We'll talk about how things are going at our meeting tomorrow.

What's happening: The teacher highlights two solutions that she thinks everyone can agree to and that will promote safety. She helps children see what they need to do to begin translating their solutions into practice. Only now does she state a personal value judgment about fighting, and ends by making sure children know they will have a chance to evaluate their solutions after they've tried them.

Learning to lead this kind of give-and-take discussion is challenging, but well worth the effort. Successful dialogues on topics that are personally meaningful to them—in this case, about peace, violence, and how people should treat one another—help children work through their experiences and ideas. As they participate, children are establishing a foundation for living peacefully and responsibly on which they will build for the rest of their lives. Learning to deal nonviolently with small problems and to affect their immediate world today will give them nonviolent ways to solve bigger problems in the wider world tomorrow.

Guiding Your Group's Dialogues

There are a number of underlying principles to keep in mind whenever you engage your children in a give-and-take dialogue. Your group discussions will be enhanced if you make sure to help children in the following ways:

❖ **Define the problem as a shared one.** Young children need help focusing beyond their own wants and needs and seeing program conflicts as dilemmas shared between two or more people.

❖ **Brainstorm possible solutions to the problem.** Coming up with a range of ideas that do not involve fighting poses a challenge which young children usually learn to enjoy.

❖ **Predict how different options might work.** Young children can have a hard time focusing on more than one idea at a time or imagining how a solution will work before actually trying it out. Talking through the concrete actions involved with a solution puts them in a much better position to make informed choices.

❖ **Choose a solution that everyone can agree to try.** The goal here is to find a win-win solution where all children feel their points of view have been heard and respected.

❖ **Help children translate their ideas into practice.** Children will often need help figuring out how to get started on new ways of behaving and coordinating their own actions with those of others.

❖ **Evaluate results.** Afterward, be sure to talk with children about how their solution(s) worked and might be improved. This teaches children that problem solving is part of an ongoing process in which mistakes are okay and that they can get better and better at finding solutions to their problems. It also provides an opportunity for children to reflect on how they each have contributed to creating a safe and caring community.

Resources for Learning More about Children's Play

Carlsson-Paige, Nancy and Levin, Diane E. *The War Play Dilemma: Balancing Needs and Values in the Early Childhood Classroom.* New York: Teachers College, Columbia University, 1987.

_____. *Who's Calling the Shots? How To Respond Effectively to Children's Fascination with War Play, War Toys and Violent TV* Philadelphia: New Society Publishers, 1990.

Cherry, Clare. *Please Don't Sit on the Kids.* Belmont, Calif.: David S. Lake Publishers, 1983.

Levin, Diane E. *Teaching Young Children in Violent Times.* Cambridge, Mass.: Educators for Social Responsibility, 1994.

_____. *Remote Control Childhood? Combating the Hazards of Media Culture.* Washington, D.C.: NAEYC, 1998.

Paley, Vivian Gussin. *Boys and Girls: Superheroes in the Doll Corner.* Chicago: University of Chicago Press, 1984.

Segal, Marilyn and Adcock, Don. *Play Together, Grow Together: A Cooperative Curriculum for Teachers of Young Children.* Published by the authors, 1993.

Slaby, Ron; Roedell, Wendy; Arezzo, Diana; and Hendrix, Kate. *Early Violence Prevention: Tools for Teachers of Young Children.* Washington, D.C.: National Association for the Education of Young Children, 1995.

Encouraging Courtesy and Manners

Courtesy and manners stem from an environment that values caring for others. Children need to learn how to communicate with each other in ways that are respectful, caring, and that recognize the needs of others. Establishing routines and systems that model these attitudes is the most powerful means of helping children learn courtesy and manners. Courteous behavior is also promoted when children feel secure. When children feel safe they can begin to care about others.

This section includes tips and teachable moments for promoting courtesy and manners.

Tips and Teachable Moments: Promoting Courtesy and Manners

Consider how the different routines in your room lend themselves to caring or courteous behavior. Look for ways to give children opportunities to "take care" of each other and behave in ways that show consideration for others.

- ❖ One child could be in charge of opening doors each day or each time the group leaves a room. Choosing the first child in line for this job is sometimes the easiest way to make this work.

- ❖ Children can help hand out materials or check to see if everyone has materials. This system also works at snack time.

- ❖ A helper chart (see "Helper Chart" on p. 2-38) gives the children specific ways to help their peers if the adult in charge is busy.

Hand Hugs

Sometimes children can benefit from having a physical connection with each other. An activity like the hand hug can be used to end an activity or before children leave to go home. These kinds of brief contact experiences can restore good feelings to a group and remind children that they are part of a community.

Have the children stand in a circle with you, holding hands. Squeeze the hand of the child on your right. Have that child squeeze the hand of the child on his or her right, and so on, passing the hand hug around the circle. The hand hug stops when it comes back to you.

Put-Ups

Put-ups are a way of helping everyone feel appreciated and of promoting caring and courteous behavior. At the end of a day or a week, ask children to share a put-up or nice thing someone did for them. This sharing makes a nice closing circle for the end of the program day.

Communication

Children can learn about courteous communication by experimenting with different ways of communicating and seeing which way feels better. It is important for children to learn that courteous communication takes more than adding a "please" or a "thank you." Though these are good words to use, the tone of the voice and the way people ask for things can make a difference in what happens next.

Use the Peace Puppets (or any other puppets) to role-play how one child asks for the markers (or any item) from another child. One version should emphasize a friendly voice as well as a careful choice of words: "Could I please use the markers?" Or, "Are you finished with the markers? Could I have a turn?" Then model an unfriendly demanding version, saying, for example, "I need those markers. It's my turn!"

Ask children:

*   How does the first voice make you feel?
*   How would you answer that request?
*   How does the second voice make you feel?
*   What would you say back?
*   What do you think could happen next?

Ask children to take turns role-playing with the puppets making different kinds of requests.

The Peace Puppets can be used to model a variety of daily communications. The most meaningful role-playing skits will spring from the actual interactions or experiences of the children in the group. (See "Peace Puppets" on p. 8-19.) Regularly observe the way children speak to each other and use negative exchanges as the focus of some of the skits. Some themes to watch for include:

*   Are children inclusive?
*   What are ways to ask if you can join an activity?
*   What are friendly ways to tell someone that it is not possible for him or her to join an activity?
*   How do children behave when they need to take turns or share resources?

❖ Do children know how to support each other or do you observe frequent put-downs?

When children forget to ask for things, or communicate in a way that does not sound courteous, an appropriate response might be: "The way you are asking for the . . . does not make me feel like doing . . ." Or "Could you make your voice friendlier?"

Adult Modeling

You play a key role in modeling the kind of behavior and communication that happen in a courteous and caring environment. You can model good communication skills by:

❖ Looking children in the eyes

❖ Paraphrasing what children say to show that you are trying to understand them

❖ Using encouragement

❖ Redirecting questions back to the group, demonstrating that you want them to share their ideas with each other

❖ Describing behavior in nonjudgmental ways, modeling openness and willingness to see someone else's point of view

❖ Sharing some personal information about yourself, building trust, and encouraging children to feel safe sharing

❖ Using body language that does not contradict your verbal language

❖ Respecting what a child is saying by not interrupting

❖ Using "please" and "thank you" and making requests in ways that respect children and foster politeness

Remember, the parents of the children in your program are your partners in building a Peaceable Program. You may want to share these tips with them. See chapter 16 for more information on including parents in your program.

Developing Communication Skills

Communication skills are a key element in the Peaceable Program. Young children are just beginning to be able to put their ideas and wishes into words and to listen to what others have to say. As children develop and practice these skills, they are better able to adjust to the give-and-take of a group setting. They are able to ask for attention in appropriate ways, to resolve conflicts without shouting or hitting, and to cooperate with other children in work and play. As a result, they feel happier, more confident, and more at peace with themselves and others.

The Peaceable Program gives young children opportunities to build communication skills through games, activities, and daily and weekly routines that emphasize self-expression, vocabulary building, listening skills, and habits of courtesy and respect.

Teaching Communication Skills from a Developmental Perspective

Each child develops in her own way and according to her own timetable. The role of the caregiver or teacher is to help guide the child from one level to the next. Children need adult help to master the social skills associated with communication. Remember that children who are the same age may be at different developmental levels. Also, at moments of stress or anxiety, a child may slip back into old patterns or forget new skills and need your assistance to get back on track. Make sure every child knows you appreciate her special gifts, regardless of the level she is starting from. This helps her feel confident that she can contribute to the group and become a valued member.

1 Start at each child's level

Language is very important to **three- and four-year-olds**. By this age they typically use language to express themselves and are full of questions about the world around them. They will develop communications skills primarily through their play activities. For instance, providing play materials that vary in texture, color, or other qualities will encourage them to learn new words to describe them. Dramatic play also helps build vocabulary, as children pretend to be parents or doctors or auto mechanics. Cooperative and hands-on activities give children the chance to converse and compare notes as they work, practicing both listening and speaking skills.

Five- and six-year-olds are transitioning from being egocentric to learning to respect other members of the group. Waiting for a turn to play or to speak, or recognizing when someone else wants to speak, may represent new and challenging skills—especially since this is an age when many children are bubbling over with chatter and questions. You can model phrases such as "Excuse me" or "Thank you for waiting" to help children learn to respect each other's right to talk.

Seven- and eight-year-olds are able to reflect thoughtfully on what they hear and say. They can begin to see that there is more than one point of view in a conflict. They are ready to begin to practice "active listening"—paraphrasing or reflecting back the speaker's words and feelings. This technique is helpful in de-escalating conflicts, because it prevents misunderstanding and helps children appreciate each other's point of view. One way to begin to teach active listening skills is to ask children to paraphrase or repeat key details as you give them directions. Make sure you give them at least five seconds to respond.

2 Choose goals and skills

The goals of building communication skills are to help children express themselves clearly and confidently, to develop habits of courtesy and respect, and to negotiate solutions when their needs conflict with others'. Some of the skills young children will need to master are:

- ❖ Developing a vocabulary that allows them to communicate clearly
- ❖ Finding words and phrases that allow them to interact respectfully and confidently with others
- ❖ Taking turns talking and listening
- ❖ Recognizing when another person wants to talk or when he or she wants to remain silent
- ❖ Being able to paraphrase what another person has said and to begin to acknowledge the other person's point of view

3 Put it all together

For discrete skill building or intervention, choose a set of skills you would like to teach in your program or classroom. Use chapter 2 and the tips and activities later in this chapter to choose daily routines and practices that reinforce these skills. Use the following sample chart to set goals for children and measure their progress:

Desired Behavior: Taking turns talking and listening

Skill	Daily Routine	Activities	Observable Changes in Behavior
Waiting for a turn to talk	Use a talking stick during circle time Encourage children to say "Excuse me" before joining a conversation or "Just a minute" when interrupted	Ring, Ring! (3-17) You Say, I Say (3-20) Pop-Up Listening (3-12)	Less noise of children talking simultaneously Children say "Excuse me" before joining a conversation

Watch and listen to the conflicts and problems that occur daily. See if there is a pattern to the conflicts such as more children crying during free play time. Decide which communication skills will help reduce the conflicts. Use the daily routines and activities as teachable moments for skill development. Check on your progress by looking and listening to the patterns of conflict. Determine if the skill needs more practice and whether activities need to be made easier or more difficult. Repeat this process as you build the peaceable program.

Setting Up for Success

Monitor the noise level: It's hard for children to practice speaking and listening skills if they can't hear what anyone's saying. If you notice that the room is becoming noisy, you may want to remind children who are speaking loudly to use their "12-inch voices" (voices that can be heard no more than a foot away) or their "indoor voices." Or teach the children that a raised hand is a signal for silence: when they see you raise your hand, they should stop talking and raise their hands until the whole room grows silent.

Keep activity groups small: Playing together fosters conversation among children—but a crowded table or play space can lead to shouting and shoving. Children need opportunities to negotiate with the teacher about how to use the space and how many can use the space at once.

Model respectful communication: The way you talk to children is as important as the things you say. For instance, addressing each child by name reinforces her sense that she is special. Making "excuse me," "please," and "thank you" a part of your daily routine not only sets an example for children, it makes them feel respected and valued. Modeling is also one of the best ways to teach complex communication skills such as asking follow-up questions, getting attention in appropriate ways, or accepting compliments or criticisms.

Use signs: Many teachers find it helpful to learn a few hand signs that represent common concepts, such as raising your hand to signal "stop" or cupping your hand around your ear to signal "listen." Hand signs provide visual cues that reinforce what the teacher is saying. This can be especially helpful for children who are easily distracted or have trouble grasping the main point of information when it is presented verbally.

Bringing It Home: Send home Parenting Connections #3 and #4 after completing some of the activities in this chapter.

Tips for Daily Practice

Notice the positive: Make a point of commenting when you notice one child speaking politely to another. You may say, "Elena, I heard you say 'thank you' to Jill." This helps children become more cooperative and highlights the kind of communication you want to encourage.

Extend children's language: Look for opportunities to extend children's language. For example, when children are struggling over shared materials, you could intervene by prompting: "You could say, 'I want the glue stick, not the glue bottle.'" By helping to clarify communication, you will reduce the number of conflicts that occur.

Teach attentive listening: Use a puppet or another adult to role-play poor listening. Have the character fidget, interrupt, change the subject, and seem distracted. Ask the children: "How do you know she is not listening?" Then ask one of the children to show a better way to listen. Brainstorm a list with the children of what good listening looks like. Put the chart on the wall where you can refer to it often. For young children put pictures next to words. (For more information about the uses of listening and responding see p. 2-25.)

Provide scripts: Provide children with words and phrases for specific occasions that are part of the regular routine of the program. For example, during circle time, when a child isn't ready to speak but still wants a turn, you can prompt her by saying, "You could say, 'I'm still thinking . . .'" and then return to her before moving on to another activity. During a group discussion, some children need more time to respond than others. It is important to allow a child that extra three to five seconds to formulate a response and to teach the other members of the group to respect different needs.

Clarify directions: Classroom conflicts often arise because children are having trouble following directions. Some of the reasons a child may not follow directions include:

* He or she does not understand the directions.
* He or she is not capable of following them.
* He or she does not intend to follow them.

Most children will want to do what you ask. If they don't follow your directions, it's probably because the directions are complicated or confusing. It is especially difficult for young children to receive directions in a large group. Try reframing the directions to make them easier to follow. Ask yourself:

* Are the directions clear?
* How many steps do the directions require? (Most young children cannot follow directions involving more than three steps.)
* Which steps are familiar to the child? Which are new?
* Do the children have the skills to accomplish the new steps?

Guidelines for Giving Directions

Here are some strategies to keep in mind when giving directions either to individuals or a group:

1. Get the children's attention. Observe their body language to gauge readiness. Say: "I will know you are listening when I can see you looking at me."

2. To keep the class focused, use a hand signal, cardboard stop sign, or some other visual cue that tells them to "wait" while you give them directions. You can then give another visual cue to signal "go ahead."

3. Model the directions for them. Use a volunteer from the group to demonstrate what you mean, or act out the steps yourself.

4. Break the directions into simple steps. You may want to provide a visual cue for each step by counting the steps on your fingers. Repeat the steps while showing your fingers. Have the children repeat each step.

5. Use visual cues—miming, pointing, or formal signs—whenever possible. This extra input highlights the most important parts of your message and helps children retain and process the information you provide.

6. Check for understanding. You might use the Thumbs-Up, Thumbs-Down process (p. 8-13) to confirm understanding. If the children don't understand, try rephrasing the directions. Ask for a Thumbs-Up, Thumbs-Down after each step.

7. Once most of the children seem to understand, check to see if there's anyone who may need extra help.

Try to anticipate which children may have trouble following the directions. You may want to consider matching children with partners so that they can help one another. Try to make sure each pair has at least one child who understands the directions clearly. Emphasize that helping does not mean doing it for each other.

When It's Not Working

Ask appropriate questions: If children do not respond to your questions, make sure the type of question you are asking is appropriate to the child's developmental level. You may need to modify the question. Children begin by being able to answer only "yes or no" questions or make concrete choices ("Is it hot or cold?"). The range of questions young children are able to understand and answer follows this sequence (from easiest to hardest): Yes or No? This or That? What? Where? Whose? Who? Why? How many? How? When?

Paraphrase: Many conflicts arise because communication itself is unclear. One way to find out where the breakdown in communication occurred is to paraphrase what you hear a child saying and check it out to be sure you are understanding her intent. For example if a child hits another child you might say: "You hit Michael because your feelings got hurt when he called you a baby." Once you have an accurate understanding of what the child is trying to say, you can provide the specific words or phrases she needs to make herself understood. For example: "Next time, try saying, 'Please don't call me a baby,' instead of hitting him." Teaching young children appropriate verbal responses enlarges their repertoire of skills and decreases unnecessary conflict.

Teach that asking for help is okay: At moments of miscommunication, teach children multiple ways to signal that they need help. For example, if a child seems confused, say: "You could say, 'I don't understand,' and I will try to be clearer." Or when a child asks for clarification spontaneously, you can seize that opportunity to comment on it for the benefit of the others. For example, "Kendra just asked a question that may be important to several of you. Kendra, can I share it?" If it is okay with her, repeat the question and answer it for the group. It is extremely important for children to learn that it is always okay to ask for help.

Avoid communication roadblocks: With good communication, people grow. With poor communication, conflicts grow. Sometimes children hear things differently than we mean to say them. For example, you might say "I want that art corner cleaned up before we go out to the playground." You might intend simply to give children a direction and a time frame, but the children might perceive it as a threat. Words, tone of voice, and body language are all important elements in clear communication. A tone or posture that children perceive as threatening may cause them to "clam up" or become defensive and angry.

Three Roadblocks to Communication with Young Children

1. **Asking Why:** "Why" questions can be perceived as attack questions. They are also developmentally difficult for young children. Children react by shutting down emotionally, lying, making excuses, or denying personal responsibility. Some examples of "why" questions are: "Why are you doing this?" "Why didn't you do that?" "Why can't you do what you're told?"

   Instead, state specifically what behavior you want from children. Give directions clearly. Look around you, notice who needs more coaching, move to that area of the room, and supportively repeat directions.

2. **Being Vague:** Vague or arbitrary commands give children no way to choose to do the "right thing." They have the effect of cornering kids and putting them on the defensive. For example: "Do it right this minute!" "Stop that right now!" "Get over here right now!" While these might be appropriate types of statements in dangerous situations where a child's safety is at stake, you don't want them to become typical interactions with children.

   Instead, give children one or two choices and a chance to follow through on their decisions. For example: "It's clean up time, Maria. Which toys would you like to clean up first, the paints or the blocks?"

3. **Scolding:** Scolding or moralizing and lecturing can make children feel stupid, "bad," guilty, and embarrassed. These responses do not teach children how to become more skillful or motivate them to be more cooperative. Some examples are: "You know better than that." "You never listen." "How many times do I have to tell you this?"

   Instead, coach children with specific responses and model for them the skills they need. For instance, instead of "Don't hit, be good." You might say "Hitting hurts. I can't allow you to hurt anyone." Instead of "Don't ever say that to me." You might try, "I don't like it when you say that. It hurts my feelings." Or instead of "Put your head down," try "You'll feel better if you rest a minute."

Activities in This Chapter:

Other Activities That Teach Communication Skills

- ❖ Stick Up For Yourself (p. 9-14)
- ❖ King of the Playground (p. 9-15)
- ❖ Come Join in the Circle (p. 10-10)
- ❖ Two in a Fight (p. 10-15)
- ❖ Shake, Shake, Freeze (p. 10-17)
- ❖ Smoky Night (p. 11-7)
- ❖ Rainbow Fish (p. 11-9)
- ❖ Mama, Do You Love Me? (p. 11-16)
- ❖ All the Colors of the Earth (p. 11-19)
- ❖ Mrs. Katz and Tush (p. 11-25)
- ❖ The Big, Big Carrot (p. 13-37)
- ❖ Discussion Pictures 1, 4, 8, 9 (chapter 14)
- ❖ Parachute Activities (chapter 15)

Pop-Up Listening

Children play alternating roles as speakers and listeners

Age 3 and up

Objective
- ❖ To build community
- ❖ To practice identifying oneself as a speaker or listener

Materials None

Procedure

1. Have the children kneel in a circle with you.

2. Make a sign for speaking, such as placing your hands by the sides of your mouth in the form of an open O.

3. Have the children practice the sign for speaking.

4. Make up a sign for listening, such as cupping one hand around your ear.

5. Have the children practice the sign for listening.

6. Count off the children in the circle so that some are designated as speakers and others as listeners. Children who are speakers make the speakers' sign. Children who are listeners make the listeners' sign.

7. Tell children that when you call out "Speakers!" the children designated as speakers should pop up and make the speakers' sign while shouting their name. When you call out "Listeners!" the listeners should pop up and make the listeners' sign, but stay silent.

> **tip**
>
> To encourage children to practice careful listening, call out the same group two or three times in a row.

8. Vary the activity by having the children trade roles from speaker to listener.

Hand Hugs

Children give "hand hugs" around a circle

● ●

Age　　　3 and up

Objective
- ❖ To build community
- ❖ To experience waiting for a turn

Materials　None

Procedure
1. Have the children stand in a circle holding hands.
2. Squeeze the hand of the child on your right.
3. Have the child squeeze the hand of the child on his or her right.
4. The hand hug stops when it returns to you.

> **note** You should explain that the squeeze should be gentle. You could say that they should squeeze their neighbors' hand the same way they would want to have their hands squeezed.

Barnyard

Children form groups by making different animal sounds

● ●

Ages 4 and up

Objective
- ❖ To form small groups

Materials
- ❖ 3" x 5" index cards (one for each child)
- ❖ Pictures of the animals you choose in step 1 (one picture is needed for each child)

Procedure

1. Make yourself a list of common farm animals. Put as many animals on your list as the number of groups you want to form. For example, if you want five groups you will need five animals. The animals should be ones that make sounds children can both identify and repeat easily. Try the following: dog, cat, duck, cow, sheep, pig. Collect pictures of the animals on your list and put them on index cards. Make enough cards so that there is one for each child. There should be about the same number of cards for each kind of animal.

   > **tip**
   >
   > This activity can be used either to form groups for small group activities or as a game in itself.

2. Have the children form a circle. Explain that you are going to give each child a card with a picture of an animal. Demonstrate the sound that goes with each animal, for example, a cat says "meow" and a cow says "moo." Explain that when you give the signal they will then make their animal's noise and try to find the other children making that noise.

3. Go around the circle, passing out the cards. Then give the starting signal at which the children begin making their noise and finding others who are making that noise.

4. After a few minutes all the children will be in groups. You can then give instructions for a small-group activity, or just play this game again.

note To extend this activity, try a more challenging version of the game. Instead of giving the children cards, whisper the name of their animals in their ears.

Remembering What You Did

Children receive time each day to
"remember what they did."

● ●

Age 4 and up

Objective
- ❖ To build trust in the group.
- ❖ To practice clear communication skills
- ❖ To help children accept feedback from their peers.

Materials
- ❖ Play phone

Procedure

1. Have the children sit in a circle.

1. Explain that you are going to call someone on the phone. When you call out that child's name, he or she should go to the center of the circle to answer it.

> **tip**
>
> Do this activity as soon after an activity period as possible. Don't ask a child to remember what she did two hours ago. Be specific.

2. Call one child. "Is Megan here today?" When she answers the phone say, "Hello, Megan, what did you do during free play time today?"

3. You will most likely need to give the children "starters." For example, "I saw you in the block area. I wonder what you were building?" or "You started at the math table doing _____. Where did you go after that?"

4. Thank the child and tell her you'll call again. Call on 3 or 4 children each day. Make sure the others know they will have a turn another day. Keep track of which students you've called on and which you haven't.

Ring, Ring!

Children communicate through a telephone
made out of juice cans and string

● ●

Ages 5 and up

Objectives
- ❖ To explore communication
- ❖ To work cooperatively

Materials
- ❖ 8′ lengths of string
- ❖ Empty frozen juice cans
- ❖ Paper clips

Procedure

1. Show children how to make a string telephone. Make a hole in the middle of the closed end of one can. Pull string through the hole and tie it to the paper clip to stop the string from slipping back through the hole. Repeat with the other can.

2. Divide the group into pairs. Help each pair make a string telephone. Be sure children know their "telephone line" must be stretched taut to work. However, the line shouldn't be so tight that they break it or pull it away from the child on the other end.

3. Demonstrate hand signals that indicate who is talking and who is listening. For example, raising your hand above your head would mean you're the listener and putting your hand on your head could mean you're the talker.

4. Have the children take turns talking and listening through the cans. One child talks into one can while another child holds the other can to his or her ear. Have them use the hand signals to indicate who's talking and who's listening.

3-17

Discussion Starter

Through a simple story, children learn
about engaging in a discussion

● ●

Ages   5 and up

Objectives
- ❖ To encourage discussion
- ❖ To model how disagreements can lead to discussion

Materials
- ❖ Talking stick■ or designated object such as a stuffed animal■

Procedure

1. Children sit in a circle or in front of you on the rug.

2. Tell the children you are going to tell a story and you need their help.

3. Tell them the story is about a discussion with another adult they know, perhaps another adult in the room. The children can help by filling in their ideas about what each person might say next. Any child who wants to add to the story needs to be holding the talking stick before beginning to talk.

4. Tell a story about a pretend discussion you had, leaving pauses for the children to fill in. For example:

   > Mrs. Lopez and I were discussing things to think about when you play safely on the playground. I said that the most important thing was _____.
   >
   > She said, "No, the most important thing is _____. "
   >
   > I said, "What makes you think that? "
   >
   > She said, "_____."
   >
   > I said, "I wonder what else is important?"

She said, "Something else that's important is _____."

Then Mrs. Lopez said, "When they're in the playground, children like to play on _____."

I said, "And children in the playground also like to play on _____."

Mrs. Lopez said, "I wonder how they can play on them safely?"

I said, "They can _____."

We talked some more and decided that children could help us with this discussion by telling us what they like to play on and how they could play safely in the playground. What else do you like to play on? How can you play safely?

You Say, I Say

Children share opinions on a topic and repeat what others have said

● ●

Ages   5 and up

Objectives
- ❖ To improve listening skills
- ❖ To encourage tolerance of differing opinions

Materials:
- ❖ Talking stick or designated object such as a stuffed animal

Procedure

1. Have the group sit in a circle. Tell the children to think of something they like to do, especially

   > **tip**
   >
   > This activity works best with older children (ages six and seven).

   - ❖ on the playground
   - ❖ after school
   - ❖ on trips

2. Hand the child on your left the talking stick or special object and ask that child to begin by saying, "When I'm at the playground, I like to _____ ." Ask the child to hand you the stick/object next.

3. Model reflecting what the child said by saying, "You say you like to use the swings when you're at the playground; I say I like to look for ladybugs."

4. Hand the talking stick or object to the child on your right and continue around the circle, with each child responding to the topic after restating what the previous child has said.

House and Telephone Line Mural

Children learn about the telecommunications network and the connection among communities by making a mural

• •

Ages   6 and up

Objectives
❖ To learn about communication between communities
❖ To explore community
❖ To explore other cultures

Materials
❖ Large piece of paper
❖ Cut-outs of houses, a satellite, and "rays" (lightning shapes)
❖ Yarn or string
❖ Popsicle or craft sticks
❖ Glue

Procedure
1. Beforehand, you can cut out shapes of houses and apartment buildings of varying styles and sizes or clip pictures from magazines. Older children may cut their own pictures from magazines. Cut out a picture or outline of a satellite and lightning shapes for rays.

2. Have children select buildings similar to their own houses and glue them on the large sheet of paper.

3. Next, children may take turns gluing sticks between the houses to represent telephone poles. String yarn between the houses and poles to connect the houses.

4. Repeat the process the next day to build a different town, city, or village that children know. Connect this community to the existing telephone lines.

5. The following day, create another community, this one from another part of the world. Connect the homes with more telephone wires. Glue the satellite in the sky between the communities and connect communities to the satellite using the rays.

6. Add more communities as children desire.

Reflection

❖ What are some of the ways people communicate?

❖ How do you communicate with each other? With your parents? With me?

Barrier Game

Children work in pairs with a barrier between them and attempt to make identical creations

● ●

Ages   7 and up

Objectives
- ❖ To practice clear communication
- ❖ To improve listening skills
- ❖ To work cooperatively

Materials
- ❖ Blocks or pattern blocks or shapes

Procedure

1. Create a barrier on a table or floor between two children so they can't see the other side of the table or floor. Barriers can be created with big books or album covers.

2. Give identical materials to each child. For example, if you give five different shapes and colors of pattern blocks to one child, give the identical shapes and colors to the other child.

   > **tip**
   >
   > This game needs to be carefully taught and supervised at first. After children become more familiar with it, they can try it independently.

3. One child leads the pair by creating a pattern or structure that the other child cannot see. Then the leader gives directions by talking to the other child and explaining, step by step, exactly how to create an identical pattern or structure with the same materials.

4. The listening child works to create an identical pattern with the directions given. This child can speak only to ask the leading child questions in order to better understand the directions. He or she cannot look over the barrier to check.

5. When the listening child is ready, the leading child removes the barrier and they both look at their work.

6. Children then switch roles and create new patterns with the same or different materials.

Cooperation

Cooperation is at the heart of the Peaceable Program. When children cooperate, the classroom functions as a community. They learn to appreciate the strengths that each child brings to the group, which creates an atmosphere of acceptance and respect. When children play and work together, the environment is less competitive, because the goal of cooperation is the success of the group rather than the individual.

Working together is a new experience for young children, and they will need to develop and practice new skills in order to feel comfortable relying on one another. The Peaceable Program gives young children opportunities to build cooperation skills through games, activities, and daily and weekly routines that encourage sharing, taking turns, and helping others.

Teaching Cooperation from a Developmental Perspective

Each child develops in his own way and according to his own timetable. The role of the caregiver or teacher is to help guide the child from one level to the next. Children need adult help to master the social skills associated with cooperation. Remember that children who are the same age may be at different developmental levels. Also, at moments of stress or anxiety, a child may slip back into old patterns or forget new skills and need your assistance to get back on track. Make sure every child knows you appreciate his special gifts, regardless of the level he is starting from. This helps him feel confident that he can contribute to the group and become a valued member.

1 **Start at each child's level:**

Three- and four-year-olds view the world from an egocentric perspective. They may not understand that other people are affected by their behavior. You can help them make this connection by reflecting back how their behavior affects other members of the group. ("When you take all the blocks, Jose has nothing to build with!") Learning to take responsibility for their actions is an essential first step in learning to cooperate.

Five- and six-year-olds are often easily frustrated by the struggle to master new skills. Cooperation skills are particularly challenging. Children who are stressed out or frustrated may act out in negative ways. If they become frustrated they may revert back to a previous level of development. If a child does act out in frustration, try to look for the underlying causes, rather than seeing the child as the problem. As the child's skill level increases the child will feel more comfortable and better able to cope with conflict and stress.

Seven- and eight-year-olds are in transition from being adult-centered to being peer-centered. They care passionately about their friendships and are very sensitive to what other children think of them. One way they try to test their abilities and establish a place among their peers is through competition. Teachers can minimize the conflicts that arise from this recurring drive by encouraging groups, rather than individuals, to compete. By collaborating to beat an external goal, such as a time limit, children can feel empowered by their accomplishments without having to engage in personal power struggles.

2 Choose goals and skills:

The goal of teaching cooperation skills is to give children the tools to build a caring, respectful learning community in which they can resolve conflicts peacefully. Some of the skills young children need to develop in order to cooperate are:

- ❖ Listening skills
- ❖ Taking turns
- ❖ Responding positively to others
- ❖ Contributing ideas
- ❖ Asking for help
- ❖ Helping others
- ❖ Learning to accept help
- ❖ Staying with their partners or groups
- ❖ Taking responsibility for their actions
- ❖ Working together toward a shared goal

3 Put it all together

For discrete skill building or intervention, choose a set of skills you would like to teach in your program or classroom. Use chapter 2 and the tips and activities later in this chapter to choose daily routines and practices that reinforce these skills. You may also find helpful the cross-referenced activities from other chapters. For example, in chapter 3 you'll find activities that build communication skills. These may also be helpful in fostering cooperation skills.

Set up a timeline for your goals and check back at regular intervals to measure your progress. You may wish to use the following chart as a guide:

Desired Behavior: Taking turns in play

Skill	Daily Routine	Activities	Observable Changes in Behavior
Taking turns	Hold a class meeting to talk about why taking turns is important. Have children take turns performing classroom chores. Post a chart to make sure each child gets a turn.	Me-You-Lisa (4-13) Send home Parenting Connection #2 and ask parents to help children practice taking turns at home.	Children are willing to wait for their turn to talk or use a toy.

Look and listen to the conflicts and problems that occur daily. See if there is a pattern to the conflicts. Decide which cooperation skills will help reduce the conflicts. Use the daily routines and activities as teachable moments for skill development. Check on your progress by looking and listening to the patterns of conflict. Determine if the skill needs more practice or whether the activities need to be made easier or more difficult. Repeat this process as you build the peaceable program.

Setting Up for Success

Group size: Children will find it easier to cooperate if groups are small. To start teaching cooperation skills and activities, divide the children into pairs. As children become more skilled, they can work in groups of three or four.

Matching pairs and groups: You may want to assign partners to ensure that each pair or group works smoothly. When forming pairs or small groups, try to match children with strong cooperation skills with others whose skills are just emerging. To prevent problems, avoid grouping the most active children together. Keep small-group activities short and focused.

Sharing materials and supplies: When using cooperative activities that involve special materials, decide what your goals are. One goal is for children to cooperate in order to produce something special, like a quilt or a mural. A different goal is for children to learn to share materials. Sometimes it's hard for children to try to accomplish both things at once. If they are concentrating on sharing, they may not be able to focus on the project as a whole or learn the skills that will allow them to use the new material effectively.

If your focus is on teaching children to use a new material, be sure each child has enough. If your focus is on sharing, explain to the children that this is the purpose of the activity. Brainstorm with the group about how to share materials. For example ask, "Can you think of a way to share the crayons and paper in your group so that everyone gets to do a part of the project?"

Providing space: You can modify the physical environment to support and promote cooperative activities. For instance, you can push tables or groups of desks together to enhance opportunities for sharing and cooperation.

When planning a cooperative activity, be sure that there is enough room to do it. Sometimes it may be necessary to allow a group of children to use the hallway or to take the whole group outside. If there are no large spaces available, try doing the activity with half the group while children in the other half are engaged in an independent activity. Stop the activity after one or two turns and rotate the groups.

 Bringing It Home: Send home Parenting Connections #1 and #2 after completing some of the activities in this chapter.

Tips for Daily Practice

Evaluate your routines: You can use classroom routines to create opportunities for children to work cooperatively in small groups, to help each other in concrete ways, and to work out problems and differences when they occur. To identify these opportunities, observe all the different activities and routines that take place during a week-long period. Ask yourself:

- ❖ Are there certain activities that could be done in small groups or pairs?
- ❖ Can children take turns with certain tasks, such as cleaning up or distributing materials?

❖ Which activities and routines are adult directed? Which of these could be more child directed? For example, when a child needs help completing a task or activity, could another child provide it?

Start with the familiar: Use familiar activities to begin teaching cooperation skills. That way, you and the children can focus on mastering the unfamiliar skills without having to master the rules of a new activity at the same time. As the children develop their skills, introduce new activities to reinforce them. Reminding them to apply their cooperation skills during the activity.

Provide examples: Children often hear adults use words like "helpful," "responsible," or "cooperative," but they do not always understand how these concepts translate into practice. Caring and helpful behaviors need to be defined behaviorally. One way to make concepts like these more concrete for young children is through demonstrations or role-plays. For instance two puppets can work together to build a tower out of blocks. Remember that children under six need adults or puppets to role-play.

For older children, you can create charts that list what "caring," "helpfulness," or "respect" look and sound like. Post these charts in the room and use them as reminders.

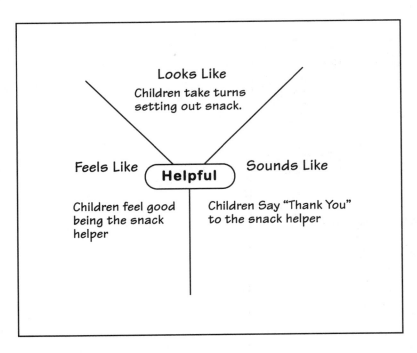

Offer opportunities for helping: Giving children opportunities to help each other not only alleviates some of the demands on the teacher, but also helps children work together toward a common goal. For example, "Zeni, Joe needs some help finishing his book. Could you put the pages in order so he can staple them?"

Use group problem-solving: Use the Peace Puppets to present a problem to the class and ask for ideas. For example, "We have a problem. Amanda and Jessie both want to sit by Nina. They got into a fight when they bumped into each other. What could we do to help them solve their problem?" Allow all the ideas to be treated as possibilities. To choose a solution, ask how children think each solution would feel to the children involved.

Give positive feedback: Look for opportunities throughout the day to comment on examples of cooperation as you see and hear them. For example, "Matt, I really appreciate the way you helped Avi zip his coat." "Kelly and Susan, you put the whole puzzle together by yourselves. Now that's cooperation!"

Use visual cues: To reinforce your positive comments, use visual cues, such as signing "good work" or "thank you" when you catch students working together.

When It's Not Working

Observe: If children don't comply with instructions or perform tasks properly, observe them closely to figure out what the problem is. They may lack a specific skill that you need to demonstrate for them, or they may need to be reminded to use a skill they already have (for example, taking turns). You may need to stop the activity and give directions again.

Recognize silliness and horseplay: In older children, silliness and horseplay may be a signal that children are confused, bored, or frustrated. You may need to stop the activity, redirect the children, or adapt the activity—for instance, by making it simpler or more challenging, quieter or livelier.

Turn the problem over: Whenever possible, turn the problem over to the group. This works best with seven- to eight-year-olds. When a child needs help, you can have him ask another child, or have one group ask another group. You can have a rule: "Ask three before you ask me," meaning that they should ask three other children for help before coming to an adult.

Slowing It Down

Slowing down an interaction as routine as sharing classroom materials can help children focus on the steps involved in sharing and cooperation. For instance discussion on sharing paints might sound like this:

- ❖ What kinds of things do children like to paint?

- ❖ What do you need to do a painting? (space, paper, paint)

- ❖ How many paint boxes does the room have? Are there enough for everybody or do we need to share the paint boxes?

- ❖ Where should we keep paint boxes so people can find them easily?

- ❖ What would be a good way to take turns using the paint boxes?

- ❖ How does it feel when you get a paint box that is dirty or is missing a paintbrush?

- ❖ What kinds of things need to be done to put a paint box away carefully?

Name the problem: Discuss behaviors that make cooperation difficult—whining, quitting, leaving the group, interrupting, disagreeing, or arguing. Use role-plays with people or puppets to lead discussions of these behaviors. Help children suggest reasons why these are not good ways of working together. End by role-playing behaviors that make cooperation easier.

Correct misbehavior: Be directive when necessary. You may need to remove a child from a group, but offer that child a way to get back in. For example, "I'll know you're ready to work again when you tell me you are quiet."

Help a child that is left out: If there's a child that no one wants to be partners with, set the stage for inclusion by saying, "We are all learning how to take turns and listen. Jerry is, too. You are all getting really good at it, and I know you can help him remember how, too." You may need to offer an incentive and lots of positive reinforcement to the children who try to help an excluded child. It is important to acknowledge that a child like Jerry has difficulty joining in the group and to use this dilemma as an opportunity to teach empathy, point of view, and compassion.

Activities in This Chapter:

Cooperative Activities and Initiatives

Activities that Encourage Caring, Helpfulness, and Respect

Other Activities That Teach Cooperation Skills:

- ❖ Rhythm Sticks (p. 10-6)
- ❖ Orchestra (p. 10-8)
- ❖ Parade (p. 10-9)
- ❖ Rainbow Fish (p. 11-9)
- ❖ Now One Foot, Now the Other (p. 11-14)
- ❖ Photo Book (p. 12-3)
- ❖ Monster Book (p. 12-6)
- ❖ Our Community Book (p. 12-7)
- ❖ Cooperative Journal (p. 12-14)
- ❖ Discussion Pictures 1, 2, 4, 6, 7, 8 (chapter 14)
- ❖ Any of the parachute activities (chapter 15)

Cooperative Games and Initiatives

Storming

Children create the sounds of a rainstorm

● ●

Ages   3 and up

Objectives

❖ To encourage careful watching and listening

❖ To demonstrate the beauty of working together

Materials   None

Procedure

1. Ask the children, "Have you ever heard a rainstorm? Let's make our own rainstorm!"

2. Have the children sit in circle.

3. Explain to the group, "We are going to create the sounds of a rainstorm by using our hands and feet. When I wave my hand over each of you, one by one you will begin rubbing the palms of your hands together and continue until everyone has joined in." Beginning in one spot, travel around the circle and wave your hand over every child.

4. Repeat, having the children snap their fingers.

5. Repeat, having the children slap their hands against their laps.

6. Repeat, having the children stomp their feet.

7. Reverse the sequence of these storming sounds to create the effect of the storm dying out.

Me-You-Lisa

Children practice each other's names

● ●

Ages   3 and up

Objectives
- ❖ To improve listening skills
- ❖ To build a sense of community by helping children learn each other's names

Materials
- ❖ A soft ball such as a foam ball.

Procedure

1. Have everyone sit in a circle including yourself.

> **tip**
> This activity is best done at the beginning of the year or when several new children have joined the program.

2. Explain to the children, "Today we're going to practice learning each other's names. It's really important that you listen and make eye contact when someone in the group says his or her name. Then try to remember it!"

3. Explain that when the ball is rolled to a child, that child should say his or her name and then roll the ball back to you. Randomly roll the ball to each child around the circle. Try it again!

> **note**
> Simplify this activity for younger children by having them pass the ball in a clockwise direction and by having children say their own names when they're holding the ball.

4. For older children, explain that you will be going around the circle again, but this time will be different. When the ball is rolled to you, you should say your name, then roll it back not to the adult, but to another child, saying his or her name. Model this with one child.

5. Begin and then repeat!

Follow Me Freeze

Children follow the leader's movements
and freeze when the music stops

● ●

Ages   3 and up

Objective   ❖ To build a feeling of community

Materials   ❖ Cassette player or record player

  ❖ Music cassettes 💼 or records

Procedure   1. Explain to the children: "This game is just like 'Follow the Leader,' but instead of just following what the leader does, you'll copy the leader's movement until I stop the music. Then everyone freezes."

> **note** Simplify this activity for younger children by letting them move in any way when the music is on and having them stop when the music is off.

2. Designate one child as the leader. Then play music while the other children follow the leader.

3. The round ends when you stop the music and children freeze. Have the leader pick another child to be the next leader and start the music again.

4. Repeat, being sure to rotate leaders so that everyone who wants to lead has a turn.

Jump Over the River

Children try to jump
across an imaginary river

● ●

Ages   3 and up

Objectives   ❖ To energize a group

❖ To build community by successfully completing a group challenge

Materials   ❖ Masking tape or two long lengths of rope

Procedure   1. Lay down two parallel lines of masking tape approximately six inches apart. These are the banks of the river.

2. Have the group line up along one side of the river and hold hands. Ask them to jump across the river as a group when you say "One, two, three, over the river!"

3. Give the signal and have everyone jump!

4. Variations on this include having children jump with a buddy, making the river wider in some places, and having children jump one at a time in quick succession.

Sticky Popcorn

Children pretend to be popcorn kernels
in this fun change-of-pace activity.

● ●

Ages   4 and up

Objectives
- ❖ To change pace
- ❖ To build community

Materials   None

Procedure
1. Have the children crouch down, pretending to be kernels of popcorn. Slowly, have the popcorn begin to pop.

2. Once the popcorn begins popping, have them start to "stick" to each other by grabbing hold of the person or people nearest to them. Within a minute or two, the entire group will be hopping and popping in one big bunch.

Pass the Shoes

Children pass their shoes around a circle to the beat of a chant

● ●

Ages   4 and up

Objectives   ❖   To increase cooperation in the group

   ❖   To build a feeling of community

Materials   None

Procedure   1.   Have everyone sit in a circle and remove one shoe. Explain that they will be passing the shoes around the circle to the beat of a chant. The goal is to get one's own shoe back.

> **note** It takes young children a few tries to get the knack of this cooperative activity, but they have fun trying. When they finally get it, they have a wonderful sense of accomplishment.

2.   Teach the chant: "We pass the shoe from me to you. We pass like this and we never, never miss." Then demonstrate the first part of the game:

> We (put your hand on the shoe in front of you)
> pass (pass the shoe to your right)
> the (put your hand on the new shoe in front of you)
> shoe (pass the shoe to your right)
> from (put your hand on the shoe in front of you)
> me (pass the shoe to your right)
> to (put your hand on the shoe in front of you)
> you (pass the shoe to your right)

Give the children plenty of time to practice this before you introduce the second part.

3. With older children you can introduce a second sentence to the chant. In the second sentence, the passing pattern gets a little tricky:

> We (put your hand on the shoe in front of you)
> pass (pass the shoe to your right)
> like (put your hand on the shoe in front of you)
> this (pass the shoe to your right)
> and we (put your hand on the shoe in front of you)
> never (pass the shoe to your right, but don't let go)
> never (bring the shoe back in front of you)
> miss (pass the shoe to the person on your right and let go)

4. This game takes practice. You always know when the group has made a mistake because someone will have a pile of shoes in front of him or her. When a mistake is made, have everyone claim their shoe, then start over.

Mirror, Mirror

Pairs of children mirror each other's movements

● ●

Ages   4 and up

Objective   ❖ To develop cooperation and communication skills

Materials   None

Procedure

1. This activity can be a little confusing, so you may need to demonstrate with a partner first. Tell the children: "Each of you will have a partner. First one of you will lead, and the other will try to copy those movements like a reflection in a mirror. Then you'll switch places and the other will lead. Now you try it!"

2. Have the children form two equal lines facing each other. They'll look across at their partners.

3. Younger children should place their palms together, pretending they're stuck together and have to follow each other's arm movements. For older pairs, the follower can try to copy the movements and facial expressions of the leader without touching. Mirroring is easiest when partners maintain eye contact and move slowly.

4. After a few minutes, ask children to switch leaders. Continue until the two partners move together comfortably and can easily alternate leadership.

5. Create some new partnerships by occasionally shifting someone from one end of a line to the other end.

Reflection   ❖ What was easy or difficult about the activity?

❖ What did you like or dislike?

4-19

Snail, Snail

Children hold hands and form a chain to make a "snail shell"

● ●

Ages 4 and up

Objective
❖ To build community and practice cooperation skills.

Materials
❖ Masking tape

Procedure

1. Tape a circle on the floor about four feet in diameter. The size of the circle will vary depending on the group size—try to make the circle big enough so that each child can sit closely but comfortably.

   > **tip**
   > The song "Snail, Snail" on the *Linking Up!* CD 📀 is a good accompaniment to this game once children understand how to play it.

2. Have the children find a seat in the circle on the tape. Stand in the middle of the circle.

   > **note** To extend the activity try to make the taped circle smaller and smaller while still having everyone work cooperatively with no bumping as they find a seat in the circle

3. Explain that when you give the signal, the children should stand up and form a line by standing side by side holding hands. Have the line move around the circle. Encourage children not to let each other's hands go if they can help it, but also not to hold hands too hard.

4. Once children are able to move in a line without letting go of hands, catch the hand of the child at the end. Explain that the group is going to make a snail by wrapping the line around you. Have the line leader walk slowly around the circle, wrapping the line around you in a spiral. When no one is left moving the snail is complete.

5. Create a signal that means that children should stop and go back to the circle and find a seat.

Touch Red!

At a signal, children touch colors on other children

● ●

Ages   4 and up

Objective
- ❖ To practice identifying colors
- ❖ To practice touching others gently

Materials
- ❖ Masking tape

Procedure

1. Mark a circle on the floor with masking tape. Have the children find a place to stand on the circle.

2. Demonstrate the signal you will use to start and stop the activity:

   - ❖ Clap four times: two slow claps followed by two quick claps.

   - ❖ Children respond by stomping their feet four times: two slow stomps followed by two quick stomps.

> **tips**
>
> ❖ This game can be a good starting point for a discussion about touching, such as where it is appropriate to touch another person.
>
> ❖ If your children are too rough during this game, tell them to touch each other the way they would touch a small kitten.
>
> ❖ The activity "Sleeping Birds" on p. 10-22 also teaches gentle touching.

3. When children hear the start signal they should mill about the play area. When you say "Touch red!" have them find someone wearing red and touch the red. When everyone is touching some red, give the signal and have them return to the circle.

4. When the children have all returned to the circle, give the start signal again. This time try announcing another color such as "Touch blue!"

5. Try having children touch body parts ("Touch elbows!") or articles of clothing ("Touch shoes!")

Cross the River

Children work together
to get everyone across the river

● ●

Ages   5 and up

Objectives
- To encourage cooperative and helping behavior
- To build a feeling of community

Materials
- "Lily pads" made from 8" x 12" pieces of green grip liner▪ or construction paper
- Masking tape

Procedure

1. Use the masking tape to make two parallel lines approximately 12 feet apart. Explain that these are the banks of the river. The goal of this game is to get everyone across the river without anyone falling in. Have the group gather on one side of the river.

> **tip**
>
> This activity is a nice introduction or follow-up to reading the book *It's Mine!* by Leo Lionni. ▪

2. Show the green squares and explain that they are the lily pads. The children will use them to cross the river. Put the lily pads in the river and show how the lily pads can be used as stepping stones to get across the river.

3. Remind them that the goal is to get everyone across the river and encourage them to follow you, but to do it carefully so that no one falls in or steps in the river. If anyone does, the whole group has to start again.

4. The first couple of times you play this game it is enough simply to cross the river this way. You can then create variations like leap frogging from pad to pad.

Fabric Braid

Children work together to create
giant fabric braids that are used to decorate the room

● ●

Ages   5 and up

Objective   ❖ To work cooperatively

Materials   ❖ Fabric strips or ribbons (8′ long)

Procedure   1. Help the children form groups of three.

2. For each set of three children, knot three strips or ribbons together at one end. Fasten the knotted end to a chain link fence or chair.

note This activity works best with older children. If possible, let each child pick the colors they would like to braid.

3. One child takes the free end of each strip, holding it taut.

4. A child on one side lifts her strip over the head of the child in the middle, then moves to his other side. Meanwhile, the child in the middle moves to the vacated side.

5. Repeat the process on the other side. Continue alternating sides until the braid is complete. Knot the end. Braids can hang in the doorway like a walk-through curtain or frame pictures on walls. If they're braided tightly enough, braids make great jump ropes!

Popsicle Sticks

Children work cooperatively to make pictures
with Popsicle sticks

● ●

Ages　　5 and up

Objective　❖ To practice simple cooperation skills

Materials　❖ Wooden Popsicle sticks

Procedure:

1. Explain the task to the children. Say: "You will be working with a partner. I will give you and your partner a pile of Popsicle sticks. I want you and your partner to make a picture of a house using the sticks. There are only two rules: (1) both of you help decide what your house will look like, and (2) both of you help make it. I will help you if you need it."

> **tip**
>
> Adapt this activity for younger children by giving each pair of children a small stuffed animal. Ask the children to use the Popsicle sticks to make a picture of a house for their stuffed animals.

2. Divide children into pairs and give each pair approximately 20-25 sticks. Tell children they may have more sticks if they need them. As the groups are working, circulate and name the cooperative skills you see children using, e.g.: "Jamal and Warren are talking about their ideas," "Shannon and Courtney are taking turns putting their sticks down." Also help children who are stuck or having problems.

3. When everyone has finished, give them all a chance to see the creations of the other groups. Then help the children reflect on their process for a minute or two. Ask the following questions:

   ❖ What was most fun about this activity?

❖ What's something you and your partner did well?

❖ What could you say to your partner to let him know he did a good job?

4. You can repeat this activity many times using the sticks or other materials such as toothpicks, Tinker Toys, or clay. Ask the children to make pictures (or sculptures) of different things each time you do this activity. As children get more skillful, you can begin to allow them to decide what they are going to make. Finally, with older children, you can also use groups of three or even four. They will need lots of practice.

Cooperative Monster-Making

Children work on creating monsters,
with each child assigned a specific role

● ●

Ages   5 and up

Objective   ❖ To work cooperatively

Materials   ❖ Construction paper

❖ Crayons

❖ Scissors

❖ Tape

❖ Role cards (one set per group), see p. 4-27.

Procedure   1. Divide children into groups of four. Explain that each
group is to create a monster and come up with a
description of the monster. The rules are simple: everyone
in the group helps decide what the monster will be like
and everyone in the group helps make the monster. Each
child is in charge of drawing and cutting out a body part.
Each child can make the body part look however he or she
wants it to look.

2. Explain that you will be giving role cards to the group.
Everyone in the group will have a specific job to do. Give
each group a set of cards, face down, and have the group
members pick cards.

3. Give each group the materials they need to create their
monsters and have them begin. Circulate to help those
groups who need it.

4. When each group has finished its monster, have them tape
the body parts together and share their monster with the
other groups.

Monster
Role Cards

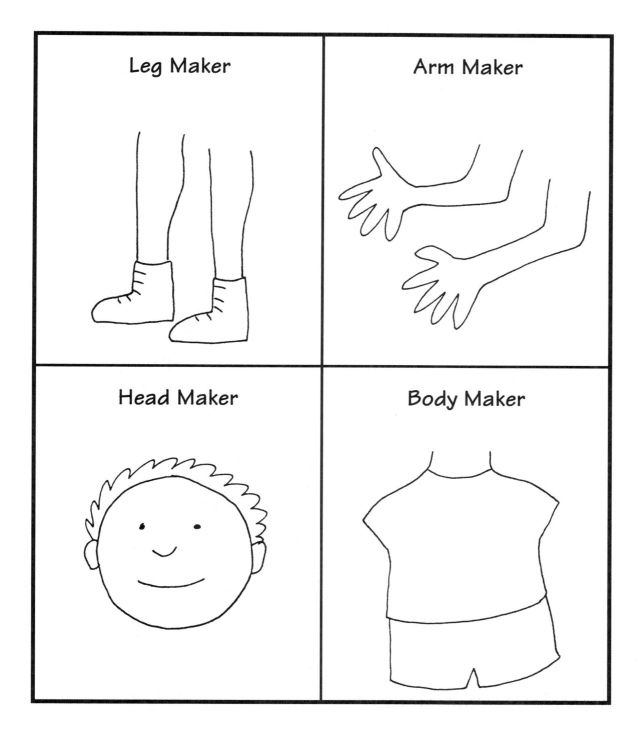

| Leg Maker | Arm Maker |
| Head Maker | Body Maker |

Cooperative Painting

Children give each other directions
in this painting activity

● ●

Ages   6 and up

Objectives
❖ To encourage cooperation

❖ To encourage careful communication as part of helping others

Materials
❖ Paper and crayons

❖ Easels and easel paper

❖ Tempera paint

❖ Paint brushes

Procedure
1. Give each child paper and crayons. Model the activity by giving directions for what they should draw as you draw it yourself, e.g., "I am drawing a green triangle in the center of the paper. You draw one too. Next to it I am putting a red square. You put one too. On the top of the square, I am drawing a blue circle. You put one on your paper."

2. Next, set up the easels so that the children will be working on opposite sides of the easel. Divide the children into pairs and assign them to an easel. Designate one child in each pair as the leader.

3. Have the leader paint a "shapes painting" and give directions to his or her partner, such as, "I am drawing a green triangle. I am painting the inside of the triangle blue." As the leader gives directions, the partner follows, trying to reproduce the leader's painting. Encourage the partners to ask their leaders questions when they don't understand something.

4. After a few minutes have the leaders and the partners change roles. When everyone is finished, let them compare and talk about their paintings.

Reflection

❖ What helped you make your painting?

❖ What's something that would make this activity easier if you did it again?

Activities that Encourage Caring, Helpfulness, and Respect

Caring comes naturally to young children. Studies show that even infants exhibit behavior that is altruistic and caring in nature. But cruelty also comes natually to young children. In working with children, we have the opportunity to nurture and develop their caring impulses as we discourage their cruelty.

Caring, helpfulness, and respect are the cornerstones of cooperation. Children learn how to be caring and respectful primarily through example. Young children are natural observers and are aware not only of how they are treated, but how adults around them respond to others. From a child's point of view, the way you speak, behave, and handle your own mistakes does more to set the tone in the room than any other course of action. Caring or respectful behavior goes beyond simple courtesy. Qualities such as empathy, respecting differences, and learning to communicate with others contribute to being a caring individual.

Frozen Bean Bag

Children help each other move around
the room with bean bags on their heads

● ●

Ages   4 and up

Objectives
- ❖ To experience helping others as a part of cooperation
- ❖ To develop social skills

Materials
- ❖ One bean bag for each child
- ❖ Cassette player with lively dancing music

Procedure

1. Explain that the object of this game is for children to help each other so that everyone can keep moving throughout the song.

> **tip**
>
> You can adapt this game for younger children by pairing the children and then playing. Partners are responsible for helping each other or other pairs who might need help.

2. Demonstrate how to bend at the knees to keep a bean bag on your head and pick up one for a friend.

3. Give each child a bean bag to put on her head.

4. Start the song and encourage the children to dance around the room.

5. If the bean bag slips off a child's head, he or she is "frozen" and must stop moving. Children who see someone frozen should try to help that person by picking up the bean bag and replacing it on the frozen child's head. If the helper's bean bag should fall off during this, then she is frozen as well. Soon everyone will be frozen.

Reflection
- ❖ What things helped you keep the bean bag on your head?
- ❖ How can you ask someone for help when you need it?
- ❖ What are some of the ways you help people in your class?

The Kindness-Catcher Camera

Children learn to identify acts of kindness by seeing
photographs of their classmates being kind

● ●

Ages   4 and up

Objective
- ❖ To encourage acts of kindness and cooperation

Materials
- ❖ Camera and film
- ❖ Display space

Procedure

1. Show the camera to the group and explain that it is your Kindness-Catcher Camera. You will be looking for children performing acts of kindness and you will catch those kind acts by taking pictures with the camera. Show the display space and give it some type of label, such as "Kindness Corner" or "Kids' Random Acts of Kindness." Explain that this is where you will display the pictures you take.

2. For the next few days, take pictures whenever you see children sharing, working cooperatively, or helping each other. It's important to try to get at least one photograph of every child, and preferably more. Post the pictures in the display space. You may want to label the act of kindness that is being performed.

3. Use the Kindness-Catcher Camera throughout the year. As you add new pictures to the display, give children the old pictures to take home. Again, be sure you take enough pictures so that everyone gets to take one home.

Musical Shapes

Children help each other in playing
this cooperative variation on musical chairs.

● ●

Ages   4 and up

Objectives
  ❖ To experience cooperation by playing a game
  ❖ To experience helping others as a part of cooperation
  ❖ To develop social skills

Materials
  ❖ Masking tape
  ❖ Music cassette
  ❖ Cassette player

Procedure
  1. Using the masking tape, make large geometric shapes on the floor of the play area. Make two circles, two squares, and two triangles. The shapes should be about three feet across. (The size will vary depending on the number of children playing the game. You want the shapes to be big enough to hold most of the children, but not so big that it easily holds all of them. Otherwise there is no challenge to the game.)

  2. Have the children identify each shape. Then explain that you will play music and they will march around in a circle until the music stops. When the music stops, they should stop moving and listen. You will say the name of a shape and they will try to stand in that shape. Emphasize that the goal is for everyone to fit inside the shapes.

  3. Play the music and have the children begin marching. Stop the music and name one of the shapes, such as "circle." The group must then find a circle to stand in. Encourage them to help everyone fit inside a circle. Compliment the

group on their helpfulness, then start the music again and keep playing the game.

Reflection

❖ How did you help everyone fit into the shapes?

❖ What were some of the things you did that didn't help others?

❖ What will you try to remember the next time you play this game?

Paper Flowers

Children make paper flowers and give them as gifts

• •

Ages   5 and up

Objective
- ❖ To work cooperatively on an art project
- ❖ To express affection by making and giving a gift

Materials
- ❖ Liquid water colors (cups of water with watercolors in them)
- ❖ Round coffee filters
- ❖ Pipe cleaners or twist ties
- ❖ Eyedroppers
- ❖ Cups
- ❖ Newspaper

Procedure
1. Cover the table with newspaper. Lay cups out on the table and fill them with liquid watercolors. Lay out eyedroppers next to the cups.

2. Divide the children into pairs and give each a flattened coffee filter and an eyedropper. Instruct children to carefully drop color on the filter and watch color spread. Slowly add more drops until the filter is completely colored. Colors can be mixed on the filter—wherever edges meet, the colors will blend.

3. Set the filters aside to dry.

4. Once they are dry, have one child grab the center of a filter, twisting the center to form a cone. Meanwhile, another child can wrap a pipe cleaner or twist tie around the twisted end. You may need to give younger children some assistance with this step.

4-35

5. When all pairs of children have finished their flowers, put them together to make a bouquet. You could offer it with a note of thanks or concern to someone special to the group: a janitor, the curator of a museum the group has visited, or a sick friend.

Reflection

❖ What are some times you've given gifts?

❖ Who have you given gifts to?

❖ Who will you give your flower gift to?

Measure Yourself

Using a piece of yarn,
children help each other measure common objects

● ●

Ages   5 and up

Objective   ❖ To encourage helping behavior

Materials   ❖ Yarn

❖ Scissors

Procedure   1. Divide children into pairs. Give each pair a long piece of yarn. Have each child lie down while her partner measures the child with the piece of yarn. Have each child cut the yarn so that it is as long as her partner.

2. Next have the children reverse roles, so that each child ends up with a piece of yarn as long as him or herself.

3. Take the children outside and have each child bring along his yarn. Have the children use their yarn to find out which things are bigger or smaller than themselves. Encourage the children to help each other by helping others hold the yarn straight, etc.

Reflection   ❖ What are some of the things you and your partner found that are bigger than you are?

❖ What are some of the things that are smaller? The same size?

❖ What are some of the ways you and your partner helped each other?

Who Do You Help?

Children make a mobile that identifies the people they help and how they help them

● ●

Ages   5 and up

Objective: ❖ To encourage helpfulness by displaying the ways children already help others

Materials: ❖ Camera and film

❖ Plastic or wire hangers

❖ Yarn

❖ Hole punch

❖ Paper plates with a hole punched near the edge

Procedure: 1. Discuss helping with the children. Ask them, "What is helping? How have you been helped by others? How are you helpful to people at home? In school? Where else?"

> **note** With younger children, simplify this activity by having them make just one drawing of a helpful or kind act, and skip step three.

2. Give each child three paper plates. Have the children draw a picture of themselves helping someone on each of their plates. For each illustration, have the child dictate to you who she is helping and how she is helping them, for example: "I help Grandpa move things in the garage." Write this below the illustration.

3. Thread the yarn through the hole in the paper plate and attach it to the hanger. Take a photo of each child with the camera and tape the picture of the child to the hanger.

4. Older children may want to add more paper plates to their mobile.

Expressing Emotions

Emotions dominate the world of young children. Because they live so much in the moment, children are easily caught up in the sweep of powerful feelings. They may feel overwhelmed by disappointment or frustration, or become overexcited at moments of joy or celebration. To cope with the emotions they experience, children need to be able to recognize and name their feelings and find ways to express them appropriately. As they become fluent in the language of emotions, able to interpret their own and others' behavior, they will also learn to empathize with others.

Recent research shows the importance of emotional intelligence—both intrapersonal intelligence (being in touch with one's own feelings) and interpersonal intelligence (being perceptive and empathetic toward others). The Peaceable Program emphasizes both of these emotional intelligences. Teaching young children to express and manage their emotions will help create a calmer, more caring classroom environment. .

The Peaceable Program places feelings at the center of the curriculum. The matter-of-fact acceptance of feelings helps children feel secure and often defuses classroom conflicts. At the same time, children learn to distinguish between appropriate and inappropriate ways of expressing their emotions. They learn this through the feedback of the teacher and peers. Through daily routines, activities, and games, children develop the skills to name their feelings and share them in a safe way.

Teaching Emotional Expression from a Developmental Perspective

Each child develops in her own way and according to her own timetable. The role of the caregiver or teacher is to help guide the child from one level to the next. Children need adult help to master the social skills associated with emotional expression. Remember that children who are the same age may be at different developmental levels. Also, at moments of stress or anxiety, a child may slip back into old patterns or forget new skills and need your assistance to get back on track. Make sure every child knows you appreciate her special gifts, regardless of the level she is starting from. This helps her feel confident that she can contribute to the group and become a valued member.

1 Start at each child's level

Three- and four-year-olds view the world in terms of their own feelings. Adults need to help them learn that when they bite, hit, or say mean things, it is hurtful to others. Most children this age also have a limited vocabulary for describing feelings—"mad," "sad," "glad," and not much more. As they learn new words—

"furious," "disappointed," "delighted"—they may feel more able to make themselves understood without having to use their bodies.

Five- and six-year-olds may feel stressed by the challenges of "not being a baby" any more, especially when they find themselves grouped with older children. Rapid changes in maturity and ability often put them on a roller coaster of emotions as they plunge from confidence and exuberance to ambivalence and insecurity. They need help learning to cope with these mixed feelings. By modeling compassion, teachers can help children this age accept themselves and stand up for themselves with other children.

Seven- and eight-year-olds are tough on the outside but soft on the inside. Their feelings are hurt easily and they need the support of others to help with their fears and worries. This is the age when "put-downs" become common; it's a perfect opportunity to help them learn to use "put-ups" instead.

2 Choose goals and skills

The goals of emotional expression are to help children learn to recognize the wide range of emotions that they are feeling, navigate the ups and downs of intense feelings, and express feelings appropriately in connection to others. Some of the discrete concepts and skills that help children reach these goals are:

- ❖ Appreciating the range of human emotions
- ❖ Developing a vocabulary of feelings
- ❖ Gaining the ability to express different feelings in positive ways
- ❖ Learning self-control
- ❖ Responding compassionately when others are expressing emotions

3 Put it all together

For discrete skill building or intervention, choose a set of skills you would like to teach in your program or classroom. Use chapter 2 and the tips and activities later in this chapter to choose daily routines and practices that reinforce these skills.

In helping children develop the skills associated with emotional intelligence, it is important to assure them that whatever feelings they bring to the group are okay. For example, when one child says to another, "You're a baby, because only babies cry," you can take the opportunity to explain that all of us feel sad and hurt sometimes and that it's okay to cry. Use the following sample chart to set your goals for children and measure their progress:

Desired Behavior: Developing a vocabulary of feelings words

Skill	Daily Routine	Activities	Observable Changes in Behavior
Learn two new words for happiness	Model new words during circle time	Read *Chrysanthemum* (9-11)	Children use the word joy and delight

Setting Up for Success

Materials and space: Provide materials and spaces that set the stage for social and emotional learning. For example, a dramatic play area well stocked with dress-up clothes and props can provide the setting for a youngster to become a concerned doctor or anxious patient, a courageous firefighter or terrified victim awaiting rescue, a bossy parent or a whiny child. By changing the clothes and props regularly you can allow for a variety of themes and even suggest new ones.

Security objects: You may wish to allow young children to keep security objects such as blankets or toys with them until they feel safe. You can also provide familiar toys to ease the transition from home to the new setting.

Teach self-control: There are lots of games and activities that can help children develop self-control. Examples include stop-and-go games, such as Red Light, Green Light or Shake, Shake, Freeze; or games like Simon Says and Mother, May I? You can also try alternating fast and slow music as children dance.

Make a feelings chart: Make a "feelings chart" and post it at the front of the room. To start a "feelings chart," write the word "happy" at the top of a sheet of newsprint. Draw a happy face to provide a visual cue for nonreaders. You can also take pictures of your children demonstrating the emotion. Ask children to suggest other words they know that mean "happy." List these words under the happy face. Extend the chart to include lists of words for other emotions, such as "sad" or "mad." Students can add new words as they learn them. You can define other words for them by giving examples. For instance, you might say, "'Frustrated' is the way you feel when you are trying really hard to do something and it won't work, like when you can't find a piece for a puzzle." If you give a concrete example, you can draw a symbol, such as a puzzle piece, to remind children of the association between the word and the feeling. There are many "feelings" posters available, such as "How Do You Feel Today?" from Frank Schafer Publications (1-800-421-5565).

Use role-plays: Role-plays are good way to demonstrate feelings and then match words to them. Remember, children under five or six need help to participate in role-playing. Use puppets, dolls, or another adult to do role-plays with this age group. Gradually include one or two children in pantomimes and role-plays as they become familiar with the format.

You may want to give guidelines for audience behavior during these activities. For example, you might say, "I want you to use good listening skills. Keep your eyes on the speakers; no talking; save your applause for the end." You can also take this opportunity to model giving feedback: "I like the way you said your part. I could really tell you were feeling sad."

Use stories: Use stories and books to help children learn new words for feelings. When reading stories or books, look for new words that describe feelings children are already familiar with ("thrilled," "petrified," "miserable," etc.) After reading the book, provide the sentence starter, "A time I felt _____ was_____." Children can use this as the launching place for a discussion or a journal entry. Writing or drawing in a journal is a good outlet for emotional expression. (Children too young to write can dictate as they draw.) The activity can also lay the groundwork for developing empathy, as children realize that other people sometimes feel the same way they do.

 Bringing It Home: Send home Parenting Connection #5 after completing some of the activities in this chapter.

Tips for Daily Practice

Build a feelings vocabulary: Take every opportunity to help children learn new words to describe their feelings. Make sure you give words for positive emotions at least twice as often as negative ones. For instance, "Sam, you must feel proud of helping Ewan tie his shoes," or "Ellen, your face looks so cheerful this morning!"

Encourage discussions at circle time: Exploring different feelings at circle time allows children to take a more neutral view of emotions. The atmosphere created by this matter-of-fact discussion may have a calming effect on children who are fearful of the intensity and power of their own feelings. One concrete place to start is by focusing on the behaviors and expressions associated with feelings. Ask children:

- What do you do when you're happy?
- How does your face look?
- What does the rest of your body do?
- How do you sit?
- How do you sound?

You can repeat this discussion using different feelings, such as sad, proud, or worried.

Pay attention to children's moods: You can help children make the connection between feelings and behavior by noticing and giving words to their moods and feelings. You might say, "You look like you're feeling happy today, Mina. Did anything special happen?" or "Michael, your tone of voice sounds angry. I wonder why."

Model: Show children how to label feelings by naming your own feelings during the day. When you do this, it not only helps children recognize feelings but gives them permission to talk about their own feelings.

Provide materials: Provide art and building materials that offer an outlet for emotional expression. For example: clay or playdough, drawing and painting materials, building materials, water or sand tables. Children may also use dolls or toy figures to explore emotions.

Promote reflection: Use the reflection questions and topics at the end of each activity to help children reflect back on their feelings. For example, "How did we feel when we played Shake, Shake, Freeze? What did we do to show that we enjoyed ourselves?" This will help them identify their feelings and encourage them to think about why they feel the way they do.

When It's Not Working

Clarify their feelings: When children are in the grip of emotion, it helps if an adult can clarify what is going on for them. Some useful phrases are:

- ❖ It seems like you might be feeling . . .
- ❖ Could it be that you feel . . .
- ❖ Does this [situation] make you feel . . . ?
- ❖ You look like you feel . . .
- ❖ You sound like you feel . . .

Asking these sorts of reflective questions helps children connect their behavior to their feelings. Children also feel more secure sharing their feelings when they know you are attentive.

Support children's empathy: When children sense that another child is sad, lonely, or upset, they are often curious about what is going on. These situations can be used to build empathy. Encourage children who are involved in the situation to look for physical cues that will help them identify how the other child is feeling. This may help them understand their own role in creating the situation or think of ways they can help.

You can also encourage children to ask questions about how the other child is feeling. Explain that assuming we know how someone else feels can sometimes lead to problems. You can suggest they ask, "Are you mad?" or "Are you okay?"

Provide outlets and strategies: Provide outlets for children when they are frustrated, overexcited, or sad. Allow them to choose (with your guidance) cooling-off activities, or set aside quiet places for them to be alone and regroup. (See chapter 6 for cooling-off techniques.) You can also teach children specific strategies, such as taking deep breaths, that help them regain control of their emotions. (See "Anger Cues, Triggers, and Reducers" on p. 6-6.)

Trace the cause: When a child is calm enough to discuss his or her feelings, you can help him figure out the source of the outburst and plan a more appropriate response. One way to do this is to ask questions. Once children have linked their feelings to the specific situation, you can initiate a problem-solving discussion.

Activities in This Chapter:

- ❖ Feelings Share (p. 5-10)
- ❖ Good News (p. 5-11)
- ❖ Feelings Soup (p. 5-12)
- ❖ Helping Hands (p. 5-13)
- ❖ Feeling Cube (p. 5-15)
- ❖ Feeling Cards (p. 5-17)
- ❖ Mashed Potatoes (p. 5-18)

Other Activities That Teach the Expression of Feelings:

- ❖ Hand Hugs (p. 3-13)
- ❖ Storming (p. 4-12)
- ❖ Jump Over the River (p. 4-15)
- ❖ Pass the Shoes (p. 4-17)
- ❖ Touch Red! (p. 4-21)
- ❖ Cross the River (p. 4-22)
- ❖ Cooperative Monster-Making (p. 4-26)
- ❖ Concentration (p. 7-13)
- ❖ Skin Tone Mural (p. 7-12)
- ❖ Family Pictures (p. 7-14)
- ❖ Oh Give Me a Home (p. 7-16)
- ❖ Same/Different (p. 7-18)
- ❖ Colors, Beautiful Colors (p. 7-19)
- ❖ Name Cards (p. 9-8)
- ❖ Chrysanthemum (p. 9-11)
- ❖ Group Agreement (p. 9-13)
- ❖ King of the Playground (p. 9-15)
- ❖ Shakers (p. 10-3)
- ❖ Parade (p. 10-9)
- ❖ Come Join in the Circle (p. 10-10)
- ❖ Two in a Fight (p. 10-15)

❖ It's Mine! (p. 11-2)

❖ Smoky Night (p. 11-7)

❖ Rainbow Fish (p. 11-9)

❖ Someone Special, Just Like You (p. 11-12)

❖ Now One Foot, Now the Other (p. 11-14)

❖ Mama, Do You Love Me? (p. 11-16)

❖ All the Colors of the Earth (p. 11-19)

❖ I Like Me (p. 11-21)

❖ Mean Soup (p. 11-23)

❖ Mrs. Katz and Tush (p. 11-25)

❖ Our Community Book (p. 12-7)

❖ Feelings Book (p. 12-9)

❖ Mike, The Lonely Dog (p. 12-12)

❖ Story Pictures (p. 13-9)

❖ The Sun and the Wind (p. 13-17)

❖ The Big, Big Carrot (p. 13-37)

❖ Discussion Pictures 2, 3, 4, 5, 6, 7, 9, 10, 11, 12

Feelings Share

Children describe their feelings about a recent group activity

● ●

Ages   3 and up

Objectives
- ❖ To build community
- ❖ To recognize feelings
- ❖ To experience waiting for a turn

Materials
- ❖ 1-3 special objects, such as polished stones or shells. (Safety note: pick objects that are larger than the opening of a 35 mm film canister.)

Procedure

1. Have the children sit in a circle with you and teach them the following rhyme (modeled on "Mary wore a red dress"):

   Michi was excited, excited, excited
   Michi was excited about seeing lions today!

2. Have them hold their hands in their laps with palms open.

3. Explain to children that when you pass by you will pat each child's hands.

4. Put a special object in three students' palms as you pat their hands.

5. Give each of the three children a turn to share his or her feelings about recent activity that the group participated in.

6. Have the group repeat the rhyme by substituting the name and feeling in the "Michi was excited" rhyme.

7. Make the activity part of your routine after group activities. Keep track of which children you've called on to make sure that each child eventually gets a turn.

Good News

Children sit in a circle making positive statements
and sharing their feelings

● ●

Ages   3 and up

Objectives
- ❖ To promote communication
- ❖ To express positive feelings

Materials
- ❖ Talking stick or designated object such as a stuffed animal

Procedure
1. Have children sit in a circle so they can make eye contact with each other. Children may talk only when they have the talking stick or stuffed animal in hand.

2. Begin by saying, "Let's share some good news!" Model saying something positive to the group and tell how you feeling about it. Then hand the talking stick or stuffed animal to the first child.

3. The first child says something positive and says how he or she is feeling. Then that child hands the talking stick to the child on the right and so on, until the stick travels around the entire circle.

Feelings Soup

Children add ingredients to "soup" in the form of different emotions

● ●

Ages   4 and up

Objective   ❖ To explore the expression of feelings

Materials   None

Procedure
1. Designate an area as the "soup bowl." An area rug is perfect, but any space large enough to hold all the children standing will do. Have the children form a circle around this area.

2. Explain that you are making "Feelings Soup" and you want to add different feelings. Choose a feeling, such as happiness. Ask the group to show you how happiness looks.

3. When everyone is looking happy, take three of the children from the circle and add them to the soup by bringing them into the center of the soup bowl space. They should continue their happy looks and movements, even when other ingredients are added to the soup.

4. Choose another feeling and have the remaining children show you how it looks. Then choose a few children and add them to the soup. Continue until all the children are in the soup.

Helping Hands*

Children make a rainbow out of pictures of their hands
labeled with times that they were kind and helpful

● ●

Ages   4 and up

Objective:
- ❖ To encourage kind and helpful behavior by identifying helpful acts

Materials:
- ❖ Colored construction paper cut into 4"x 4" squares (you will need a red, orange, yellow, green, and blue square for each child participating)
- ❖ Scissors
- ❖ Pencils
- ❖ Paste
- ❖ Large sheet of mural paper

Procedure:
1. Begin by spreading out the mural paper. In pencil, draw one large arch on the paper to form a rainbow. Continue drawing arches below or above this one until you have a rainbow with five arches. Label each section of the rainbow with the words "red," "orange," "yellow," "green," and "blue." Use colored markers for children who cannot read. Hang the rainbow on the wall where children will be able to reach it.

2. Give each child one of construction paper squares and a pencil. Have children trace their hands on the paper and label the paper with their names. (You can help younger children write their names.)

3. Have each child tell you of an act of kindness he or she performed. Write this on the palm of the paper hand,

---

* Adapted with permission from William J. Kreidler, *Elementary Perspectives* (Educators for Social Responsibility: Cambridge, MA, 1990.)

making sure the child's name and act of kindness are written within the hand outline. If the children are able, have them cut the hands out. If your children cannot manage scissors, skip this step and go right to step four.

4. Have children paste their "Helping Hands" on the appropriate color of the rainbow. Repeat the process over the next several days until all the rainbow is filled in with helping hands. Then post it where parents will be able to see it.

Feeling Cube

Children use a special die to play a game
that involves acting out and identifying feelings

• •

Ages   5 and up

Objective
❖ To identify feelings

Materials
❖ Feeling Cube model (p. 5-16)

❖ Glue

❖ Paper

❖ Cardboard

Procedure
1. Make your cube by starting with the model on p. 5-16. Copy the model onto a sheet of paper and glue the sheet to cardboard. Cut the cardboard along the outer edges of the copied model. Score and fold covered cardboard along the lines of the model to form the cube. Secure the edges with tape.

2. Children roll the cube like a die. When a picture comes up, have them name the emotion and make a face to demonstrate it.

3. Make the cube more interesting by asking children to try these variations:

❖ Make a sound to go with the feeling.

❖ Use your whole body to demonstrate the feeling.

❖ Tell one thing someone might do if they felt this way.

❖ Say something someone might say if they felt this way.

Feeling Cube Model

Feeling Cards

Children use special cards to play a game
that involves acting out and identifying feelings

● ●

Ages   5 and up

Objective
- ❖ To identify feelings

Materials
- ❖ Feeling Cube model (p. 5-16)
- ❖ Paper
- ❖ Cardboard
- ❖ Glue

Procedure
1. Begin preparation as in the Feeling Cube activity. After you've mounted the sheet on cardboard, cut the various faces into separate squares instead of folding it into a cube.

2. Place cards face down and mix them up.

3. One child picks a card and looks at it without showing it to others. Have this child act out the feeling on the card, while other children guess which feeling is being acted out.

Mashed Potatoes

Children say "mashed potatoes" expressing different emotions

● ●

Ages   5 and up

Objective   ❖ To explore the communication of feelings

Materials   ❖ Talking stick■ or designated object such as a stuffed animal■

Procedure   1. Have children sit in a circle. Tell the children, "We are going to take turns saying 'mashed potatoes.'"

▶ **note** You can make this activity more difficult by alternating tones within the circle. For instance, the first child uses a happy tone, next sad, then shy, angry, etc.

2. Explain that the person holding the talking stick or frog is the only one speaking.

3. Hand the talking stick to the child to your left and ask her to say "mashed potatoes" in a happy way.

4. After the first child has said "mashed potatoes" she should pass the stick to the next child in the circle. This continues until the last child speaks.

5. Choose a different emotion and go around the circle again.

Understanding Anger

Anger is one of the most difficult emotions for children to manage. It can flare up very quickly, catching them unprepared. When children are angry, it's hard for them to think clearly and make good choices. That's why it is important for them to develop and practice skills for coping with anger.

Children have many images of how to manage anger. Unfortunately they are not all positive. Many adults have problems with anger management and children may mimic what they see the adults in their lives doing. Media images also reinforce poor anger management by presenting characters whose anger often results in violence. Being aware of the influences outside of your program will help you understand why children might act out in particular ways.

The Peaceable Program focuses on giving children the skills to manage their anger so that they can resolve conflicts peacefully. Children learn to recognize "anger cues" and practice ways of calming down. This helps them understand that it is okay to feel angry and that they can find safe, fair ways to express their anger. And knowing that no one will be allowed to hurt anyone else through words or actions reinforces that every member of the group is important.

Teaching Anger Management from a Developmental Perspective

Each child develops in his own way and according to his own timetable. The role of the caregiver or teacher is to help guide the child from one level to the next. Children need adult help to master the social skills associated with anger management. Remember that children who are the same age may be at different developmental levels. Also, at moments of stress or anxiety, a child may slip back into old patterns or forget new skills and need your assistance to get back on track. Make sure every child knows you appreciate his special gifts, regardless of the level he is starting from. This helps him feel confident that he can contribute to the group and become a valued member.

1 Start at each child's level

Three- and four-year-olds have a limited vocabulary. As a result, they tend to overgeneralize their feelings. When they are angry, they may say something like, "I hate you!" You can respond effectively by acknowledging the child's feeling ("I know you're really angry") and stating the child's underlying wish ("You really want to bounce that ball now"). You can then help the child figure out a way to fulfill the wish ("We're going outside in five minutes and you can play with the ball then. Do you want to set the timer so you know when five minutes is up?"). It's important for adults to listen for what the child means and not react to the specific words he or she is using. When a child says, "I hate you!" an adult should hear "Can you help me?"

Five- and six-year-olds are beginning to develop self-control. Therefore, when they have a clear understanding of their physical reactions to anger they can practice different techniques to calm themselves. It is important for them to understand what anger looks like in order to monitor themselves and focus on calming down.

Seven- and eight-year-olds have not learned how to pace themselves. When they are tired, they may become grumpy and find themselves easily frustrated by a task that they could otherwise do. At the same time, they do not want to lose face with their peers by appearing less than capable. You can help them by checking in to gauge their activity level and suggesting alternatives if they seem likely to become frustrated or angry.

2 Choose goals and skills

The goal of understanding anger is for children to find safe and appropriate ways to express anger. Some of the discrete skills that support this goal are:

❖ Developing a vocabulary for anger

❖ Recognizing the physical cues that accompany anger

❖ Understanding anger management techniques

❖ Finding acceptable ways to express anger

3 Put it all together

For discrete skill building or intervention, choose a set of skills you would like to teach in your program or classroom. Use chapter 2 and the tips and activities later in this chapter to choose daily routines and practices that reinforce these skills. (Many activities from chapter 5, "Expressing Emotions," are appropriate for this chapter.)

Choose a skill set that you want to teach in your program or classroom. Use the following sample chart to set goals for children and measure their progress:

Desired Behavior: Recognizing physical cues that accompany anger

Skill	Daily Routine	Activities	Observable Changes in Behavior
Recognize that when they are angry, their hearts may beat faster or faces grow warmer.	Comment on the connections between physical actions and emotions throughout the day	Mean Soup (11-23) Feeling Cube (5-15)	Children use Peace Place to calm down

Different children have different thresholds for frustration; some get mad quickly, while others are slow to anger. For nearly all children, managing anger is a learned behavior. Many children have learned inappropriate ways to handle anger, such as hitting. They need adult help to learn to name feelings, calm down, and direct their behavior appropriately.

Dealing with children's anger poses a special challenge for adults. Many of us are not comfortable with anger. We may respond by becoming angry ourselves. You may find it helpful to develop your own techniques for calming down so that you can continue to respond effectively in these difficult situations.

Setting Up for Success

Materials and space: Provide ample materials in good working order in order to reduce opportunities for conflict or frustration. In addition, set up the room to allow for a comfortable flow of traffic. Children are less likely to get into anger-provoking situations if they have sufficient personal space.

Transitions: Many children have difficulty managing the transition from one activity to another. They may become angry at being interrupted or anxious about moving into a new situation. This can be a time when fights or tantrums erupt. Prepare children for transitions by announcing them five minutes and then one minute ahead of time. Allow plenty of time for them to change from one activity to the next, and provide support by helping them to pick up and move to the next thing. For example: "I know you were having a really good time with the blocks. It's time to pick up so we can go to snack. I will help you."

Saving work: Children are invested in their projects. If someone crumples up their art work or knocks down their tower, they will get mad. You can prevent hurt or angry feelings by providing name cards to place on unfinished work or work that children want to save and show. When it is cleanup time, place the name cards on the work and remind children not to clean up other people's materials without asking first. You can also provide a place children can store their unfinished work.

Pay attention: When observing children, keep anger cues, triggers, and reducers in mind. (See chart on p. 6-6.)

Bringing It Home: Send home Parenting Connections #6 after completing some of the activities in this chapter.

Tips for Daily Practice

Build an anger vocabulary: To help children recognize that there are different degrees of anger, help them learn words to express a range of angry feelings: annoyed, irritated, furious, etc. For example, you can use these words to reflect back to them how they are feeling or to describe the feelings of a character in a story. Being able to differentiate between mild and extreme anger helps children monitor their own anger levels and lays the groundwork for helping them understand how conflicts escalate.

Provide scripts: Often children will try to gain someone's attention by hitting. You can help them find words instead. Provide scripts for children when they are in a potentially anger-provoking situation—for example, "You could tell Mario, 'I get mad when you bump my elbow. Please stop.'" Children respond well to scripting, and with few reminders, will begin to use these phrases appropriately. Teaching them to use "I" statements instead of "you" statements ("I don't like it when . . ." or "I wish you would . . ." instead of "You're always . . .") encourages self-awareness and provides a useful skill for defusing conflict. You could also use "Flying Feathers" Puppet Script (p. 8-27).

Teach strategies that prevent hitting: Teach strategies that remind children not to hit. For example, tell children: "When you feel like hitting, pull in your arms like a turtle." Children can remind each other to "be a turtle."

Anger Cues, Triggers, and Reducers

Anger Cues: Ask the following questions in order to help children recognize anger in themselves and other children:

- ❖ How does your body feel when you are angry?
- ❖ What do your hands do? (e.g., make fists)
- ❖ What does your face do?
- ❖ How does your voice sound?
- ❖ Do you walk differently? Sit differently? Stand differently?

Anger Triggers: Talk about what bugs, irritates, annoys, or infuriates class members. Make a list using the statement "I get angry when _____" and have the children do an art project after they share their answer with the group. Make a bulletin "bug" board listing things that "bug" children in the class. This will remind children of each other's triggers.

Anger Reducers: Help children think about ways to calm down when they are upset. Explain that when we're angry we sometimes do and say things that make the situation worse. In order to solve a problem, we need to know how to calm down. As a group, have the children brainstorm ideas of "Things I Do to Calm Down." Make a list and then go back over the ideas and use the visual cues of thumbs up or thumbs down to decide whether each idea will make things better or worse.

Ask children to help you create an anger-management poster to remind them to Stop, Calm Down, Talk It Out, and Make a Choice. They can brainstorm a list of cooling-off techniques to write or illustrate.

When It's Not Working

Acknowledge children's feelings: The first step to helping children when they are angry is to acknowledge their feelings. Try using phrases such as:

- ❖ "I can see you are angry."
- ❖ "It looks like you feel pretty angry/mad about . . ."
- ❖ "I see we have a problem."

Many children calm down almost immediately when they feel someone recognizes how they feel. Acknowledging their feelings helps them in a number of ways:

- ❖ They feel safe knowing someone is there to help.
- ❖ They feel that the problem has been recognized and their feelings noticed.
- ❖ They learn that being angry is okay and that learning what to do is important.

Model acceptance: Children are often frightened by the force of their rage. You can help them feel safe by showing that you are not afraid of anger and by modeling acceptance of angry feelings. Make sure this message is consistent: for example, to respond to girls' anger the same way as boys' or to use the same tone with a difficult child as with a child who you find easier to handle.

Help children calm down: Generate a list of ways to calm down (see "Ideas for Cooling Off" below). When children get upset, refer them to this list of choices and help them find a quiet place or materials to work with.

Ideas for Cooling Off

- ❖ Popping bubble wrap
- ❖ Doing jumping jacks
- ❖ Blowing on a pinwheel
- ❖ Counting to ten or one hundred
- ❖ Pretending to blow out candles
- ❖ Turning a tornado tube

- ❖ Listening to Music
- ❖ Sorting buttons
- ❖ Getting a hug
- ❖ Sitting quietly
- ❖ Ballooning

Helping Kids Calm Down Is Not "Time Out"

Using a Peace Place to help children calm down is not the same as using "time out." Time out is a common disciplinary technique in which children who are being disruptive are isolated from the group. They are not allowed to talk, play, or reenter the group until a fixed amount of time is up. Some early childhood educators feel that time-outs punish children for their angry behavior and do not give them the skills to learn how to handle their anger constructively.

In the Peaceable Program, adults use a multi-step process to help children cope with angry feelings. When a child is overwhelmed or disruptive, she may need some time in a quiet place to calm down. But instead of isolating the child, you can go together to the Peace Place or another quiet corner. There, you can redirect her energy by suggesting a calming activity or task. Once the child is calm, you can help her sort out the cause of her anger and think of safe, acceptable ways to express hurt, anger, or frustration. Direct adult intervention and guidance are critical when children are overwhelmed by their emotions.

Focus on underlying needs: Anger surfaces when underlying needs aren't met. Once a child is calm enough to discuss his or her feelings, you can try to figure out the source of the feelings. Follow up by discussing the problem with everyone involved and looking for a constructive solution. (See chapter 8, "Conflict Resolution".)

Activities in This Chapter:

- Cooling-Off Choices (p. 6-10)
- Calming-Down Process (p. 6-11)
- Ballooning and Draining (p. 6-14)
- The Anger Suit (p. 6-15)
- Hanging Up the Anger Suit (p. 6-17)

Other Activities That Teach Anger Management:

- Remembering What You Did (p. 3-16)
- Storming (p. 4-12)
- Sticky Popcorn (p. 4-16)
- Mashed Potatoes (p. 5-18)
- Brainstorming (p. 8-15)
- Talk It Out Together Process (p. 8-16)
- Two in a Fight (p. 10-15)
- Smoky Night (p. 11-7)
- Mean Soup (p. 11-23)
- What Can I Do When . . . ? (p. 12-11)
- Discussion Pictures 5, 9 (chapter 14)

Cooling-Off Choices

Children chart activities that help them to cool off

● ●

Age　　　　3 and up

Objective
- ❖ To learn ways to cool off

Materials
- ❖ Poster paper and markers

Procedure

1. Explain that sometimes anger makes people say and do things that will make a problem worse. In order to solve a problem, we need to feel calm. So children need to figure out ways to cool off when they are upset.

2. As a group, have children share their ideas for activities that help them cool off. Write these ideas on a chart (for young children, draw a symbol to represent each idea). When the list is complete, go back and cross out ideas that they should not use because they might hurt someone or something. Remind children how important it is to have safe choices for things to do when they are angry. (For suggestions see "Ideas for Cooling Off" on p. 6-7.)

3. When you have a list of five to ten cooling-off ideas, post the chart in the Peace Place for easy reference.

Calming-Down Process

A four-step process for
helping children regain self-control

• •

Ages 3 and up

Objectives
- ❖ To help children learn a process for regaining self-control
  when upset
- ❖ To develop social skills

Materials
- ❖ A Peace Place
- ❖ The Calming Down chart (p. 6-13)
- ❖ Materials to manipulate such as buttons to sort, a tornado
  tube to turn, or a pinwheeel to blow on.

Procedure
1. Tell children you are going to help them learn a process for
   calming down when they are upset.

2. Present the Calming Down chart. Review the steps.
   - ❖ Step 1: Stop
   - ❖ Step 2: Go to the Peace Place
   - ❖ Step 3: Cool Off
   - ❖ Step 4: Take Time for Feelings

3. Walk the group through the
   Calming Down method,
   using the Peace Puppet Script
   4: The Ow! (p. 8-31) Stop the
   puppet script where
   indicated. Explain that

   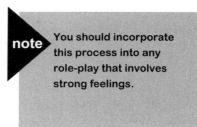

   note You should incorporate
   this process into any
   role-play that involves
   strong feelings.

   sometimes we need to calm down before we think about
   resolving the conflict. Use the puppets to demonstrate the
   Calming Down Process.

   - ❖ Step 1: Stop. The puppets face each other.

> ❖ Step 2: Go to the Peace Place. Remind the students that the Peace Place is there for them to calm down during a conflict.

> ❖ Step 3: Cool Off. Go through the chart of cooling-off choices you generated in the previous activity (p. 6-10). (If you haven't done this activity you can use "Ideas for Cooling Off" on p. 6-7.) Have the puppets act out some of the cooling-off activities, such as sorting buttons or blowing on a pinwheel.

> ❖ Step 4: Take Time for Feelings. Begin the conflict resolution process by having the puppets explain how the conflict made them feel.

4. After you have explained the process, post the chart in the Peace Place. You may want to illustrate the chart so that young children can identify the steps.

5. Post the Calming Down chart (p. 6-13) in the Peace Place.

Calming Down

Step 1: STOP!

Step 2: Go to the Peace Place.

Step 3: Cool Off.

Step 4: Take Time for Feelings.

Balloning and Draining[*]

Children are introduced to two simple techniques
to help them cool off their anger: deep, slow breathing
and conscious muscle relaxation

● ●

Ages   4 and up

Objectives   ❖ To learn cooling-off techniques

Materials   None

Procedure   1. "Ballooning" is basically deep breathing. Have the
                   children stand and tell them to take slow (not deep)
                   breaths and fill themselves up with air as if they were
                   balloons. Then have them slowly let the air out of the
                   "balloons." Repeat a few times and have the children note
                   how they feel.

                2. "Draining" is consciously tensing and relaxing the
                   muscles in the body. Again, have the children stand. Ask
                   them to tighten all the muscles in their bodies and hold
                   them tight until you say to relax. After a few seconds, say,
                   "Now relax slowly and let all the anger drain out of you.
                   Imagine a puddle of anger at your feet."

                   ❖ How did you feel when you finished ballooning/
                      draining?

                   ❖ When might you use this technique?

                   ❖ How could you balloon or drain in a less obvious way?

---

[*] Adapted with permission from William J. Kreidler, *Creative Conflict Resolution* (Glenview, Ill: Scott
Foresman and Co., 1984).

The Anger Suit

Children wear an old suit to act out
what it looks and feels like to be angry

● ●

Ages   5 and up

Objectives   ❖ To explore the nature of anger

Materials   ❖ An old suit, dress, or T-shirt (slightly larger in size than the children in the group)

❖ Chart paper and markers

Procedure   1. Explain that the first step to learning how to control anger is being able to identify it when we see or feel it.

2. Hold up the Anger Suit and explain that a tailor friend of yours made this suit especially for this group. This suit makes the person who wears it act very, very angry. We will use it to learn some of the signs that tell us that other people are angry, and we will use it to learn some techniques to help other people and ourselves calm down when we're feeling angry.

3. Ask for a volunteer to try on the Anger Suit. Warn him that it may feel strange at first to be so angry with no apparent reason. You may need to pull the volunteer aside to prompt him to really exaggerate the emotion.

4. Ask the audience to suggest something that might happen to the volunteer to make him angry. Ask the volunteer to show the group how he might react, in a really angry way, to that situation.

5. Draw three columns on a piece of chart paper. At the top of the first column, write "Anger looks like . . ." On the top of the second, write, "Anger sounds like . . ." And the third column, "Anger feels like . . ." Fill in the chart as a group,

considering what the volunteer did, said, and felt like in the Anger Suit.

6. Hang the Anger Chart up and store the Anger Suit for later use. Follow up with the "Hanging Up the Anger Suit" on p. 6-17.

Reflection

❖ Why might it be important to be able to tell what anger looks and sounds like?

❖ Why do we need to know how anger feels?

Hanging Up the Anger Suit

The group tries to help a person
who wears the Anger Suit figure out how to get out
of it by suggesting ways to calm down

● ●

Ages   5 and up

Objective
- ❖ To brainstorm ways to calm down when angry

Materials
- ❖ Anger Suit (see previous activity for description)
- ❖ Chart paper and markers

Procedure

1. Have a volunteer wear the Anger Suit. Remind the group that this suit has magical powers and makes whomever puts it on instantly and intensely angry.

2. Review the Anger Chart that your group created in "The Anger Suit" activity, identifying the way that anger looks, sounds, and feels.

3. Explain that the task for the group today is to help the volunteer who has put on the Anger Suit figure out how to get out of the suit and hang it back up. The only way that he can do this is by following the advice of the audience—anger management experts—who will each offer tips that help us all calm down when we are angry.

4. You may need to help the "experts" come up with anger management techniques. You can do this by reminding them about how anger looks, sounds, and feels. For example, you might refer to the anger chart, where it says that "Anger feels like . . . your heart is beating really fast" and suggest that taking deep, slow breaths will change this.

5. Make an illustrated chart of the anger diffusion techniques that the group of experts come up with. As they suggest

things, have the volunteer act them out, slowly taking off the Anger Suit as he calms down, until he has taken it off, hung it up, and returned to normal.

6. Give other children a chance to try on and take off the Anger Suit, as the experts suggest techniques from the list.

Reflection

❖ How did it feel to wear the Anger Suit? How did you feel when you were calming down?

❖ When might we need to remember the list of things to do to hang up the Anger Suit in our daily lives?

Appreciating Diversity

Young children are trying to build an understanding of the world around them. Their interest in learning who they are makes them aware of the differences and similarities they share with those around them. They notice differences in gender, color, and physical ability. More important, they are able to absorb the often unspoken attitudes that the people around them hold toward those differences.

The Peaceable Program helps children appreciate diversity in an unself-conscious way. By learning to acknowledge differences without bias, children help to create an environment in which each child can feel comfortable about the ways he or she is different from others. They can feel safe taking risks or standing apart from their peers. Children's own concerns—refining their understanding of the world, establishing their identity, and finding their place—provide the context for developing skills that will help them question and challenge prejudice in the world around them.

Teaching the Appreciation of Diversity from a Developmental Perspective

Each child develops in her own way and according to her own timetable. The role of the caregiver or teacher is to help guide the child from one level to the next. Children need adult help to master the social skills associated with appreciating diversity. Remember that children who are the same age may be at different developmental levels. Also, at moments of stress or anxiety, a child may slip back into old patterns or forget new skills and need your assistance to get back on track. Make sure every child knows you appreciate her special gifts, regardless of the level she is starting from. This helps her feel confident that she can contribute to the group and become a valued member.

1 Start at each child's level

Three- and four-year-olds often see the world in absolute terms. They are eager to figure out and master the rules of the world and can be very inflexible about them! Because they tend to overgeneralize, they may need help refining and testing their ideas. For instance, one child may tell another that "the grandmother always dies before the grandfather." Children this age will also play out ideas they pick up from adults around them. By observing their play and listening to their conversation, teachers can notice when children are misinformed and gently empower them to test their ideas.

Many of the rules and generalizations of the age focus on gender as children explore what it means to be a boy or a girl. Thus it is common to hear a boy say,

"Girls can't drive trucks," and even use it as a reason to exclude girls from the sandbox where he and his friends are playing with trucks. This gives the teacher the opportunity to say: "Girls and boys are able to choose what they want to drive." You can even teach the words to the song "Ballet Dancing Truck Driver" from the Changing Channels kit.▪ (For more information or to order, call ESR at 1-800-370-2515.)

Five- and six-year-olds want to grow up and become powerful, like adults. They are especially apt to imitate superheroes like those they see in Saturday morning cartoons. Take time to learn about the shows children watch and the heroes they admire. Many cartoon heroes are aggressive or violent in their actions. Discuss with children the differences between what's real and what's pretend and talk about the consequences of hurtful and violent behavior. You can also ask questions about how the heroes' enemies are portrayed and what the story might look like from their point of view.

Seven- and eight-year-olds value the opinions of their peers. Issues of inclusion and exclusion are very important to them. They are also ready to explore notions of fairness. The ability to distinguish between "fair" and "unfair" will help them learn lessons about personal responsibility.

Many children will need help to develop the skills to make friends and join others' play. To help foster a sense of inclusion, take time to celebrate each child as an important member of the group. By discussing ways that friends may be alike or different, you can create an atmosphere of tolerance rather than conformity.

2 Choose goals and skills

The goal of appreciating diversity is to help children learn to view differences without bias, understand the value of diversity, and begin to develop the skills to recognize and stand up against prejudice when they encounter it. (See "Creating an "Anti-Bias Curriculum" on p. 7-4.) Some of the skills young children will need to master are:

❖ Identifying differences and similarities in a nonjudgmental way

❖ Using appropriate language to acknowledge or ask questions about physical differences

❖ Checking out the accuracy of their own ideas and assumptions

❖ Learning to stand up for themselves and for others

❖ Recognizing that all people have feelings

Creating an Anti-Bias Curriculum

Many early childhood teachers and caregivers adopt a multicultural approach to appreciating diversity. To expose children to a variety of cultures, they use images and activities that emphasize their foods, holidays, and traditions. Some early childhood educators, however, feel that children learn more from an *anti-bias* approach to diversity issues. According to Louise Derman-Sparks, author of *The Anti-Bias Curriculum: Tools for Empowering Young Children* (Washington, D.C.: NAEYC, 1989) the goals of an anti-bias curriculum are to make the value of diversity relevant to the child's own experience and to use children's questions and beliefs as a springboard for challenging prejudice.

In a multicultural approach, activities relating to cultural diversity are rarely integrated into the rest of the curriculum. In addition, these activities may not directly address assumptions and behaviors children bring into the classroom that may prevent them from valuing and appreciating diversity.

By contrast, an anti-bias approach percolates through the curriculum, as caregivers listen and respond thoughtfully to the things children say and do. They help children explore the everyday differences between themselves and their friends and use teachable moments to encourage children to evaluate the generalizations they are beginning to form about gender, race, physical ability, and other issues. Can girls be firefighters? Is dark skin "dirty"? Questions like these may make adults uncomfortable, but they are part of children's struggle to make sense of their world. By starting with children's own experience and by creating an environment in which children feel safe, comfortable, and free to explore their differences, teachers can give children the ability to recognize the biases they encounter as their world grows larger and the courage, compassion, and responsibility to challenge prejudice wherever they find it.

Put it all together

For discrete skill building or intervention, choose a set of skills you would like to teach in your program or classroom. Use chapter 2 and the tips and activities later in this chapter to choose daily routines and practices that reinforce these skills. You may also find helpful the cross-referenced activities from other chapters. Use the following sample chart to set goals for children and measure their progress:

Desired Behavior: To comment appropriately on differences

Skill	Daily Routines	Activities	Observed Change in Behavior
Practicing objective observation	During circle time, snack time, and play time, comment on physical differences in nonbiased ways: "Eric moves fast with his feet and Joe moves fast in his wheelchair."	Skin Tone Mural (7-12)	Children use a variety of descriptions and nonbiased words to talk about skin color

Your program goals may not reflect the values prevalent in children's homes and communities. If the children in your program encounter or observe acts of intolerance on a regular basis, work toward giving children ways to check on the accuracy of such ideas. Your activity selections and skill development will help them connect the concrete words and actions of their parents, siblings, TV, and other influences with those of the Peaceable Program.

Setting Up for Success

Posters: Post pictures around the room that reflect diversity. Look for images that show children, families, and adults of different races, ethnicities, and genders. Some sources for these kinds of images include: Unicef, the Children's Defense Fund, the National Black Child Development Institute; magazines such as *Indian Artist*, *Ebony*, and Latino *Today*; and advertisements showing ethnic diversity. Images of people doing everyday things make diversity more meaningful to young children than photos featuring traditional costumes or exotic settings, which may reinforce stereotypes ("All Japanese girls wear kimonos"). It's also helpful to display pictures showing people with a variety of body types or different physical abilities.

Play area: Children often associate various forms of play with specific genders. One way to break down this kind of stereotyping is to arrange the classroom so that play areas associated with different genders are located near each other. For instance, the kitchen could be next to a tool area or sandbox. Dress-up clothes and hats also encourage children to explore different gender roles through dramatic play—for instance, children of both genders can dress as ballet dancers, nurses, or police officers.

Toys and materials: Dolls, figures, and other toys should represent people of diverse races and genders. It can be challenging to find a diverse selection that does not reflect stereotypes. Two mail order catalogues that contain a wide variety of dolls and playthings are Kaplan (1-800-334-2014) and Constructive Playthings (1-800-448-4115).

Art supplies: Provide the children with markers, crayons, and paints in a wide variety of skin colors. Mix paints to create different shades. Engage the children in finding shades that match their own skin colors. This provides an occasion casually to compare and contrast the different colors represented in the group.

Accessibility: Many classrooms and play spaces are not accessible to children with special needs. To ensure that a program can meet these children's requirements, it may be necessary to modify equipment or reorganize the room so that all children have access to materials. For example, are all children able to use the climbing structures? Children using wheelchairs may need extra-wide spaces so they can maneuver easily; trays or tables can give them access to them to blocks or puzzles that other children play with on the floor. You can also add Velcro to make it easier to pick objects up.

Groups: Make a conscious effort to set up small groups that integrate children across racial, ethnic, and gender lines. Research shows that working in a small, cooperative group is a powerful way for children to overcome any fears or stereotypes they have already formed.

> **note** **Bringing It Home:** Send home Parenting Connections #7 and #8 after completing some of the activities in this chapter.

Tips for Daily Practice

Observe and discuss: Observe which children are using which materials. Are girls playing with blocks and trucks? Do boys play in the housekeeping area? Are some children excluding others from play, and if so, what seem to be their reasons? Use your observations to guide casual conversations or group discussions about issues such as gender roles, fairness, and rules for playing together.

Acknowledge differences: Neutral observation helps children see differences in a nonjudgmental light. For example, if children are playing with one another's hair, a teacher might give them words to describe the texture of each: "Julia, your hair is curly, isn't it? Anna, your hair is straight." The more children see that you are comfortable with differences and that you talk about them with ease and respect, the more they will be able to accept differences.

Use culturally diverse teaching materials: Curriculum materials can reinforce the message of appreciating diversity. For example, if you are teaching the alphabet, children over six can play matching games with pictures of letters from different alphabets. They can learn to count in other languages or compare various words for colors. Many will enjoy singing simple songs like "Happy Birthday" in more than one language or signing along as they sing. You can also play tapes and CDs with songs in different languages, such as *Linking Up!* 💼 ,(For more information about *Linking Up!* or to order call ESR at 1-800-370-2515) and read books or stories featuring children from diverse backgrounds.

Involve families: Parents, grandparents, or aunts and uncles will have good ideas about ways to bring their home cultures into the classroom. Perhaps they will be willing to collaborate in planning projects and activities for your classroom, not only during holidays but at other times as well. You can also ask if they prefer you to use the child's "home" name at school, rather than an anglicized version of it, and ask them to teach you the proper pronunciation so you can share it with the class.

There are also many ways to acknowledge that children come from different kinds of families. For example, pictures in the classroom may depict single-parent families, extended families, multi-generational living situations, children of same-sex couples, and so on. Create a class book, "All About Our Families," with a page devoted to each child. Children can take turns bringing the book home to read with their families. They may also enjoy sharing stories about how each child got his or her name. It may be helpful to check in with the parents or guardians before introducing this topic to make sure you handle it in a way that is comfortable for the family.

Can Boys Use the Play Kitchen?

When children make comments that reflect biases or stereotypes, you can use questions to encourage them to re-examine their beliefs. For example:

Child: Boys can't use the play kitchen.

Adult: What makes you say that?

Child: Boys don't like cooking and stuff.

Adult: Have you ever seen a boy cook?

Child: No.

Adult: Sure you have. Remember how we made cookies on Monday? Jamal and Eric did most of the work.

Child: That's different. That's here. I mean at home.

Adult: Have you ever seen a boy cook at home?

Child: No.

Adult: Let's ask the kids at group meeting if anyone has seen a boy cook at home.

At the group meeting you could expand it out to include images of men cooking on television or in movies.

When It's Not Working

Intervene to prevent exclusion: Be prepared to intervene when you hear children making comments that exclude a child on the basis of gender, race, or physical ability. Instead of changing the subject or tackling it head-on, try asking why a child made that comment. For example: "I wonder why you think girls can't be firefighters?" Then help them find a new way to look at their assumptions. (See "Can Boys Use the Play Kitchen?" on previous page.)

Correct, but don't punish: Children who use offensive language or gestures should not be reprimanded for their behavior, nor should they be told directly that their thinking is wrong. Instead, help them to see what they are doing and why it is hurtful. For example: "You may not use those words about other people. It hurts them." Use the opportunity as a teachable moment to address how words can hurt.

Empower children: Help the offended child stand up for herself. Support her hurt feelings and give her suggestions of words to say. For example: "I'm proud that I'm a girl, and I can play where I want to."

Meet with parents: If a child in your room consistently uses words or behaviors that are hurtful to others, it may be helpful to meet with the parents. Explain why you think this is an important issue and discuss how you are dealing with it in the classroom. Ask them for suggestions for managing their child's behavior and encourage them to reinforce anti-bias messages and practices at home. If parents support their child's words and actions, make clear that in your class you will not allow children to act out of prejudice.

Activities in This Chapter:

- ❖ Footprint Mural (p. 7-11)
- ❖ Skin Tone Mural (p. 7-12)
- ❖ Concentration (p. 7-13)
- ❖ Family Pictures (p. 7-14)
- ❖ Bread, Bread, Bread (p. 7-15)
- ❖ Oh Give Me a Home (p. 7-16)
- ❖ Same/Different (p. 7-18)
- ❖ Colors, Beautiful Colors (p. 7-19)
- ❖ Wrappers (p. 7-20)

Other Activities That Teach Appreciating Diversity:

- ❖ Remembering What You Did (p. 3-16)
- ❖ You Say, I Say (p. 3-20)
- ❖ Good News (p. 5-11)
- ❖ Helping Hands (p. 5-13)
- ❖ Name Cards (p. 9-8)
- ❖ Once Upon a Time Game (p. 9-9)
- ❖ Chrysanthemum (p. 9-11)
- ❖ Stick Up For Yourself (p. 9-14)
- ❖ Come Join in the Circle (p. 10-10)
- ❖ Chocolate (p. 10-13)
- ❖ Anansi the Spider (p. 11-5)
- ❖ Smoky Night (p. 11-7)
- ❖ Rainbow Fish (p. 11-9)
- ❖ Someone Special, Just Like You (p. 11-12)
- ❖ Mama, Do You Love Me? (p. 11-16)
- ❖ All the Colors of the Earth (p. 11-19)
- ❖ Mrs. Katz and Tush (p. 11-25)
- ❖ Books of Their Own Stories (p. 12-5)

Footprint Mural

Children step in paint trays, then walk across paper to make a mural out of their footprints

● ●

Ages   3 and up

Objective
- ❖ To foster an appreciation of diversity
- ❖ To nurture a sense of community

Materials
- ❖ Large roll of paper
- ❖ Paint
- ❖ Three or four dishpans or aluminum trays
- ❖ Washcloth or sponge
- ❖ Towel
- ❖ Chairs

Procedure
1. Lay a long sheet of paper on the ground and place the pans, each containing a shallow coating of a different color of paint, at one end. Set chairs at the other end, along with a pan of water, a washcloth, and a towel.

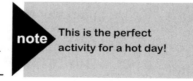

note This is the perfect activity for a hot day!

2. Have the children take off their shoes. Have each child step in the paint color he chooses and walk the length of the paper. Then have each child sit and wash, rinse, and dry his feet.

3. Write each child's name by his footprints.

Reflection
- ❖ What can feet do?
- ❖ Besides people, who else has feet?
- ❖ How are feet alike and how are they different?

Skin Tone Mural

Children select strips of painted paper
that match their skin tone and make a mural

● ●

Ages   3 and up

Objectives
   ❖ To explore differences and similarities
   ❖ To explore and discuss racial diversity

Materials
   ❖ Strips of paper painted in various shades of skin tones
   ❖ Crayons in various skin tones.▪
   ❖ Large poster board

Procedure

1. Lay out strips of paper painted in various skin tones. Have each child pick the strip that most closely matches her skin tone. Or have children use the crayons to create their own strips.

> **tip**
>
> Read the book *All the Colors of the Earth* ▪ by Sheila Hamanaka (New York: Morrow Junior Books, 1994).

2. Have each child glue a strip onto the poster and write her name on it. You can write names for younger children. Help older children to arrange strips by colors and shades.

Reflection
   ❖ What gives skin its color? Does anyone know what melanin is?
   ❖ Look at the colors on the board. Is anyone actually white or black? Why do you think some people are called white or black or brown or yellow or red?

Concentration

Children play a card game
using photographs of their families

● ●

Ages   4 and up

Objective   ❖ To explore similarities and differences between children's
                     families

Materials   ❖ Photos of the families of the children in the group

                ❖ Cardboard or poster board

                ❖ Lamination or glue

Procedure   1. Ask the children to bring in
                    a photo of their family. For
                    each photo, cut a piece of
                    cardboard to the same size.
                    Laminate or glue each photo
                    onto the cardboard to make
                    a set of cards.

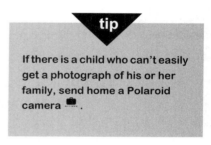

tip

If there is a child who can't easily
get a photograph of his or her
family, send home a Polaroid
camera 📷 .

2. These cards can be used for several variations of the game
    Concentration. Lay out all the cards face up. Have the
    children take turns at finding cards with certain
    similarities. Examples include finding all the cards with
    mommies, with daddies, with two people, with one
    person, with a grandparent. Children's observations can
    allow for discussion about families who have dark skin,
    light skin, who live with one parent or two, or whose
    families include grandparents.

3. With older children, also try the more traditional version
    of Concentration where the cards are placed face down
    and children try to match cards from memory.

Family Pictures

Children use sponges and paint to make portraits of their families

• •

Ages   4 and up

Objective   ❖ To develop a sense of belonging by identifying one's place in one's family

Materials   ❖ Compression sponge paper ■

                  ❖ Paint

                  ❖ Markers

                  ❖ Large sheets of paper

Procedure   1. Prepare for this activity by cutting the compression sponge paper into people shapes. Cut out the shapes of adults and children. When you have finished cutting the shapes, put the shapes in water to expand them into thick sponges. (You may need to practice this process with one shape to learn how to cut the sponge paper so that the shapes are recognizable when the sponges have expanded.) Make several sets of these people shapes.

> **tip**
>
> Give your children an extra challenge by asking them to write, or perhaps dictate, stories about their families. They might also enjoy drawing and discussing pictures of animal families.

                  2. Distribute paper to each child. Have the children dip the sponges in paint and press them on their own paper to represent the members of their families.

                  3. Now identify family members and help to the children to write names under each figure.

Reflection   ❖ What do you like about your family?

                  ❖ Does everyone in a family always live together?

Bread, Bread, Bread

Children taste and examine different kinds of bread

● ●

Ages   4 and up

Objectives: ❖ To explore how various cultures prepare bread

Materials: ❖ Several loaves of bread of different types, such as Italian bread, bagels, pita bread, French bread, challah, soda bread, matzoh, saltines, etc.

❖ Spreads for the bread, such as butter, jams, peanut butter

❖ A bread knife and table knives for the spreads

Procedure: 1. Ask the children to imagine that you have just arrived on Earth from Mars and you are very curious about things on planet Earth. For example, someone told you about something called "bread." What is "bread?" (You may want to omit this step with younger children.)

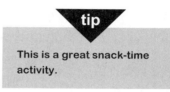

tip

This is a great snack-time activity.

2. Show the various loaves of bread and ask children to identify the ones they know. Ask some of the following questions:

note Read *Bread, Bread, Bread,* by Ann Morris, (New York: Scholastic Inc. 1989).

❖ How are these loaves of bread the same? How are they different?

❖ If you included crackers in your assortment, ask: "Are all of these called 'loaves?'"

❖ What goes into bread?

3. When you have finished discussing the breads, have children choose the ones they'd like to try. Allow the children to choose and use the spreads they would like.

Oh Give Me a Home

Children explore the concept of shelter

● ●

Ages 5 and up

Objectives:
- ❖ To help children understand the need for shelter
- ❖ To explore the wide variety of homes

Materials:
- ❖ Chart paper
- ❖ Markers
- ❖ Glue
- ❖ Scissors
- ❖ Magazines with pictures of different kinds of houses. (Try to include magazines that have pictures of different types of shelters around the world, such as National Geographic.)

Procedure:

1. Ask children to leaf through the magazines and cut out any pictures they see that show buildings people live in (apartment buildings, trailers, houses, igloos, houseboats, etc.)

2. When children have cut out the pictures, ask them what types of buildings they found. Use their discussion to create the headings for a graph. Write each category across the top of a sheet of chart paper.

3. Under each heading, glue the pictures children have cut out showing houses in that category. Ask: "Which kinds of housing do we have the most pictures of? Which do we

> **tip**
>
> As a follow-up activity, have children work in groups of four to make temporary "houses." Find a big, empty box, such as a refrigerator box and put it in your classroom. Give every child a role in decorating the "house." Fabrics, rugs, pictures, and play food help make the house more cozy and help the children think of it as theirs.

have the fewest pictures of?" You may also want to discuss which types of housing are most common in your own community and what the graph would look like if it showed only those kinds of houses. Emphasize that different types of housing are just different, not weird, funny, or wrong.

4. Lead a discussion about shelter with the children, starting with the following questions:

❖ What kinds of shelters can you think of that are not listed on our graph?

❖ What kinds of materials do people use in making shelter?

❖ How are these shelters the same?

❖ How are they different?

❖ What kinds of shelters do animals use?

Same/Different

Children practice looking for differences and similarities

● ●

Ages   5 and up

Objective: ❖ To encourage children to look for similarities as well as differences

Materials: None

Procedure: 1. Have two volunteers stand in front of the group. Ask the group to identify ways the two children are different. Next ask them to identify ways the children are the same. Record on a chart labeled Same and Different. Put the two children's names at the top of the chart. Under the word "Same" write the similarities, and under the word "Different" write the differences. (With younger children, add simple illustrations to the chart.) For example:

Kiesha and James

Different   Same
Kiesha is a girl; James is a boy   Both wearing red sneakers
Kiesha is taller than James   Both have brown skin
James wears glasses   Both are five years old

---

2. Repeat this several times with new children so that eventually all the children in the program who wanted to have participated. This makes a good quick activity when you are changing from one activity to another.

Colors, Beautiful Colors

Children name positive associations with many different colors

● ●

Ages   5 and up

Objectives: ❖ To practice color names

❖ To counter the negative associations of "black" and "brown"

Materials: ❖ Sheets of construction paper in various colors including black, brown, and tan

Procedure: 1. Hold up one of the sheets of construction paper and ask children to identify the color. Ask: "What are some things you like that are this color?" For older children, list their words on the construction paper. After they name a few things, hold up a different colored sheet. Repeat the procedure until you have used all the colors.

2. A variation of this activity is to lay the sheet of construction paper on the floor. Have children pretend to place objects of that color onto the paper. For example, with a piece of black paper children may say such things as "I like licorice and it's black," or "I like my kitty and she's mostly black."

3. Yet another variation is to have children cut pictures of objects and paste them on the appropriately colored sheets.

tip

Follow up this activity by reading the book *Mr. Rabbit and the Lovely Present* by Charlotte Zolotow (New York: Harper & Row, 1962). This book is also available in Spanish.

Wrappers

Using a large piece of cloth, children
explore ways to cover their bodies

● ●

Ages   6 and up

Objective
  ❖ To explore clothing as a basic need
  ❖ To explore cross-cultural similarities and differences

Materials
  ❖ Several lengths of fabric approximately two to three yards long (sheets and towels are good, but try to have some boldly patterned fabrics)
  ❖ Clothespins with spring hinges
  ❖ Mirror
  ❖ Magazine pictures of different kinds of clothing (try to include pictures of both conventional clothing and outlandish styles)

Procedure
  1. Discuss clothing as a basic need: "Why do people wear clothes? How do clothes protect people? How does clothing change in different kinds of weather? Besides cloth or fabric, what other materials are used in making clothing?"

  2. Hold up a piece of cloth and ask, "Could this be worn as clothing?" Ask for a volunteer to show you how.

  3. Give several children pieces of fabric and have them think of ways to drape it into clothing. The clothespins can be used to secure the fabric.

  4. Lead a discussion about clothing using the following questions:
     ❖ What changes would you make to your outfit if this were a rainy day? A cold day? A hot day?

❖ What are some of the things people use to fasten their clothes?

❖ How is the outfit you made like other kinds of clothing you wear? How is it different?

5. Once you have introduced the cloth, place it in a play area for children to use during playtime. Put the fabric in a laundry basket or a box. Place a mirror nearby (preferably a full-length one) and display the clothing pictures. As children play with ways to wear the cloth, emphasize that the various styles of clothing are just different rather than strange, weird, or wrong.

> **tip**
>
> Follow up this activity by looking at pictures of children's clothing from around the world in the book *Children Just Like Me* by Barnabas and Anabel Kindersley (New York: Dorling Kindersley, 1995). The book is also a good resource for "Oh Give Me a Home" on p. 7-16.

Resolving Conflict

Children learn to solve conflicts in many ways. The principal way they learn is by watching how adults, family members, peers, and media characters handle conflicts. Not all of this modeling is good. Adults, for instance, do not always have all the tools they need to resolve conflicts; and cartoon characters are notably poor role models. Children often need additional help to understand what conflict is and how to resolve it without violence or disrespect.

Conflict resolution builds on the other skills developed in the Peaceable Program: communication, cooperation, expressing and managing feelings, and appreciating diversity. These are the essential ingredients needed to resolve conflicts. While young children rarely engage in negotiating or conflict-solving spontaneously, they can be guided through the process so that they not only do well, they enjoy it. The pride and self-confidence they develop allows the whole group to function more smoothly, releasing the teacher from constant pressure to intervene.

Strategies and Problem Solving

Research has identified two basic approaches for teaching conflict resolution skills to young children. One is the *strategy* approach, in which children learn specific strategies for handling conflict. Sharing and taking turns are two strategies that most young children can learn. Sometimes children can come up with conflict resolution strategies themselves. Other times, they need suggestions or direct instruction from adults. Not all strategies work for all conflicts, of course, so part of the instruction is learning when it's appropriate to apply a particular strategy.

The second approach is the *open-ended problem-solving* approach, in which children confronted with a problem learn to follow specific steps to arrive at a solution. They will need adult guidance to learn and practice a sequence of problem-solving steps. This approach complements the strategy approach, since in proposing a solution children will draw on strategies they have already learned or developed.

All children have some skills and strategies for dealing with conflicts. The goal of the Peaceable Program is to add to these. Children can develop new skills and strategies in a number of ways. They may learn by watching how you, the teacher, handle problems as they arise. They may learn through direct instruction at teachable moments: "Here in preschool we don't hit when someone is bothering us. We use words and tell someone to leave us alone." And they may learn through more formal lessons: "Today we're going to talk about what to do when someone keeps bothering you."

Teaching Conflict Resolution from a Developmental Perspective

Each child develops in his own way and according to his own timetable. The role of the caregiver or teacher is to help guide the child from one level to the next. Children need adult help to master the social skills associated with resolving conflict. Remember that children who are the same age may be at different developmental levels. Also, at moments of stress or anxiety, a child may slip back into old patterns or forget new skills and need your assistance to get back on track. Make sure every child knows you appreciate his special gifts, regardless of the level he is starting from. This helps him feel confident that he can contribute to the group and become a valued member.

1 Start at each child's level

Three- and four-year-olds are apt to see things from only one point of view—their own. The three-year-old who hits, for instance, may not fully understand that the hitting hurts the other child. For the same reason, children this age often do not want to share toys and other materials and are likely to get into conflicts over them. They need active intervention and guidance to begin to appreciate other children's needs and feelings.

Five- and six-year-olds are experiencing competition for the first time. If they lose their feelings are easily hurt. When conflicts arise, they will need help finding the words to express those feelings before they can move on to resolve the conflict. This is also a good reason to introduce cooperative games and activities, which reinforce the message that every member of the group is important.

Seven- and eight-year-olds need to feel that they are in control of a situation in order to "save face" in front of peers. The best solution to conflicts for children this age is one that both parties negotiate so that both can feel like winners. The teacher can help children begin to develop the skills they need to understand and respect each other's point of view and to work out a peaceful solution.

2 Choose goals and skills

The goal of conflict resolution is to help children who are engaged in conflict to find solutions that work for everyone. Some of the discrete skills that help children reach these goals are:

- ❖ Distinguishing between Thumbs Up and Thumbs Down solutions (what will work and what won't work)
- ❖ Following a sequence of problem-solving steps, such as the Talk It Out Together method
- ❖ Suggesting their own solutions to conflicts
- ❖ Cooperating to put solutions into practice
- ❖ Calming down and getting control

3 Put it all together

For discrete skill building or intervention, choose a set of skills you would like to teach in your program or classroom. Use chapter 2 and the tips and activities later in this section to choose daily routines and practices that reinforce these skills. You can also choose activities from this chapter that help children work on the skills you are targeting. You may also find helpful the cross-referenced activities from other chapters.

Use the following sample chart to set goals for children and measure their progress:

Desired Behavior: to be able to choose a good solution

Skill	Daily Routine	Activities	Observable Change
Use thumbs up or thumbs down	At circle time and story time, ask yes/ no questions and have children practice giving thumbs-up and thumbs-down signs	Thumbs Up, Thumbs Down (8-13)	During circle time all children respond to questions with a thumbs-up or thumbs-down sign

In responding to conflicts that arise in the classroom, remember that there is a difference between teaching and preaching. Preaching is unlikely to give children new skills or understandings. Instead, use the conflict situation to help children acquire a new skill or reinforce ones they have already been taught. Look at the conflict as an opportunity for learning rather than "I told you so" moment.

Setting Up for Success

Create a peace place: A Peace Place is a corner or area of the room that is set aside for children to use when they are solving their conflicts or cooling down. (See "Setting Up a Peace Place" on p. 2-13.)

Introduce key problem-solving concepts: Prepare children for conflict resolution by introducing key concepts in advance like the Talk It Out Together method early in the year. (See p. 8-16.) Use the language of problem solving when you intervene in conflicts, for instance by asking, "Can you think of a Thumbs Up solution for this conflict?" The more you use these words and concepts, the more likely they will be able to use these terms themselves.

Posters: Copy the Talk It Out Together chart (p. 8-18) on newsprint or posterboard and display it in your classroom. With children who are not yet able to read, you will want to put some simple symbols next to the words to provide a visual reminder for each step

 Bringing It Home: Send home Parenting Connections #9 and #10 after completing some of the activities in this chapter.

Tips for Daily Practice

Practice: One way to help children become familiar with some basic conflict resolution techniques is to practice them when there isn't a conflict. Allow some time for role-playing or games when children aren't involved in a problem and can focus on how some of the techniques work.

Give starters: Try giving starters to help children talk about conflicts as they arise. For example, "I saw that you were in the housekeeping area. You were playing . . ." This provides children with a few thoughts and words to help them begin to talk about what happened.

Paraphrase: Paraphrasing is an important tool to help children hear what they are telling you reflected back to them. This will help them retell their story of the conflict. This technique also allows you to include feelings in the conversation. For example, "So you were trying to tell Justin to stop hitting and he wouldn't stop. That must have been hard. What happened next?"

Connect cause and effect: Young children tend to see conflicts in very concrete terms. When asked what the problem is, they typically remember what just happened or what is right in front of them ("He hit me!"). It is important to use techniques to help them talk back through the chain of events that led to the conflict. For example, "He was playing with the truck, you wanted it and tried to take it from him, and then he hit you. Is that right?" Become the bridge between cause and effect by helping children see the events leading to the conflict. This will allow you to better understand what really occurred as well as help children begin to understand cause and effect.

Promote creativity: Help the children find creative solutions. Ask questions like "What could you do if this happened again?" or "What could you do now to make this situation better?" Focus children's attention on inventing something new. One way to do this is by holding a one-to-one brainstorm where they can think of a few different ideas for resolving the conflict. (See "Brainstorming" on p. 8-15.)

When it's appropriate, give children responsibility for solving the problem. You will often need to supervise this, of course, but try as much as possible to let them solve it. For example, set a kitchen timer for seven minutes and ask the children to see what solutions they can create in that time. If they can't come up with anything, you will be available to help them.

Use scripts: Young children may need scripts to help them through parts of the problem-solving process. For example, suggest to a child: "You could say, 'I want to try taking turns.'" Sometimes children will come up with the idea of sharing or taking turns but won't know how to explain it. By helping them present their ideas, you can help them become better communicators in conflict situations.

Help with implementation: The most difficult part of problem solving for young children is implementing the solutions they develop. They will most likely need help. For example, if children choose sharing as a solution, ask, "How will you share the blocks?" First try guiding them by asking questions that will encourage them to create their own solutions. Allow them to try the solution even if you think it will fail. Use this as an opportunity to promote more problem solving. In the end you may need to tell them how to implement the solution.

The Basics of Conflict Resolution

Stop: Teach the stop sign (hand up). Discuss how it is important for children to say "stop" or make the sign for stop so they can walk away and gain control of their feelings. Remind them that it's okay to stop unsafe behavior by walking away from it; they don't have to resolve a conflict right away.

Talk It Out Together: The Talk It Out Together method is a problem-solving process that's easy for children as young as four to remember:

1. Get Together.

2. Take Turns Talking and Listening.

3. What Will Help?

4. Choose a Plan.

5. Do It!

This is a good example of a time you will want to focus on readiness more than mastery. Few preschoolers will master this process initially, and most will need help remembering and implementing it. By introducing it and practicing it, children will begin to acquire some of these skills, but even older children may still need help in using them or rely on adults to get the process started. (See "Talk It Out Together Process" on p. 8-16)

Thumbs Up/Thumbs Down: This simple process is used to evaluate solutions. Children decide whether all the parties in a conflict would give a particular solution a thumbs-up sign or a thumbs-down sign. Using stories or puppets to portray different scenarios, ask children to suggest solutions and have the whole group practice using the signs. Children can also use this sign to signal "start" and "stop" or "yes" and "no." (See "Thumbs Up, Thumbs Down" on p. 8-13.)

When It's Not Working

Validate their feelings: Children need some validation of their feelings before they can solve a problem in a safe and structured way. When a conflict is beginning to get out of hand, you can intervene by giving them a chance to tell you how they feel. You may need to help by providing possible descriptions and words. (See chapter 5, "Expressing Emotions" for ideas on how to help children develop a vocabulary of feelings words.)

Take time to cool off: Don't try to solve problems with children when emotions are still running high. Give them a chance to cool off. Make it clear that you are not punishing them, just giving them a chance to collect themselves. You can have them sit in the Peace Place but let them know it is not a punishment. A kitchen timer is handy for this purpose. When the bell rings, ask children if they are ready to talk about the conflict. (For more on cooling down see chapter 6.)

Bring the conflict to closure: Many conflicts are over before an adult has the chance to intervene. Children may still need to learn from the experience, however. To bring a conflict to closure, bring the participants together and ask the following questions: What happened? How do you feel? What could you do if this happened again? What could you do now to make things better? Then look for opportunities to help children do what they said they would do when similar situations arise.

Responding to Conflict: Choosing Your Course of Action

While many conflicts occur among young children, not all of them are suitable as teachable moments. You will need to consider a number of factors, including how much time you have, how much you think the children will learn from this situation, and how important the problem seems to be to the children involved. In addition, some problems cannot be handled on the spot either because of the time or situation, or because the children need to cool off before they can discuss their differences.

In deciding what to do, consider the following questions:

- ❖ Which children are involved? How upset or angry are they? What do they need from you and each other to work out the problem?

- ❖ Is there enough time to devote to the problem? Can the children deal with the problem right away or do they need some time to calm down? Is everyone in an appropriate place to hold the discussion? If problems cannot be addressed right away, it is important for children to hear the reason and to be told that the discussion will take place at a specific time (e.g., after snack, when we get back inside).

- ❖ What is the conflict about? Is it a difference over resources or a difference in opinions? Is it a problem with a clear, immediate solution or is it more complex? Is the problem one that recurs frequently or is it unique to the children involved?

- ❖ Should the discussion be private or public? Some discussions are best handled with only the children involved, especially when the conflict affects only them or is related to an immediate situation. For some children, airing a dispute in public may be too difficult. However, some problems, particularly those that involve experiences that are common to most children, provide an opportunity for group problem-solving. Some problems can also be handled privately and then discussed at a later date in more general terms.

Five Styles of Handling Children's Conflicts

Style	Description	Uses	Limitations
Direction	When you say, in effect, "Do this," you are directing. Direction is a nonnegotiating approach. An adult authority decides what needs to be done and gives the direction that it be done. It's important to recognize that directing need not be unkind or authoritarian. Children can be told nicely, but clearly, what they need to do.	When safety is at stake; when children are out of control and need help getting back into control; when there is no time to discuss or negotiate; when the problem is not important enough to spend much time or energy.	Doesn't build children's independence in problem solving; may cause resentment on the part of children; may not really solve problems.
Mediation	A third party—either a staff person or any trained person—sits with children and helps them work out their conflict by creating an environment where problem solving can take place. This is done by strictly enforcing ground rules: be honest, no interrupting, and no name calling or put downs. The mediator helps the disputants define their problem, develop solutions, and choose a workable solution.	Because the disputants are solving the problem themselves, they are invested in the solution. Also, it helps get to the root of some persistent problems.	Takes time! The conflict may not be worth the time and effort compared to the learning that comes from it.

Style	Description	Uses	Limitations
Arbitration	Also involves a third party who hears both (or all) sides, then tells the disputants how they should handle the conflict. This may be done with some input from the disputants, or by simply saying, "This is what you're going to do."	Efficient. Gives the disputants a chance to state their point of view, but doesn't spend a lot of time on problem solving.	May not get to the root of the problem. The disputants may not learn anything about solving conflicts.
Judgment	Sometimes the emphasis needs to be not on problem solving, but on determining who was right and who was wrong. Children depend on the adult to act as a judge, to listen and weigh the evidence, and then to pass a fair judgment.	When there has been clear wrongdoing and the parties involved want justice; when there is a need for consequences to be decided upon for actions.	Doesn't build independent problem-solving skills; keeps children dependent upon adults; is by nature a win-lose solution rather than a win-win solution.
Listening Sympathetic-ally	Just listening, not asking a lot of questions or giving advice or solutions, is lending a sympathetic ear. Children have a great need to be listened to regarding their conflicts. It is not uncommon for them to be able to figure out their own solutions once they have expressed their feelings and feel they have been heard.	Respects children and lets them express their feelings and opinions; helps them clarify their positions and feelings; gives them attention and support; can be combined with other methods of resolving conflict.	Takes time; may not lead to problem solving; disputants may feel problem is unresolved.

Activities in This Chapter:

Other Activities That Teach Conflict Resolution:

Thumbs Up, Thumbs Down

Children learn to evaluate solutions to problems

● ●

Ages   3 and up

Objective
- ❖ To evaluate potential conflict solutions

Materials   None

Procedure
1. Explain that when we are trying to resolve conflicts, some solutions are better than others. The best solutions are those that don't hurt anybody and allow everybody in the conflict to say "That's okay with me."

2. Show the group the thumbs-up sign and the thumbs-down sign. Discuss their meaning with the group. You may need to explain that they are ways of saying "Okay!" and "Not okay!"

3. Give the group the following conflict situation:

   In Ms. Chang's group the children love to go outside to play. Ms. Chang rings the bell for cleanup time and the children put on their coats and line up to go outside to play. Recently children have gotten hurt as others push and shove in line. Ms. Chang gathered the group and said, "We've got a problem. The pushing and shoving in line is hurting children."

4. Lead a discussion using the following questions:

   - ❖ What is the problem?

   - ❖ How does it feel to be pushed and shoved?

   - ❖ How could the children solve the problem?

5. Continue the story. Ask the children to listen to all the solutions Ms. Chang's group thought of without evaluating them. (In the next step you will ask them to

evaluate the solutions as "thumbs up" or "thumbs down.")

❖ Ms. Chang cancels outside play.

❖ Ms. Chang lets only children who do not push and shove play outside, while the pushers and shovers have to sit in the director's office.

❖ Ms. Chang calls the parents of the children who push and shove and the parents take them home while the others go outside to play.

❖ Ms. Chang lets a few children go outside with another teacher until all of the children are outside and no one has to line up.

6. Go through the list again, asking children to evaluate the solutions as either thumbs up or thumbs down using their hands. For each solution, ask the children what they think would be the outcome of the solution. Would it be thumbs up for everyone? Thumbs down for everyone? Thumbs up for some and thumbs down for others? Finish the activity by having the children say which solution seems best for everyone.

Brainstorming

Children work together coming up with ideas

● ●

Ages   4 and up

Objective   ❖ To introduce brainstorming as a way to generate ideas

Materials   ❖ An ordinary object such as a box, a wooden spoon, or a cardboard tube

Procedure   1. Explain that the purpose of brainstorming is to come up with as many ideas as possible in a short period of time. During the brainstorm no one says whether the ideas are good or bad, sensible or silly, workable or not workable. The point is simply to get out as many ideas as you can. After the brainstorm is finished, children evaluate the ideas.

2. Set the object in front of the group. Ask them to suggest all the things they can think of that they could do with that object. Write their suggestions on the board. After a few minutes, or after energy for the brainstorm runs down, end the brainstorm.

3. Review the ideas and have the children vote with a thumbs-up or thumbs-down sign to signify whether they think it is a good or unworkable idea.

4. Put a mark by each idea the majority of the group thinks is good.

5. Now have the children vote only once, giving a thumbs-up on their favorite idea.

6. Tally the marks to find the #1 favorite idea.

7. Do it!

Talk It Out Together Process*

Children learn the Talk It Out Together method of solving conflicts

● ●

Ages   3 and up

Objective
- ❖ To learn and practice the Talk It Out Together conflict-solving process

Materials
- ❖ Talk It Out Together Conflict-Solving Chart (see p. 8-18)
- ❖ Two Peace Puppets▪
- ❖ Talking stick▪ or designated object such as a stuffed animal▪

Procedure
1. Display the Talk It Out Together Conflict-Solving Chart and go over it with the group.

   - ❖ Step 1: Get Together
   - ❖ Step 2: Take Turns Talking and Listening.
   - ❖ Step 3: What Will Help?
   - ❖ Step 4: Choose a Plan.
   - ❖ Step 5: Do It!

2. Walk the group through the Talk It Out Together method, using the following puppet role-play:

   The puppets are cleaning up after an activity. Two puppets are pulling at the same toy until one of the puppets pushes the toy at the other and he falls down and starts to cry. Say, "The puppets seem to have a problem. Let's use the Talk It Out Together method to resolve this conflict."

---

* This model was developed through the collaboration of ESR's Early Childhood training team: Lisa M. Cureton, Chris Gerzon, Rebecca Johns, Kim Jones, William J. Kreidler, Carol Miller Lieber, Sarah Pirtle, and Sandy Tsubokawa Whittall.

❖ Step 1: Get Together. The puppets face each other.

❖ Step 2: Take turns Talking and Listening. The puppets take turns talking about how they felt about the toy and about the pushing and falling.

❖ Step 3: What Will Help? The puppets take turns suggesting plans that will make both parties feel okay.

❖ Step 4: Choose a Plan. The puppets suggest two different solutions that are agreeable to both of them. Ask the children to give a thumbs-up or thumbs-down to the plan they like best.

❖ Step 5: Let's Do It. The puppets pick the plan they like by signaling thumbs-up.

Talk It Out Together
Chart

Step 1: Get Together.

 Step 2: Take Turns Talking and Listening.

Step 3: What Will Help?

 Step 4: Choose a Plan.

Step 5: Do It!

Peace Puppets

Peace Puppets🝑 are an easy, fun way to help young children practice problem-solving skills. The common theme in Peace Puppet activities is that the Peace Puppets have problems. They act out these problems for the children, who then help the puppets solve the problems using the Talk It Out Together approach. The scripts included in this section will give you an idea of how a Peace Puppet session goes, but it's easy to make up your own scripts, using problems that arise in your program.

This section includes:

❖ How to make Peace Puppets

❖ How to use the Peace Puppets

❖ Peace Puppet activities

❖ Peace Puppet scripts

How To Make Peace Puppets

Begin by gathering one pair of socks,🝑 a few brightly-colored pieces of felt,🝑 glue,🝑 and scissors. Put one sock over your hand and wrist. Push the toe of the sock in between your thumb and your other fingers to form a mouth. This will be your puppet. Plan where you'd like the facial features to go. Cut shapes out of the felt for eyes, nose, eyebrows, and any other features you'd like to put on your puppet. Be creative. If you like, you can use additional materials to decorate your puppet. Check your local craft store for ideas. Glue the pieces of felt to the sock and allow to dry. Repeat this procedure with the other sock. Try to make the two puppets look different from each other.

Here are two other types of puppets that are both easy to make and easy for young children to use.

Block Puppets

Find several ordinary blocks of wood, small enough for children to hold. Attach picture of a person to the block using glue or tape. The picture can be from a set of cut-outs or cut from a magazine. Try to choose pictures that reflect a variety of ethnic and racial groups. If a picture is significantly larger than the block of wood, you may need to mount it on cardboard first so that it will stand up by itself.

Envelope Puppets

Use legal-size envelopes and seal them closed. Cut each envelope in half crosswise. This makes two puppets. Next have the children make the puppets by drawing a face or a whole body on the side. Sometimes children may want to make faces on both sides of the envelope, for example, a smiling face on one side and a frowning face on the other.

How to Use Peace Puppets

❖ During a Peace Puppet session, you should be the one to introduce and operate the puppets. Use the puppets to role-play the conflict up to the point where it has escalated and one of the puppets is ready to hit, cry, yell, or tell the adult in charge. Once this point is reached, stop and ask the children:

  ❖ What's the problem here?

  ❖ How do you think the puppets feel right now?

  ❖ What could they do to solve their problem?

  ❖ What could they do now to make things better?

❖ Name the puppets, but don't use names of anyone in the group.

❖ Have a special box or basket that is used only for the Peace Puppets. That way you'll always be able to find them when you need them. It also emphasizes the special nature of the Peace Puppets.

❖ Children enjoy using the Peace Puppets on their own. Have two ground rules for this. First, the Peace Puppets must never get to the point where they hit or bite each other. And second, the Peace Puppets must always return to the special Peace Puppet box or basket.

❖ Use the Peace Puppets to introduce or reinforce a variety of concepts and themes, based on whatever conflicts and problems are actually occurring in your program. For example, if there is a lot of trouble between children at the sand table, that can be turned into a Peace Puppet role-play.

❖ A strength of the Peace Puppet approach is that it can help young children begin to think about the consequences of actions by allowing them to witness the consequences. If children suggest an idea that you think might have negative consequences, try using the puppets to show what would happen.

❖ Children will not need much encouragement to interact with the puppets— they do this naturally. But if children start talking to you, ask them to address the puppets directly. Having the puppets respond directly to the children will facilitate this.

❖ You can use the Peace Puppets when there are actual conflicts. There are two approaches to this, both of which are described in the activities below.

❖ One note of caution: don't have puppets physically fight with each other and don't allow the children to use them in this way when they play with them. The reason is simply that children don't need any more models of aggressive behavior, and we don't want to make aggressive behavior fun.

❖ Consider sending the Peace Puppets home for an overnight visit. This way children can show their parents what they are learning about problem solving. Two visits a week is a manageable number, although you should also have extra Peace Puppets in case the puppets aren't returned promptly.

Introducing the Peace Puppets

Children are introduced to the Peace Puppets,
observe a conflict over a toy, and suggest solutions

● ●

Objectives
- ❖ To introduce the Peace Puppets and the problem-solving procedure
- ❖ To give children a chance to practice the problem-solving procedure

Materials
- ❖ Peace Puppets ▪
- ❖ Script 1: Truck Stop (p. 8-25)
- ❖ Toy truck ▪

Procedure
1. Tell the children that you would like to introduce some friends of yours. Take the Peace Puppets out of their box or basket and explain that the Peace Puppets are special puppets. They are called the Peace Puppets because they have problems and they need the children's help to solve their problems and make peace.

2. Read Peace Puppet Script 1 to the children, acting out the story with the Peace Puppets as you read. Discuss the conflict as suggested at the end of the script. Have the children brainstorm ideas for solving the problem.

3. When the brainstorm is complete, pick up the Peace Puppets again. Have them confer with each other by whispering. Then have them tell the class what they have decided to do to solve their problem. (Always have the Peace Puppets choose one of the solutions the children came up with.) Be sure to have the puppets thank the class for their help.

4. For future Peace Puppet sessions, you may use different Peace Puppet scripts.

Using the Peace Puppets with Real Conflicts

Children's conflicts are recorded and used in Peace Puppet sessions

● ●

Objectives
- ❖ To resolve actual conflicts using the Peace Puppets
- ❖ To practice the problem-solving procedure

Materials:
- ❖ Peace Puppets💼
- ❖ Notebook labeled "Peace Puppet Problems"
- ❖ Other materials as needed

Procedure:

1. Ask the children involved in a conflict what their conflict is about and have them describe it to you. Next ask if they would be willing to have this problem used in a Peace Puppet session. (The conflict may still need immediate attention from you. Scheduling it for the Peace Puppets is simply a way to bring it up before the group.)

> **note** This is an instance where it might be appropriate to name the puppets after the children involved in the conflict. Using the puppets usually provides enough distance from the problem for children to feel safe in discussing their conflict. Ask the children if they want the puppets to be named after them.

2. If they say yes, record the problem in the Peace Puppet problem book. The next time you have a Peace Puppet session, read the problem description from the book. Bring out the puppets and use them to enact the story of the conflict. Proceed as you normally would with a Peace Puppet session.

Intervening with Peace Puppets

The Peace Puppets help children involved in a conflict to work toward a solution

● ●

Objective

❖ To help children talk about their conflicts

Materials

❖ Peace Puppets

Procedure

1. Ask the children involved in a conflict what their conflict is about and have them describe it to you. Next ask if they would like to have the Peace Puppets help them.

2. If they say yes, bring out the puppets and use them to enact the story of the conflict. Proceed as you normally would with a Peace Puppet session, asking

   ❖ What's the problem?

   ❖ How do you think the puppets feel right now?

   ❖ How did you feel when you had this conflict?

   ❖ What could the puppets do to solve their problem?

   ❖ Would any of those ideas help you with your conflict?

   ❖ What could the puppets do to make things better now?

   ❖ What could you do to make things better now in your conflict?

Peace Puppet Script 1:

"Truck Stop"

Bring out the Peace Puppets and give them names, being careful not to name them after any child in the group. Explain that today the puppets have a problem that involves toys. Present the Peace Puppet skit "Truck Stop." When you've presented up to the stop point, discuss the conflict and ask how the conflict might be solved.

Props
- ❖ Peace Puppets 💼
- ❖ Toy truck

Dialogue

Puppet 1: Hi! That looks like fun. Can I play?

Puppet 2: No. I'm playing with it now. You can play with it later.

Puppet 1: But I want to play with it now.

Puppet 2: I have it now. Go away.

Puppet 1: That's not very nice. We're supposed to share.

Puppet 2: I don't want to share. Go away.

Puppet 1: You'd better let me play or . . .

Puppet 2: Or what?

Puppet 1: Or I'm going to tell on you!

STOP!

Discussion
- ❖ What is the conflict or problem the puppets have today?
- ❖ How do you think they feel right now?
- ❖ Have you ever had a problem like this?
- ❖ What could they do to solve this problem?

Conclusion   When the brainstorm is complete, pick up the Peace Puppets again. Have them confer with each other by whispering. Then have them tell the class what they have decided to do to solve their problem. Be sure to have the puppets thank the class for their help.

Peace Puppet Script 2:

"Flying Feathers"

Bring out the Peace Puppets and give them names, being careful not to name them after any child in the group. Explain that today the puppets have a problem that involves toys. Present the Peace Puppet skit "Flying Feathers." When you've presented up to the stop point, discuss the conflict and ask how the conflict might be solved.

Props

❖ Peace Puppets.

❖ Three red feathers (you can make these by drawing three feathers on red construction paper and cutting each one out)

❖ Five yellow feathers (you can make these by drawing five feathers on yellow construction paper and cutting each one out)

❖ Construction paper and crayons

Dialogue

Begin by showing the puppets working on an art project.

Puppet 1:   [Picks up the feathers] I'm going to put these on my mask.

Puppet 2:   Hey! I was going to put them on *my* mask.

Puppet 1:   I need them all for my mask.

Puppet 2:   You're supposed to share things here.

Puppet 1:   You just want them because I got them first. You can use the green ones and those sequins.

Puppet 2:   I don't want green feathers, I want those yellow and red ones.

[Puppet 2 grabs the feathers. In the ensuing struggle, the feathers are crushed.]

Puppet 1:   Now see what you did!

Puppet 2: You did it. You always wreck everything!

Puppet 1: I'm telling on you.

Puppet 2: I'm telling on you too!

STOP!

Discussion

❖ What is the conflict or problem the puppets have today?

❖ How do you think they feel right now?

❖ Have you ever had a problem like this?

❖ What could they do to solve this problem?

Conclusion When the brainstorm is complete, pick up the Peace Puppets again. Have them confer with each other by whispering. Then have them tell the class what they have decided to do to solve their problem. Be sure to have the puppets thank the class for their help.

Peace Puppet Script 3:

"I Won!"

Bring out the Peace Puppets and give them names, being careful not to name them after any child in the group. Explain that today the Puppets have a problem that involves a race. Present the Peace Puppet skit "I Won!" When you've presented up to the stop point, discuss the conflict and ask how the conflict might be solved.

Props
❖ Peace Puppets
❖ Piece of yarn to act as finish line

Dialogue
Lay the yarn on the rug as a finish line. Have the two puppets race to the line, making sure they cross the line at the exact same time.

Puppet 1: I won!

Puppet 2: No you didn't, I won!

Puppet 1: Did too!

Puppet 2: Did not!

Puppet 1: Cheater!

Puppet 2: Liar!

Teacher: Hey! What's all the shouting about?

Puppet 1: We had a race and I won, but she says she won!

Puppet 2: I did win!

Teacher: Let's ask the kids. Did you see either puppet win or was it a tie?

STOP!

Discussion   Get responses from the group. If no one can agree on who won, then what should they do next?

❖ Have you ever had a problem like this?

❖ What did you do to solve it?

❖ After getting several responses, say, "Let's ask the Peace Puppets if they think that will work for them." (The solution most children suggest is to run the race again. You may want to do so, and again have a clear tie.)

❖ Both puppets did a good job in this race and they are both good runners. How could they celebrate that?

Conclusion   When the brainstorm is complete, pick up the Peace Puppets again. Have them confer with each other by whispering. Then have them tell the class what they have decided to do to solve their problem. Be sure to have the puppets thank the class for their help.

Peace Puppet Script 4:

"Ow!!"

Bring out the Peace Puppets and give them names, being careful not to name them after any child in the group. Explain that today the puppets have a problem that involves toys. Present the Peace Puppet skit "Ow!!" When you've presented up to the stop point, discuss the conflict and ask how the conflict might be solved.

Props
- ❖ Peace Puppets
- ❖ Box with small toys
- ❖ Chair to act as a "shelf" for the box

Dialogue
Place the chair in front of you. Set the box on the seat of the chair. This conflict begins with the second puppet on the floor, by the feet of the chair, playing with a small toy.

Puppet 1: [Comes in and sees the second puppet playing.] That looks like fun. Where did you get that toy?

Puppet 2: Out of that box up there. You get one too and we can play together.

[Puppet 1 reaches up to get the box and tugs at it a few times. With the last tug it falls on the head of Puppet 2.]

Puppet 2: Ow! You hurt me!

Puppet 1: I didn't mean to.

Puppet 2: You did it on purpose. You're a big jerk!

Puppet 1: I am not. You're just a big baby!

Teacher: What's all the shouting over here?

Puppet 1 and 2: He/She started it!

STOP!

Discussion
- ❖ What is the conflict or problem the puppets have today?
- ❖ How do you think they feel right now?
- ❖ Have you ever had a problem like this?
- ❖ What could they do to solve this problem?

Conclusion   When the brainstorm is complete, pick up the Peace Puppets again. Have them confer with each other by whispering. Then have them tell the class what they have decided to do to solve their problem. Be sure to have the puppets thank the class for their help.

"The Scribbler"

Bring out the Peace Puppets and give them names, being careful not to name them after any child in the group. Explain that today the puppets have a problem that involves toys. Present the Peace Puppet skit "The Scribbler." When you've presented up to the stop point, discuss the conflict and ask how the conflict might be solved.

Props
- ❖ Peace Puppets
- ❖ One sheet of drawing paper
- ❖ Crayon

Dialogue Puppet 2 is drawing a design of circles on the drawing paper.

Puppet 1: Can I see what you're drawing?

Puppet 2: Sure!

Puppet 1: You're not drawing anything, you're just scribbling.

Puppet 2: I am not. It's a design!

Puppet 1: It looks like scribbles to me. You're a scribbler baby.

Puppet 2: I am not!

Puppet 1: Scribbler! Scribbler!

Puppet 2: You better shut up . . .

Puppet 1: Or what?

Puppet 2: Or I'm going to tell.

STOP!

Discussion
- ❖ What is the conflict or problem the puppets have today?
- ❖ How do you think they feel right now?
- ❖ Have you ever had a problem like this?
- ❖ What could they do to solve this problem?

Conclusion   When the brainstorm is complete, pick up the Peace Puppets again. Have them confer with each other by whispering. Then have them tell the class what they have decided to do to solve their problem. Be sure to have the puppets thank the class for their help.

"You're Not Listening!"

Bring out the Peace Puppets and say that today the puppets have a problem that involves listening. Present the Peace Puppet skit "You're Not Listening!" When you've presented up to the stop point, discuss the conflict and ask students to give the puppets advice on how to be better listeners.

Props
- ❖ Peace Puppets 💼
- ❖ A paper bag with the name "Meredith" on the side

Part One

Feel free to change the names of the puppets and change the name on the paper bag to avoid using the names of children in the group.

Dialogue   Puppet 1 comes in and picks up the bag.

Puppet 1:   Boy, am I hungry. I'm so happy it's snack time. [Opens bag] Hey, this isn't my snack. I had a cupcake and a banana.

Puppet 2:   [Comes in] Someone stole my snack. [Sees Puppet 1] That's my snack. You stole it!

Puppet 1:   I didn't mean to, I . . .

Puppet 2:   What a stealer you are! Give me my snack! [Grabs bag]

Puppet 1:   But I . . .

Puppet 2:   I'm going to tell everyone how you steal.

Puppet 1:   But . . .

Puppet 2:   Hey everybody, Marcus was trying to steal my snack, but I caught him.

Puppet 1:   [Shouts] Cut it out!

STOP!

Discussion
- ❖ What's the conflict here?
- ❖ How do you think the puppets feel right now?
- ❖ How are they not being good listeners?
- ❖ How could they be better listeners? What could they do differently?

Part Two

Complete the skit. If your students have some good ideas that are not in the script as written, feel free to incorporate them. The goal is to show how good listening can make a difference in how people solve problems.

Dialogue

Puppet 1: I hate it when you won't let me explain.

Puppet 2: But you took my snack.

Puppet 1: That's what I'm trying to tell you. I didn't mean to. It was a mistake.

Puppet 2: My name is on the bag.

Puppet 1: I didn't see it. I opened the bag when you walked in.

Puppet 2: Oh.

Puppet 1: It hurt my feelings when you called me a stealer. Then you told everybody and that made me mad.

Puppet 2: I'm sorry.

Puppet 1: That's okay.

Puppet 2: Want to share snacks?

Puppet 1: Sure.

Discussion
- ❖ How did the conflict change once the Peace Puppets started listening to each other?
- ❖ What did they do to become better listeners?

Preventing Bullying and Namecalling

by Carol Wintle

Bullying happens when someone is repeatedly treated unkindly by one or more people. Unkind actions can include name calling, making fun, picking on, hitting, kicking, shoving, pushing, pinching, extorting money, damaging belongings, threatening, spreading lies, and purposely excluding someone from group activities.

There probably isn't a program for children that hasn't grappled with how to stop children from calling each other names that are put-downs. Providers need to help young children build respect for the names that people have and like to be called, identify what it feels like to be called names or put down, and identify what children can do if someone makes fun of them.

This section includes information about:

- ❖ Current research on bullying
- ❖ Targets of bullying

❖ Children who bully

❖ The phenomenon of "join-ins"

❖ Tips and activities for preventing bullying and name calling

❖ Additional resources for preventing bullying and name calling

The Current Research on Bullying

Bullying involves an imbalance of power. Either a group is bullying an individual (this is known as scapegoating) or one person is bullying another. In the latter case, the person doing the bullying may be older, more popular, or physically stronger than the person being bullied. Children who bully and children who are targets of bullying can get stuck in these patterns of behavior for many years. They need caring adults to help them break out of these roles.

New information on bullying is being discovered every day, and while most of the research is done on school-age bullying, early childhood programs can benefit from these studies. Current research has revealed the following:

❖ Bullying is one of the most overlooked problems in schools today.

❖ Even in the best-administered schools, twenty-five percent of children surveyed reported that one of their most serious concerns was fear of bullies.

❖ One in ten children is regularly harassed or attacked by bullies at school.

❖ Children in primary grades report that teachers do not talk with them about bullying and that teachers try to put a stop to bullying only once in a while or almost never.

❖ In 400 hours of video-documented episodes of bullying at school, the teachers noticed and intervened in only one out of every twenty-five episodes.

❖ The aggressive behavior of children who bully starts in the preschool years.

---

* For more information see: Laura Sessions Stepp, "Getting Tough with the Big, Bad Bullies," *Washington Post*, December 1, 1992; *Set Straight On Bullies*, National School Safety Center, Pepperdine University; Dan Olweus, *Bullying at School: What We Know and What We Can Do* (Cambridge, Mass.: Blackwell, 1993); Hara Estroff Marano, "Big Bad Bully," *Psychology Today*, September/October 1995, p. 57.

Targets of Bullying

Research on bullying indicates that many children who are targets of bullying share some similar characteristics. These include:

- ❖ Having sensitive, quiet, and cautious personalities
- ❖ Being anxious and insecure
- ❖ Lacking assertiveness skills (tending to cry or withdraw when bullied)
- ❖ Having few close friends
- ❖ Being afraid, tending to blame themselves for the bullying, and developing depression
- ❖ Disliking aggression and violence
- ❖ (If male) being physically weaker than their peers

Children Who Bully

Research shows that many children who demonstrate chronic bullying behavior also tend to share certain qualities. These are:

- ❖ Having difficulty empathizing with other people's feelings
- ❖ Having impulsive tendencies and hostile feelings
- ❖ Believing that aggression is a good way to solve conflicts and that there are rewards gained by dominating others
- ❖ (If male) being physically strong
- ❖ Probably having experienced a permissive attitude towards aggressive behavior at home
- ❖ Probably having experienced a lack of affection and warmth at home
- ❖ Probably having experienced physical punishment and violent emotional outbursts at home
- ❖ Growing up to be adults who teach their children how to bully and who get in trouble with the law, with co-workers, and with peers

Join-Ins

Scapegoating occurs when a group bullies an individual. Sometimes one child initiates bullying and others join in by laughing at the targeted child, not letting him or her join their game, etc. Children may join in on bullying because it seems like fun, they want to be part of a popular group, they think the targeted child deserves to be treated poorly, or because there are no negative consequences for joining in. Much can be accomplished by teaching all children that this behavior is wrong and by giving consequences to any children who participate in bullying, regardless of whether they were the key initiators or not.

Tips and Activities for Preventing Bullying and Name-Calling*

The activities in this section will help you teach children:

❖ what bullying is

❖ what they can do if they are bullied

❖ what they can do if they see someone else being bullied

❖ what adults will do if they see or hear about anyone being bullied

In addition to these activities, there are many other things your program can do to help children who bully and children who are bullied to break out of these patterns. Here are a number of ideas you can implement in your program.

❖ Establish a range of consequences for bullying behavior. These may include: having a serious talk with one of the adults in the program; needing to do something nice for the person they hurt; involving parents/ guardians.

❖ Send a letter home to all parents about what bullying is and what your program is doing to prevent bullying.

---

* From Carol Wintle and Boston Area Educators for Social Responsibility, "Preventing Bullying At School," (Cambridge, Mass.: BAESR, 1995).

❖ Increase supervision (by well-trained adults) on the playground, in lunch and snack areas, in hallways, on buses, and in rest rooms. Set up a consistent procedure for recording any bullying incidents.

❖ Pair unpopular children with a variety of friendly, helpful buddies.

❖ Encourage children when they demonstrate thumbs-up behavior.

❖ Play cooperative games and do cooperation activities (see chapter 4) to help students get to know and appreciate each other better.

❖ If you suspect that a child in your program is being bullied, find a time to talk privately with that child.

    a. Tell the child what you have noticed and that you want to put a stop to the problem.

    b. Let the child know that if other children are picking on or excluding him, it is not his fault.

    c. Ask the child what he has experienced and encourage the child to tell you how he is feeling.

    d. Remind the child about what to do if someone treats him in an unkind way (see "Stick Up For Yourself" on p. 9-14).

    e. Help the child role-play these various options.

    f. Ask the child to let you and his parents know if the bullying happens again.

❖ Whenever you suspect that a child is bullying others, talk privately with the child. If a group of children is bullying others, it is better to speak privately with each child in the group rather than talk to the whole group at once.

    a. Describe what you have seen.

    b. Remind them of the thumbs-up rules (see "Group Agreement" on p. 9-13).

    c. Let them know that you care about them and want to help them learn how to treat other children in a thumbs-up way.

    d. Explain the consequences.

    e. Enforce the consequences.

❖ Keep a record of bullying interventions.

❖ Look for opportunities to help children who bully develop their positive potentials.

❖ Work cooperatively to solve any bullying problems with the parents/guardians of children who bully, as well as those who are targets of bullying. Parents/guardians of a targeted child can help their child develop her strengths, practice sticking up for herself, and develop a stronger friendship network. Parents/guardians of children who bully can monitor their child's behavior more closely including strictly limiting the amount of violent media their child views, generously encouraging their child for thumbs-up behavior, and giving respectful, nonviolent consequences when the child acts disrespectfully. Parents who need help implementing these strategies can be referred to agencies that provide family support services.

❖ If necessary, refer either children who bully or who are targets of bullying for counseling or other support services.

Thumbs-Up and Thumbs-Down Displays

Children illustrate kind and hurtful actions towards others

● ●

Objective
- ❖ To reinforce the concepts of thumbs-up and thumbs-down behavior

Materials
- ❖ Paper
- ❖ Crayons
- ❖ Cut-outs of a fist with the thumb sticking up and a fist with a thumb sticking down

Procedure

1. Designate two areas of wall space for the bulletin boards. Title one area "Thumbs Up" and the other "Thumbs Down."

2. Create two large book covers, one titled "Thumbs Up" and one titled "Thumbs Down." The pages in these books will contain children's illustrations and brainstormed lists.

3. Introduce or review the concepts of thumbs-up and thumbs-down behavior (see "Thumbs Up, Thumbs Down" on p. 8-13).

4. Invite them to make pictures of thumbs-up and thumbs-down actions to go on the bulletin boards or in the books.

5. Decorate the displays and books with cut-out hands (fists with thumbs sticking up or thumbs sticking down).

6. As you go through the following activities, use the bulletin board space to display children's artwork, brainstormed lists, etc., that relate to each activity. As the bulletin boards get crowded, move displayed material into the books.

Name Cards

Children learn about their own names

● ●

Objective   To help children see that the name they have is special

Materials   3″ x 5″ index cards (one per child)

Procedure

1. Tell the children that everyone's name is special. Ask them to find out what is special about their name.

   tip

   This a great activity for the first weeks of your program, or for when a new child arrives.

2. Send home a note to each child's parent/guardian asking them to provide information about what makes their child's name unique. For example:

   ❖ What do they like about their child's name?

   ❖ Does their child's name have a special meaning?

   ❖ Is their child named after someone special?

3. Print each child's name on an index card. On the back of the card write one thing that is special about that child's name. Post these cards on the "Thumbs-Up Bulletin Board" ("Thumbs-Up and Thumbs-Down Displays" on p. 9-7) and use them when playing the "Once Upon a Time Game" (facing page).

Once Upon a Time Game

Children share the meaning of their names

• •

Objective   ❖ To help children see that every child's name is special

Materials   ❖ Name Cards (see previous activity)

Procedure   1. Give each child a Name Card.

2. Sit in a circle with each child holding his or her Name Card. Decide which child will go first.

3. Instruct the children to hold their Name Cards in their laps until it is their turn. When it is their turn, they should hold up their Name Card for everyone to see.

4. Begin the game by saying, "Once upon a time a very special child was born and that child's name was . . ." At this point, the first child holds up his or her Name Card. Say the child's name. For example, "Rose."

5. Go on to the next child. Invite the children to repeat the line with you. "Once upon a time a very special child was born and that child's name was . . . Larry."

6. Go around the circle in this way until every child has been introduced.

7. Go around the circle again, this time saying the one thing that is special about each child's name. For example, "Once upon a time a very special child was born and that child's name was Rose. Rose was named after her grandmother. Once upon a time a very special child was born and that child's name was Larry. Larry's name means lion."

8. This game can be as short or as long as you like. Here are some other lines you can add.

❖ "Once upon a time a very special child was born. Her name was Rose. Rose was named after her grandmother. One day Rose was feeling . . . [e.g., happy]." Each child says how he or she is feeling that day.

❖ "One day she came to school and . . . [e.g., passed out snack]." Each child says something he or she did that day at school.

❖ "One day she came to school and said. . . [e.g., I'm hungry]." Each child says a word or sentence. If a child cannot think of anything to say, that is fine. You can end the sentence by saying, "One day she came to school and was quiet." Then go on to the next child. Come back to the quiet child later and see if he or she has thought of something to say.

❖ "One day she came to school and made a sound and it went like this . . ." Each child makes a sound, such as a cow mooing, teeth clicking, wind blowing, etc.

❖ "One day she came to school and made a movement. It went like this . . ." Each child makes a movement such as waving, squinting, clapping, etc.

Chrysanthemum

Children listen to a story
about name calling and discuss it

● ●

Objectives
- ❖ To build respect for people's names
- ❖ To identify how it feels to have someone make fun of your name

Materials
- ❖ The book *Chrysanthemum* by Kevin Henkes■

In this book a little girl loves her name until she goes to school and the children make fun of it. Mrs. Twinkle, the music teacher, helps the children see that Chrysanthemum's name is really very terrific.

Procedure
1. Read *Chrysanthemum* up to the end of the first day of school where Victoria says, "If I had a name like yours, I'd change it," and Chrysanthemum, feeling miserable, wishes she could.

2. Lead a discussion using the following questions:
   - ❖ How is Chrysanthemum feeling?
   - ❖ What happened on Chrysanthemum's first day of school?
   - ❖ What is the problem here?
   - ❖ What could Chrysanthemum do about this problem?
   - ❖ What do you think will happen in this story?

3. Read the rest of the story, then lead a discussion using the following questions:
   - ❖ Was the problem solved?
   - ❖ Do you like the way the problem was solved?
   - ❖ How does Chrysanthemum feel now?
   - ❖ Has anybody ever made fun of your name?

❖ How did you feel?

❖ Has anybody ever made fun of someone else's name?

❖ How did you feel?

4. Make up a poem with the children such as:

Our names are absolutely perfect.

We love the way they sound,

when someone else says them,

when we say them ourselves.

We love the way they look,

when they are written with ink on an envelope,

when they are written with icing on our birthday cakes,

when we write them ourselves with colored crayons.

Our names are absolutely perfect!

5. Invite children to draw pictures and tell stories of good and bad dreams (or other stories) for their Story Journals, Story Tapes, or for Story Circle Time. (See chapter 13 for descriptions of these activities.)

Group Agreement

Children listen to a story
and make a group agreement to be kind to each other

● ●

Objective To involve children in creating an agreement to treat each other in kind and caring ways

Materials

❖ Small and large sheets of paper

❖ The book *Chrysanthemum*, by Kevin Henkes

Procedure

1. Read or review the story *Chrysanthemum*. Ask the children to remember the ways the children made fun of Chrysanthemum's name. For example, they

    ❖ giggled at the way it sounded

    ❖ said her name was too long

    ❖ said, "If I had a name like yours, I'd change it," "She looks like a flower," "Let's pick her," "Let's smell her," and "I just cannot believe your name."

2. Print this list on a piece of paper and post on the Thumbs-Down Bulletin Board (see p. 9-7).

3. Print on a large sheet of paper: "In this program we treat each other in thumbs-up ways." Ask each child to sign their name to this agreement.

4. Post the agreement on the Thumbs-Up Bulletin Board. Then ask, "What if you forget, and treat someone in a thumbs-down way? What could you do?"

5. List the children's responses and add any of the following:

    ❖ Make that person an apology picture.

    ❖ Do something else nice for that person.

    ❖ Tell that person something you like about him or her.

6. Post this list on the Thumbs-Up Bulletin Board.

Stick Up For Yourself

Children listen to a story about
name calling and role-play their solutions

● ●

Objectives
- To identify ways that children can stick up for themselves
- To role play several of these options

Materials
- Paper and markers
- The book *Chrysanthemum*, by Kevin Henkes

Procedure
1. Ask, "If someone treats you in a thumbs-down way, what could you do?"

2. List the children's responses. Then ask, "Are all of these ideas thumbs-up actions?"

3. Circle the ones that reflect thumbs-up behavior. Add any of the following:
   - Ask or tell them to stop.
   - Ask or tell them to leave you alone.
   - Tell them how you feel. ("You are hurting my feelings." "I don't like it when you tease me.")
   - Ask them why they are treating you like that. ("Why won't you let me play with you?")
   - Go play with someone else.
   - Ask an adult to help you figure out what to do.

4. Read or review the story *Chrysanthemum* up to the page where children are teasing Chrysanthemum on the playground. Go around the circle and give each child a chance to pretend to be Chrysanthemum and stand up and say, "Stop teasing me," "Please don't make fun of my name," "You are hurting my feelings," "Why are you teasing me?" or "I don't want to play with kids who aren't nice."

King of the Playground

Children listen to a story
about bullying and act it out

• •

Objectives
❖ To practice brainstorming

❖ To act out a story in which an adult helps a child figure out what to do about being bullied

Materials
❖ The book *King of the Playground* by Phyllis Reynolds Naylor

In this story, Sammy is afraid to go to the playground because Kevin is there. By talking with his father, Sammy figures out how not to be bullied by Kevin.

Procedure
1. Read the book up to the point where Sammy shouts, "You can't play here! I'm King of the Monkey Bars," and then tells Kevin what he would do if he saw him there again.

2. Lead a discussion using the following questions:

   ❖ How do you think Sammy is feeling?

   ❖ What is Sammy's problem?

   ❖ How do you think he can solve this problem?

   ❖ What do you think will happen next in the story?

3. Read the rest of the story, then lead a discussion using the following questions:

   ❖ How does Kevin stand up for himself?

   ❖ Do you like how Kevin solved his problem?

4. Involve the children in a dramatization of the story. Choose one child to play Kevin, and one child to play Kevin's father. Reread the story for the dramatization. (If necessary, say each child's lines first, and have the child repeat back to you.)

5. Explain that in this story Sammy was bullying Kevin. Introduce or review the concepts of thumbs-up and thumbs-down behavior (see "Thumbs Up, Thumbs Down" on p. 8-13). Ask the children to remember all the thumbs-down things Sammy did to Kevin. Make a list for example:

   ❖ Sammy said that Kevin couldn't play on the playground.

   ❖ Sammy said he would put Kevin in a hole in the ground.

6. Post this list on the Thumbs-Down Bulletin Board (see "Thumbs-Up and Thumbs-Down Displays" p. 9-7).

7. Ask the group, "If someone was bothering you in the way Sammy was bothering Kevin, what could you do?" List the children's ideas. Then ask, "Which of these are thumbs-up choices?" Circle the thumbs-up choices. Add the following to the children's list:

   ❖ Say, "Leave me alone."

   ❖ Say, "I don't want you to bother me any more."

   ❖ Say, "Stop that."

   ❖ Tell an adult about the problem and ask that adult to help you to figure out what to do.

8. Give each child a chance to practice standing up to a bully. Have the children take turns saying one of the lines above.

9. Invite the children to draw Story Pictures or tell stories for their Story Journals, Story Tapes, or for Story Circle Time. (See chapter 13 for descriptions of these activities.)

Additional Resources

Garrity, Carla et al. *Bullyproofing Your School: A Comprehensive Approach for Elementary Schools*. Longmont, Colo.: Sophis West Inc., 1994, 1995.

"Keeping Your Child Safe From Bullies," The Violence Prevention Project, Harvard Pilgrim Health Care Foundation, 1-800-580-0660.

Olweus, Dan. *Bullying at School: What We Know and What We Can Do*. Cambridge, Mass.: Blackwell, 1993.

Paley, Vivian. *You Can't Say You Can't Play*. Cambridge, Mass.: Harvard University Press, 1992.

Music*

Music brings people together. When we make music and sing together, we have fun and feel closer to each other.

Just as children need to practice reading or counting, they need to practice social skills. Cooperative songs provide a time for young people to practice playing together and talking out problems, as well as a time for adults to give children guidance.

Six activities in this section are reprinted from *Linking Up! Using Music and Movement to Promote Caring, Cooperation, and Communication, Pre-K–3*, by Sarah Pirtle. This recording (available on cassette or CD) and the accompanying teaching guide help providers to create a Peaceable Program through music and movement activities. Sarah Pirtle's songwriting has won numerous awards, including the Oppenheim Gold Seal Best Audio Award and the Parents' Choice Classic Award. To order *Linking Up!* or for more information call 1-800-370-2515.

This section includes:

- ❖ teachable moments for using the *Linking Up!* recording
- ❖ music activities

*The introduction and teachable moments sections of this chapter were contributed by Sarah Pirtle.

Teachable Moments: Linking Up!

❖ When singing songs with your group, believe in yourself as a singer. Music belongs to everyone. You never need to apologize for your singing voice. We need to model for our children that their voices are welcome and that we don't need to judge how we sound.

❖ If you lead a regular circle time with your group, begin with a favorite song. Choose one that is upbeat, joyful, and that helps the children feel welcomed. Welcoming songs on the *Linking Up!* recording include, "Come Join in the Circle," "Good Morning to the Sky / Buenos Días Al Cielo," and "¡Hola! ¿Que tal? / Hello My Friends."

❖ Have the children take turns choosing what song the group will sing. Create a chart that lists children's names and move down the list giving each child a chance to choose a song.

❖ Look for opportunities to ask children for their suggestions. For example, ask the children:

  ❖ What do you want to sing next?

  ❖ How can we move to this song?

  ❖ What other words could we sing?

  ❖ Moving to music provides a safe setting for working on social skills. Use conflicts as learning experiences. Respond to conflicts by guiding children to solutions, rather than by punishing them. For strategies on intervening in conflicts, see chapter 8.

Shakers

Children construct instruments
and make music together

● ●

Ages   4 and up

Objective   ❖ To build community

Materials   ❖ Empty toilet paper rolls

                ❖ Beans or pebbles

                ❖ One or more staplers

                ❖ Felt-tip pens, stickers, other decorations

Procedure   1. Distribute an empty toilet paper roll to each child. Have them staple one end of their toilet paper tube closed. (Younger children will need help with this step.) Fill the tube part-way with beans or pebbles.

                2. Have children staple the opening shut and decorate the tube.

                3. Now you'll make a sound with a shaker and invite the children to copy it. Keep it short and simple: fast shakes; three slow, strong shakes; or shake, pause, shake, shake.

                4. Younger children may take turns leading the group in a rhythm. Divide older children into small groups and let each establish a distinct rhythm. Bring the large group together and see if each group can maintain its own rhythm while everyone plays.

Reflection ❖ Was this exercise hard to do? What was hard about this?

                ❖ How does it sound when we all play the same rhythm?

                ❖ How does it sound if everyone is playing a different rhythm? Is it music or noise?

Feeling the Music

Children sketch or draw while listening to music

● ● ● ● ● ● ● ● ● ● ● ● ● ● ● ● ● ● ● ●

Ages   4 and up

Objective   ❖ To recognize and express feelings evoked by music

Materials   ❖ Paper

                  ❖ Crayons or felt pens

                  ❖ Music cassettes■ or records: one selection very calm and soothing (such as selections of Debussy's "The Sea") and a lively, dramatic piece (such as Vivaldi's "Fire Dance")

                  ❖ Cassette or record player

Procedure   1. Explain to the children: "We're going to listen to some music. First, just listen to it, but when I play it again, you'll draw on your paper. Sketch or just draw lines, whatever the music makes you feel or think."

                  2. Play the slow music for the children. Then play it a second time. While they listen to the music the second time, have the children draw on their paper. Tell the children, "You can sketch a picture or just draw lines, whatever the music makes you think or feel."

                  3. Now play the lively music once just for listening. Play the same music again while the children draw.

                  4. Hold each child's fast-music picture up for all to see and allow the child to tell about his or her feelings and the picture.

                  5. Discuss similarities in the pictures.

                      ❖ What colors are used most often?

                      ❖ Are there lots of lines or swirls?

                      ❖ How does the picture remind you of the music?

6. Repeat steps 3 and 4 with the slow music.

Reflection Discuss music in movies, television, and in stores. How does it affect the way you feel? Does it excite you, scare you, sometimes slow you down?

Rhythm Sticks

Children beat sticks and learn about rhythm

● ●

Ages   4 and up

Objective
- ❖ To work cooperatively
- ❖ To make music together

Materials
- ❖ Rhythm sticks 📖

Procedure
1. Explain to the children: "Rhythm is the beat of music. We can count the beat. Let's count now and try to make a steady beat with a pattern."

2. Count "1-2-3-4" with children, inviting them to strike their sticks together on each number.

> **note** You'll want to keep the sessions short, so just do one activity per session. If children can't hold their sticks quietly until they're directed to play, be ready to collect them and bring them out another day.

3. Here are some rhythmic variations children enjoy:

   - ❖ Hit the sticks only for "1" and hold for "2-3-4."

   - ❖ Count fast, then slowly.

   - ❖ Add half notes: "1-and-2-and-3-and-4-and."

   - ❖ Sing a favorite song and use the rhythm sticks to accompany the song.

   - ❖ Start a steady rhythm and let the children join in as soon as they can pick it up. Then make a distinct change. Children will stop, pause, and then join in the new rhythm. Let children see how fast they can copy each rhythm.

   - ❖ Have each child take a turn playing a *short* rhythm. Then have the group play it back.

❖ Children face a partner. They sing a song and together beat out a rhythm. This takes coordination and is best done with older children.

Reflection

❖ Did everyone play their sticks?

❖ Was it tough joining in?

❖ Was it easier or harder working with partners?

Orchestra

Children pretend to play in an orchestra and take turns as the conductor

● ●

Ages   5 and up

Objective   ❖ To establish a sense of community and cooperation

Materials   ❖ Musical instruments 💼 (one instrument per child is ideal)

Procedure

1. Show the children a picture of an orchestra with a conductor. Tell the children, "Let's all be an orchestra, playing music together. Does anyone know what the conductor does?" Allow children to answer. "That's right. A conductor is the person who tells the musicians when and how to play. Let's give everyone a chance to be a conductor today."

> **tip**
>
> Older children can choose hand signals to represent their instruments. The conductor then learns the hand signals and uses them to designate which instruments should play. This is best done in a small group of five or six children.

2. Form a large circle and give everyone in the circle an instrument. Be sure that like instruments sit together. The first few times you should model the role of conductor. Eventually, let a child play this role. Remind the children to watch the conductor closely.

3. When the conductor points to one person or group, they should begin playing. Everyone stops when the conductor makes a grand sweep of his or her arms. When the conductor wants to signal one group to stop, have him hold up his hand.

4. Give each child a turn at being the conductor.

Parade

Children create a marching band

● ●

Ages   4 and up

Objective   ❖ To establish sense of community and cooperation

Materials   ❖ Musical instruments 💼

❖ Rolls of crepe paper

Procedure   1. Tie three-foot streamers of crepe paper on everyone's wrists.

2. Choose a leader. Have the children form a line, holding their instrument of choice and following the leader around the room or outside playing their instruments.

> **tip**
>
> Older children may like to create more elaborate "band uniforms" by taping a stripe of crepe paper down the outside seam of their pants. Or have the children dress up in any costumes that are available.

3. For older children, form rows of three or four across. One child designated as "drum major" stands in front and leads the group by marching straight ahead with knees high. If the drum major stops and turns, everyone stops, turns, and marches in that direction. The drum major may signal stops and starts with a whistle.

Come Join in the Circle*

Children gather and sing a welcoming song

● ●

Ages   3 and up

Objective
- ❖ To help children feel welcomed
- ❖ To build community

Materials
- ❖ *Linking Up!* CD 💼 by Sarah Pirtle with Roberto Díaz
- ❖ CD player

Procedure

1. Preview the song "Come Join in the Circle," to familiarize yourself with the music and lyrics:

> **note** This is a good activity to use each day at the start of your program. This joyful song helps the children feel welcome. The words also ask the children to notice each other, helping them all to feel seen and included.

> Come join the circle,
> Moon, moon, the moon and sun.
> Come join the circle,
> There's room for everyone.
> I'm so glad you're here [clap, clap].
> I'm so glad you're here [clap, clap].
> Come join the circle,
> There's room for everyone.
> Wave around the circle,
> Moon, moon, the moon and sun.
> Wave around the circle
> Wave to everyone.
> Wave the way you like,
> Wave the way you like,

---

* Reprinted from *Linking Up! Using Music, Movement, and Language Arts to Promote Caring, Cooperation, and Communication, PreK-3*, by Sarah Pirtle (Cambridge, Mass.: Educators for Social Responsibility, 1998).

Wave around the circle,
Wave to everyone.[*]

2. Gather the children in a circle. Play the song "Come Join the Circle."

3. Ask the children to wave to each other when they hear the words, "Wave around the circle." As the song repeats, ask the children to invent the kind of wave they want to use, or make suggestions about different ways to wave. For example, say to the children, "Let's try waving with our elbows." Or ask, "What's another way we can wave?"

> **tip**
>
> Invent a verse to welcome children back after they have been away from the group. For example:
>
> We're glad to see
> you're back now.
>
> You're back now,
> you're back now.
>
> You were gone
> for eight long days,
>
> We want to read you
> the big book we made.

4. Try putting your group's own lyrics into this tune. Gather information from the children about their recent activities and experiences. Ask the children, "Who has news to put in our song today?" Put this information into the song, and ask the class to echo back each sentence as you present it. For example:

Emma climbed to the top of an apple tree.
Pavel helped his grandma make pierogi.
Maisie's cat is still missing.
We hope your cat comes back.

Or create a verse about a special trip:

We took a trip to Boston,
and we rode in the swan boats.
We threw bread in the water,
and the ducks gobbled it up.

---

[*] Words and music by Sarah Pirtle copyright © 1997 Discovery Center Music

Or create a verse about activities children did that day in your program:

> Caitlin built a rocket.
> Keno cut a snowflake.
> Jessie did the circle puzzle.
> And Reggie hummed a song.

Such a verse could also be used as a guessing game. For example,

> Who built a rocket?
> Who cut a snowflake?
> Who did the circle puzzle?
> And who hummed a song?

Chocolate*

Children make hand movements
as they sing a song in Spanish

● ●

Ages   5 and up

Objective
- ❖ To sing and count in Spanish
- ❖ To increase concentration and focus

Materials
- ❖ *Linking Up!* CD 💿 by Sarah Pirtle with Roberto Díaz
- ❖ CD player

Procedure

1. Preview the traditional song "Chocolate," to familiarize yourself with the music and lyrics:

   Part I:

   > Uno, dos, tres, CHO
   > Uno, dos, tres, CO
   > Uno, dos, tres, LA
   > Uno, dos, tres, TE

   Part II:

   > Chocolate, chocolate,
   > bate, bate, chocolate.
   > Chocolate, chocolate,
   > bate, bate, chocolate.

2. Describe to the children the background of the song. In Mexico, *chocolate* (pronounced "cho-co-LA-

> **tip**
>
> Simplify this activity for younger children by instructing them to rub their palms together for all or most of the song.
>
> This activity is useful when the group needs to become more focused.
>
> The following bilingual resources include the song "Chocolate" and provide illustrations of how the molinillo (the beater) is used to make chocolate:
>
> Orozco, Jose-Luis. *De Colores and Other Latin-American Folk Songs for Children.* New York: Dutton, 1994.
>
> Griego, Margot et al. *Tortillas Para Mama and Other Nursery Rhymes in Spanish and English.* New York: Henry Holt & Co., 1981.

---

* Reprinted from *Linking Up! Using Music, Movement, and Language Arts to Promote Caring, Cooperation, and Communication, PreK-3*, by Sarah Pirtle (Cambridge, Mass.: Educators for Social Responsibility, 1998).

tay") is a common beverage made of chocolate and hot milk. Traditionally, it is mixed using a carved wooden beater called a *molinillo* (in Mexico the beater would be pronounced "mo-li-NEE-yo"). The *molinillo* is spun by rubbing the handle between your palms. To help children follow your description, José-Luis Orozco suggests leading a pantomime of pouring in the milk and chocolate and then stirring the beverage using a *molinillo*. (Note that on the recording the words are pronounced are they are said in Puerto Rico.)

3. Teach motions to accompany the song. In Part I, begin by counting one, two, three with your fingers on "Uno, dos, tres." Then, at each syllable—cho, co, la, te—tap one fist on top of the other.

   During Part II, tap your fists as you sing "chocolate, chocolate." Then rub your palms together, like you're using the beater to stir the *chocolate* as you say, "Bate, bate, chocolate." (On the recording it says, "Rub your hands together like you're twirling the beater, the *molinillo*.")

4. Adapt the motions to fit the needs of your age group. Younger children may be most comfortable rubbing their palms together for all or most of the song, while older children enjoy the alternation of movements.

   If children hit their hands hard, encourage them to treat themselves in a friendly way: "We can make the motion strong without hurting our hands."

Two in a Fight*

Children act out a song about fighting

● ●

Ages   4 and up

Objective   ❖ To improve communication and problem-solving skills

Materials   ❖ *Linking Up!* CD by Sarah Pirtle with Roberto Díaz
                 ❖ CD player

Procedure   1. Preview the song "Two in the Fight," to familiarize
                    yourself with the music and lyrics:

> There were two in a fight
> And the little one said, "I'm angry, I'm angry."
> But the other one started to run away.
> "Come back and hear what I have to say."
> Keep talking, keep talking.
> Come on back, (click, click)
> come on back, (click, click).
> We can figure this out.
> Come on back, (click, click)
> come on back, (click, click).
> We can figure this out.
> There were two in the fight
> And the other one said, "I'm angry, I'm angry."
> But the little one did not run away.
> "Tell me what you have to say."
> Keep talking, keep talking.
> Talk it out, (click, click),
> Talk it out, (click, click).
> We can figure this out.
> Talk it out, (click, click),

---

* Reprinted from *Linking Up! Using Music, Movement, and Language Arts to Promote Caring, Cooperation, and Communication, PreK-3*, by Sarah Pirtle (Cambridge, Mass.: Educators for Social Responsibility, 1998).

Talk it out, click, click).
We can figure this out.[*]

2. Use your index fingers to act out this story.

---

[*] Words and music by Sarah Pirtle copyright © 1997 Discovery Center Music

Shake, Shake, Freeze*

Children alternate between moving and freezing

• •

Ages   3 and up

Objective
- ❖ To alternate movement and self-control
- ❖ To respect personal boundaries

Materials
- ❖ *Linking Up!* CD🖴 by Sarah Pirtle with Roberto Díaz
- ❖ CD player

Procedure
1. Preview the song "Shake, Shake, Freeze," to familiarize yourself with the music and lyrics:

   Shake, shake, shake, shake, shake and FREEZE.
   Shake, shake, shake, shake, shake and FREEZE.
   Shake, shake, FREEZE.
   Shake, shake, FREEZE.
   Shake shake shake and FREEZE.†

> **tip**
>
> Choose motions according to the following principles:
>
> ❖ Work within the abilities of the group. For example, if you notice that children lose self-control while seated, wait until another day to progress to standing.
>
> ❖ Build up at a pace that suits the group. For example, if they are eager and able to go directly to full-body movement, use only one seated motion. If they need more structure and guidance while moving through the space, try slow, sustained movements like "swimming" through the space with hands pressed together.
>
> ❖ Provide contrast. For instance, after hopping change to waving movements, or use blinking the eyes to provide a moment of rest.

---

* Reprinted from *Linking Up!:Using Music, Movement, and Language Arts to Promote Caring, Cooperation, and Communication, PreK-3*, by Sarah Pirtle (Cambridge, Mass.: Educators for Social Responsibility, 1998).
† Words and music by Sarah Pirtle copyright © 1997 by Discovery Center Music

2. Gather the children in a circle. The movements for this song develop in increments. Begin with the children seated. Have the children all make a movement when they hear the word "shake." Suggest movements that are easy to do while seated, such as blinking the eyes, wiggling the fingers, lifting the shoulders up and down, waving the elbows, rocking back and forth, and bouncing. Have the children stop their movements when they hear the word "FREEZE."

> **▼ tip**
>
> Choose motions according to the following principles:
>
> ❖ Consider the types of movements that might benefit your group that day. For example, if the group needs strong, forceful expression, have the children stomp. If the group needs to look at each other more or make connections, have them shake hands as they walk.

3. For the next round, have the children stand up. Suggest movements that are easy to do while staying in place. Some examples are twisting the upper body from side to side, stretching to the ceiling, shaking the whole body, jumping up and down, stamping the feet, and bending over. Again, have the children stop their movements when they hear the word "FREEZE."

4. For the next round, have the children move around the space. Tell the children that it is very important not to bump into each other. Suggest movements such as walking, skipping, galloping, and leaping. Also suggest that children try to interact as they move through the space by waving and shaking hands. Again, have the children stop their movements when they hear the word "FREEZE." Be sure to take time to pause and notice whether children are holding the freeze and whether boundaries are being respected.

5. At the end of the song, the music slows down and the lyrics are:

> Moving slow like you're going through peanut butter.
> Moving slow like you're going through peanut butter.
> Moving slow, moving slow, and end up in your place.

Have the children slow down their movements at this point.

My Roots Go Down*

Children act out a song about nature

● ●

Ages 4 and up

Objective
- ❖ To collaborate with others
- ❖ To create new words or movements

Materials
- ❖ *Linking Up!* CD 💼 by Sarah Pirtle with Roberto Díaz
- ❖ CD player

Procedure
1. Preview the song "My Root Go Down," to familiarize yourself with the music and the lyrics:

   My roots go down,
   down to the earth.
   My roots go down,
   down to the earth.
   My roots go down,
   down to the earth.
   My roots go down.[†]

2. Have the children stand with enough room to move in place without bumping into others. Have them keep their feet anchored in place, swinging their arms as if their arms were branches of a tree. During the chorus of the song, encourage children to

> **tip**
>
> Here is an idea for an additional activity using this song:
>
> 1. Divide the children into small groups of three to five children. Ask these groups to sit or stand in a circle.
>
> 2. Have the groups move together to the song. Each group does not have to move in the same way, but have them watch each other and try each other's ideas.
>
> 3. Sample verses:
>   - ❖ I am a whale swimming with my friends.
>   - ❖ We are a stream with swirling ripples.
>   - ❖ We are a flower opening to the light.
>   - ❖ We are beavers building a new lodge.
>
> 4. Then let the groups decide together what they want to be and have them develop their own dance.

---

* Reprinted from *Linking Up! Using Music, Movement, and Language Arts to Promote Caring, Cooperation, and Communication, PreK-3*, by Sarah Pirtle (Cambridge, Mass.: Educators for Social Responsibility, 1998).

† Words and music by Sarah Pirtle copyright © 1997 Discovery Center Music

feel the earth under their feet. Notice whether children's movements indicate that they are feeling rooted and anchored. Ask the children, "Can you feel your feet firm on the ground as if roots connect you to the earth?"

3. Have the children add different movements as they sing the same words. For example, have them add stomping.

4. Ask the children for a suggestion. Ask, "What shall we put in the song today?" A child could answer, "Jumping beans." Then the group can jump as everyone sings:

    I am a jumping bean, jumping to the sun.

    My roots go down.

5. Suggest new verses that connect children to animals, trees, and places in nature. Some examples of possible verses are:

    *   I am a pine tree on a mountain side.
    *   I am a waterfall skipping home.
    *   I am a willow swaying in a storm.
    *   I am a wildflower pushing through stones.

Sleeping Birds*

Children pretend to be sleeping birds and gently pat each other on the back

● ●

Ages 3 and up

Objective
- ❖ To learn to give and receive gentle touch
- ❖ To care for others

Materials
- ❖ *Linking Up!* CD ▪ by Sarah Pirtle with Roberto Díaz
- ❖ CD player

Procedure

1. Preview the song "Sleeping Birds," to familiarize yourself with the music and lyrics:

   ▼ **tip**

   This is a good activity to use before a rest period or before circle time.

   We see the birds
   sleeping. We see the birds sleeping.
   We'll pat you, we'll help you feel safe in your nest. Safe in your nest, safe in your nest.
   We'll pat you, we'll help you feel safe in your nest.
   Los pajaritos duermen, quietos en sus nidos
   Acariciarlos los hace dormir
   Seguro estaran, seguro estaran
   Me gusta mimarlos, hacer los dormir
   Despierten, pajaritos[†]

2. Select a place where children can lie down. Place a rug or blanket in that area.

3. Play the song once so that the children can learn it. As children learn the song, have them gently pat their own

---

* Reprinted from *Linking Up! Using Music, Movement, and Language Arts to Promote Caring, Cooperation, and Communication, PreK-3*, by Sarah Pirtle (Cambridge, Mass.: Educators for Social Responsibility, 1998).

† Words and music by Sarah Pirtle copyright © 1997 Discovery Center Music

hands. Tell the children to pat their hands and pat each other as softly as they would pat a kitten.

4. Have each child decide which role he or she wants to play: the sleeping bird or the person who pats. You will be one of the patters.

5. Play the song and have the children play the roles they have chosen. Make sure all children are patted.

6. Repeat, having the children switch roles.

Children's Books

Children's books are one of the most powerful tools you have for teaching conflict resolution and other social skills. They are also one of the easiest to use. The books in this section are only a few of the possibilities. They have been successfully used by early childhood programs around the country. The lesson plans included here for these books will give you a good idea of how to use other children's books in your program.

In many ways, children's literature is an ideal vehicle for teaching conflict resolution and other social skills. Books can be used to:

- ❖ Introduce, model, and reinforce skills
- ❖ Develop understanding and concepts about conflict and peacemaking
- ❖ Develop core themes and values in your program
- ❖ Involve parents by sharing books with them for use at home

This section includes activities that teach conflict resolution and social skills through children's books.

 note **Bringing It Home:** Send home Parenting Connections #3, #5, #7, and #8 after completing some of the activities in this chapter.

It's Mine!

● ●

Ages   3 and up

Summary   Three frogs bicker all day long, saying "It's mine! It's mine! It's mine!" But when a bad storm arrives, they realize that they need to share to survive—and it's more fun besides.

Themes
- ❖ Conflict resolution
- ❖ Sharing
- ❖ Helping others

Materials
- ❖ The book *It's Mine!* by Leo Lionni 💼

Procedure
1. Read the children the story *It's Mine!*

2. Lead a discussion using the following questions:
   - ❖ How did the frogs talk to each other?
   - ❖ Have you ever had that kind of argument with a friend? Tell us about it.
   - ❖ If you were a fish, what would you say to the frogs?

Three On An Island

A follow-up activity to *It's Mine!*

● ●

Materials   ❖ Carpet squares or masking tape

Procedure
1. Lay out carpet squares or make squares with the masking tape. Make the squares small enough so that they are a bit too small for three children to stand on one of them.

2. Divide the children into groups of three and assign each group to a particular square. The challenge is to figure out a way all three children can fit onto their square the way the frogs in the story fit onto the rock.

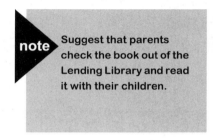

note Suggest that parents check the book out of the Lending Library and read it with their children.

Take the Frog Home

In the kit you'll find a small tote bag containing a stuffed frog, a copy of *It's Mine*, and a blank journal (we included extra journals in case one becomes full). Have children take turns taking the frog and *It's Mine!* home using the tote bag. The child who takes the tote bag home should use the blank journal to record, in words and drawings, the adventures the frog has while visiting the child's home. Parents can do the writing while children dictate the stories. Parents can also read *It's Mine!* to the child. Below is a sample letter to parents explaining the project. (If you don't have the kit, you can match a stuffed animal you already have with a children's book.)

Dear Family:

Today is your child's turn to bring home our Frog Friend!

In the tote bag you will find a stuffed frog, a copy of the book *It's Mine!*, as well as a journal notebook. Please read the book to your child and have your child tell you a story about the frog's adventures while visiting your house. Write your child's story in the journal for the rest of us to enjoy. Be sure to write your child's name or have your child sign the story.

Please have your child bring back the frog, the book, the journal, and the tote bag on the morning of _____. And thanks for your help with this project. I hope you will enjoy it as much as we do!

Sincerely,

Anansi the Spider

● ●

Ages 5 and up

Summary *Anansi the Spider* sets out on a long, difficult journey. Threatened by Fish and Falcon, he is saved by his sons. But which of his sons should Anansi reward? Nyame, the God of All Things, comes up with a resourceful solution.

Themes
❖ Caring
❖ Helpfulness
❖ Individual strengths

Materials
❖ *Anansi the Spider* by Gerald McDermott

Procedure
1. Before you read the story, ask the children to tell you some of the things they are good at. Ask if there have ever been times when they needed to use the skills they have. Explain that Anansi the Spider has children who are good at many things, and they help Anansi when he is in trouble.

2. Read the story *Anansi the Spider.*

3. Lead a discussion using the following questions:

   ❖ Which character would you like to be? How are the characters alike and how are they different?

   ❖ How are we alike and how are we different?

   ❖ What is your special talent? How can you use it to help someone in the class?

   ❖ Can you tie shoes? Are you good at finding misplaced things? Can you be a friend to someone who is sad?

Act It Out

A follow-up activity to *Anansi the Spider*

● ●

Materials None

Procedure:

1. (Read the story to the children several times before attempting to perform it, so children are familiar with it. You might make it a regular for story time.)

2. Choose children to play Anansi, his six sons, Fish, and Falcon. Leave out Fish and Falcon if you're working with a smaller group and have Anansi just pretend to be swallowed by Fish and picked up by Falcon.

3. While you read the story, children will act out their parts: Anansi will fall, Stonethrower will pretend to throw a rock, Fish will gently put its arms around Anansi to swallow him, Game Skinner will pretend to split the hands apart, etc. If children want to deliver their lines, let them.

> **note** ▶ Suggest that parents check the book out of the Lending Library and read it with their children.

Smoky Night

● ●

Ages   5 and up

Summary   *Smoky Night* is a story about the Los Angeles Riots in 1992. It helps children understand conflict and how common emotions, such as love for a pet, can bring people together.

Themes
❖ Conflict resolution
❖ Appreciation for diversity

Materials
❖ *Smoky Night,* by Eve Bunting
❖ Talking stick or designated object such as a stuffed animal

Procedure
1. Have the children sit in a circle. Ask: "Do any of you have a pet?" Pass around the talking stick and have each child respond to the question when he or she is holding the talking stick. Explain that *Smoky Night* is a book about a time when two cats are lost during an apartment fire and how their owners are worried about their safety.

2. Begin *Smoky Night.* Stop reading at the end of the page that begins, "Across the street from us people are dragging . . ." Ask the children why Mother doesn't shop at Mrs. Kim's store. Discuss why Mrs. Kim yells at Daniel's cat. Have the children identify what the conflict is and what makes it worse. Continue reading the story, saying, "Let's see if Daniel and Mrs. Kim can resolve their conflict."

3. Lead a discussion using the following questions:
   ❖ What did Daniel think but not say? Did it make the conflict better or worse that he didn't say it?
   ❖ How did Daniel and Mrs. Kim begin their friendship?
   ❖ Have you ever been afraid of someone because they yelled at your pet? What happened?

What Can You Do?

A follow-up activity to *Smoky Night*

● ●

Materials
- ❖ Colored markers
- ❖ Paper for each child

Procedure
1. Remind the children that Mrs. Kim and Daniel started their friendship because their cats shared a bowl of milk. Ask the children to draw a picture about what they did to begin a friendship with someone different.

2. Have the children share their pictures with the whole group or with an adult in the group.

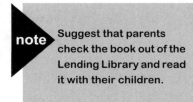

note Suggest that parents check the book out of the Lending Library and read it with their children.

Rainbow Fish

● ●

Ages   3 and up

Summary   *Rainbow Fish* is a story about sharing. It helps children understand conflict and how common emotions, such as loneliness and caring, can foster friendship.

Themes
- ❖ Conflict resolution
- ❖ Sharing
- ❖ Jealousy
- ❖ Loneliness
- ❖ Community

Materials
- ❖ *Rainbow Fish*, by Marcus Pfister ▪
- ❖ Talking stick ▪ or designated object such as a stuffed animal ▪

Procedure
1. Before you read the story, have the children sit in a circle. Explain that *Rainbow Fish* is about a fish who felt special because he had beautifully colored sparkling scales. Ask this question: What about you makes you feel special? Pass around the talking stick and have each child respond to the question when he or she is holding the talking stick.

2. Explain that Rainbow Fish would not share his special scales with any of the other fish in the ocean. Explain that he had no friends because he wouldn't share.

3. Read the story *Rainbow Fish*. Stop reading at the end of the page that begins, "You want me to give you one of my special scales . . ." Ask the children what happens to the Rainbow Fish. Discuss why the Rainbow Fish does not want to share his scales. Have the children identify what the conflict is and what makes it worse. Continue reading

the story, saying, "Let's see if the Rainbow Fish can resolve his conflict."

4. Lead a discussion using the following questions:

   ❖ Whom did the Rainbow Fish ask for help? Did the advice make the conflict better or worse?

   ❖ What happened to make the Rainbow Fish want to give away his scales?

   ❖ Have you ever been asked to share and you refused? What happened?

How to Give a Compliment

A follow-up activity to *Rainbow Fish*

• •

Materials

❖ Colored markers

❖ Paper

❖ Colored shiny stickers

Procedure

1. Remind the children that the Rainbow Fish had lots of friends when he shared his beautifully colored shiny scales with the other fish. Ask the children to draw a picture about a time when they shared something with someone else. Give them the colorful shiny stickers to decorate their pictures.

2. Have the children share their pictures with the whole class and have them take turns giving each other compliments on their pictures. You may need to model the behavior first. For example, "Jose, I like the way you put all your stickers in a row."

   note Suggest that parents check the book out of the Lending Library and read it with their children.

Someone Special, Just Like You

● ●

Ages   4 and up

Summary   *Someone Special, Just Like You* celebrates the inclusion of all children. Photos show boys and girls with a range of physical abilities enjoying everyday activities. The book shows that the pleasures of childhood are common to all.

Themes   ❖ Expression of feelings

❖ Appreciation of diversity

Materials   *Someone Special, Just Like You* by Tricia Brown 💼

Procedure   1. Have the children sit in a circle.

2. Ask the children to think of different ways they can move their hands. Ask two or three children to demonstrate their ideas for the group. Then have everyone do their own hand movements. Use a thumbs-up sign to signal "start" and a thumbs-down sign to signal "stop."

3. Tell them you are going to read a story about the different ways children have fun and ask them to look for any ways the children are like them or ways that they are different.

4. Read *Someone Special, Just Like You.*

5. Lead a discussion using the following questions:

❖ What did you notice about the children in the pictures?

❖ How are the children in the book like you?

❖ What did they do that you like to do?

❖ What were three things everyone could do?

Move, Move, Freeze

A follow-up activity to *Someone Special, Just Like You*

● ●

Materials   A chalkboard, white board, or flip chart and marker

Procedure

1. Have the children list some of the things that the children in the book did. Write the list on the board. Whatever they can easily remember is fine for starting this activity. The list will grow as you repeat the activity.

2. Have the children give a "thumbs up" for activities they like to do.

3. Make up movements to go with each activity, e.g. holding a pretend ice cream cone and pretending to lick the ice cream.

4. Have each child pick his or her favorite activity from the list.

5. Explain that a thumbs-up sign signals "start" and a thumbs-down sign signals "stop."

6. Teach the rhythm: move, move, freeze. For instance, with the pretend ice cream cone you could say, "Lick, lick, freeze."

7. Give the start signal and have everyone do his or her favorite activity.

8. Give the freeze signal after two moves. Everyone should stop. Repeat the activity a couple of times.

9. Ask a few children to explain why they chose the activity they chose.

10. Point out that everyone was doing different things because we all enjoy different activities and that's okay.

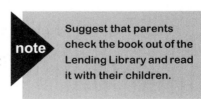

note Suggest that parents check the book out of the Lending Library and read it with their children.

Now One Foot, Now the Other

● ●

Ages   5 and up

Summary   *Now One Foot, Now the Other* is a story about the unconditional love between a grandfather and his grandson. The story shows how the young and old can learn and share together. The grandfather teaches the toddler to walk, and later the boy teaches the grandfather to walk after a stroke.

Themes
❖ Expression of feelings
❖ Appreciation of diversity

Materials
❖ *Now One Foot, Now the Other* by Tomie dePaola
❖ Small wooden blocks
❖ Pictures of senior citizens

Procedure
1. Pass around pictures of senior citizens and talk about things children can do with older friends and family.

2. Read *Now One Foot, Now the Other*. Stop reading at the page that begins, "Bob sounded like a monster!" Ask the children if they have ever been afraid of someone because of the way they sounded. Have the children use a thumbs-up or thumbs-down sign to answer. Continue reading the story saying, "Let's see what happens next."

3. Lead a discussion using the following questions:
   ❖ What did Bob teach Bobby to do?
   ❖ How did Bobby feel when they made the block tower together?
   ❖ How did Bobby feel when Bob had a stroke?
   ❖ What scared Bobby the most?
   ❖ How did Bobby help his grandfather?

Sharing, Caring, and Building Friendship

A follow-up activity to *Now One Foot, Now the Other*

● ●

Materials ❖ Small building blocks

Procedure 1. Have each child pick a partner.

2. Give each pair about eight small blocks.

3. Have them decide which block will go last on the tower.

4. Remind them that the grandfather always sneezed when he and Bobby put the elephant block on top. Help each pair make up their own physical gesture to use when they put the last block on the tower.

5. Have the pairs build the block tower together. Tell them if it falls it's okay to try again.

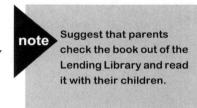

note ▶ Suggest that parents check the book out of the Lending Library and read it with their children.

Mama, Do You Love Me?

● ●

Ages 3 and up

Summary *Mama, Do You Love Me?* is a story about the unconditional love between a mother and her child. The child, called Dear One, plays with different emotions—love, sorrow, anger, worry, sadness, surprise, fear—to test Mama's love. Mama's response is: "You would still be you, and I would love you."

Themes
- ❖ Expression of feelings
- ❖ Testing the limits of expected behavior
- ❖ Appreciation of diversity

Materials
- ❖ *Mama, Do You Love Me?* by Barbara Joosse 💼
- ❖ An ice cube
- ❖ Pictures of a whale, a walrus, and a polar bear

Procedure

1. Have the children sit in a circle. Pass around an ice cube and ask the children to tell you how it feels to hold it.

2. Show pictures of the whale, walrus, and polar bear, and tell the children that the story you are going to read takes place in northern Alaska, where it is so cold that some people make houses of ice, called *igloos*, and where whales, polar bears, and walrus live.

3. Read the story *Mama, Do You Love Me?* Stop reading after the child asks, "What if I threw water at our lamp?" Ask the children if they have ever done something to make someone angry. Have the children give a thumbs-up or thumbs-down sign as an answer.

4. Continue reading the story, saying, "Let's see what happens next."

5. Lead a discussion using the following questions:

❖ If Dear One had dropped the eggs by accident would it make Mama mad?

❖ If Dear One put water on the fire on purpose would it make Mama mad?

❖ What did Mama tell Dear One? What do you say to someone you love?

Animal Calls

A follow-up activity to *Mama, Do You Love Me?*

• •

Ages　　3 and up

Procedure

1. Pick a few animals from the book. Use the age of the children as a guideline for deciding how many animals to pick. For instance, choose three animals or less for a group of 3-year-olds.

2. Make up a sound for each animal you've chosen. For example:

   ❖ Raven = Caw Caw

   ❖ Dog = Woof Woof

   ❖ Whale = Ooooor

   ❖ Puffin = Howl

   ❖ Ptarmigan = Screeech

   ❖ Salmon = Swish

   ❖ Wolf = Awooo

   ❖ Walrus = Arrh

   ❖ Polar Bear = Grrr

3. Teach the animal sounds to the children.

4. Use the thumbs-up sign to signal the children to start the sound and the thumbs-down sign to signal an end. Practice each sound.

5. Read the story interactively by having the children make each animal sound when they encounter that animal in the story.

note Suggest that parents check the book out of the Lending Library and read it with their children.

All the Colors of the Earth

● ●

Ages   3 and up

Summary   *All the Colors of the Earth* compares skin colors to the colors found in nature. The story helps children understand that differences in skin color are part of being human.

Themes
   ❖ Appreciation of diversity

Materials
   ❖ *All the Colors of the Earth*, by Sheila Hamanaka.▪

Procedure
   1. Have the children lie on their stomachs in a circle and have each child stretch one arm into the circle.

   2. Ask the children if all their hands look the same. After the children have named some of the differences they observe, tell them you will be reading a story about how our skin colors are like the colors of nature.

   3. Read aloud *All the Colors of the Earth*.

   4. Lead a discussion using the following questions:

      ❖ Do you know anything about a person from the color of her skin?

      ❖ Do you know anything about someone from the length or style of his hair?

      ❖ What color is love?

What Color is Nature?

A follow-up activity to *All the Colors of the Earth*

● ●

Materials
- Multicultural crayons
- Some of the following objects (or pictures of them):
  - yellow grass
  - red fall leaves
  - pink sea shells
  - spices such as cinnamon, ginger, sugar
  - walnuts
  - wheat
  - amber
  - ivory
  - caramel
  - chocolate
  - honey
  - sand
  - butterflies

Procedure
1. Talk about the objects and their colors that are mentioned in the book.

2. Pass out the objects and pictures.

3. Pass out the multicultural crayons.

4. Ask the children to match the objects and pictures with the crayons.

5. Ask each student to find a crayon or object that matches his or her skin color.

6. Conclude by rereading the pages that begin, "Children come in all colors of love, In endless shades of you and me."

I Like Me

• •

Ages   3 and up

Summary   *I Like Me* helps children understand that each of them is unique and special. The story describes ways for them to care for themselves, such as by brushing their teeth or learning how to try again after making a mistake.

Themes
- ❖ Positive self-image
- ❖ Expression of feelings

Materials
- ❖ *I Like Me*, by Nancy Carlson▪

Procedure
1. Have the children sit in a circle.

2. Pass a hand mirror around the circle. As children take turns holding the mirror, ask each to tell the group one thing he or she likes about him/herself. After the children have had an opportunity to name their special qualities, tell them you will be reading a story about how one special pig sees herself.

3. Read aloud *I Like Me*.

4. Lead a discussion using the following questions:
   - ❖ What do you do to take care of yourself?
   - ❖ What can you do when you make a mistake?

You're Special Because . . .

A follow-up activity to *I Like Me*

● ●

Materials   None

Procedure
1. Ask the children to form two lines facing each other.

2. Have one child identify what she likes about herself.

3. Have the child walk slowly down the space between the two lines and let each child in line take a turn gently patting her back and repeating, "I like _____ (whatever positive quality the child identified) about _____ (child's name)."

4. Repeat the activity until each child has had a turn or continue the activity with three to five children each day until all the children have taken a turn.

Mean Soup

● ●

Ages   3 to 4

Summary   *Mean Soup* is about how a sympathetic mother teaches her son a coping strategy for dealing with a bad day.

Themes
- ❖ Anger management
- ❖ Compassion

Materials
- ❖ *Mean Soup*, by Betsy Everitt

Procedure

1. Have the children sit in a circle. Ask, "Have any of you ever had a bad day, where everything seemed to go wrong?" Ask a few children to tell what went wrong.

   > **note** The purpose of this activity is to validate the wide range of children's feelings. Children should know that all feelings are okay, but that they need to act on them appropriately.

2. After a few children have responded, explain that *Mean Soup* is about Horace's bad day and how his mother helped him deal with it.

3. Begin to read *Mean Soup*. Stop reading at the end of the page that begins, "His mother said, 'Hello.' And Horace hissed." Ask the children why Horace is having a bad day.

4. Say, "Let's see if Horace's mother can help Horace with his bad day." Finish reading the story.

5. Lead a discussion using the following questions:

   - ❖ What did his mom do to make Horace feel better?
   - ❖ What did Horace do that made him feel better?
   - ❖ What is the difference between yelling in a pot of water and yelling at a person?

What Makes You Angry?

A follow-up activity to *Mean Soup*

● ●

Materials
- ❖ Large empty soup pot
- ❖ Wooden spoon
- ❖ Paper
- ❖ Colored markers

Procedure

1. Remind the children that Horace had different things happen at school that made it a bad day for him. Ask the children to draw a picture of some things that have happened to them at school or at home on a bad day.

2. Have the children share their pictures with the whole group or with an adult in the group by coming up to the large pot and putting in their "bad day" picture.

3. Let the children scream or stick their tongue out at the pot as they put their picture into it.

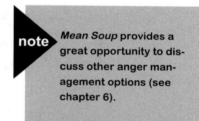

note *Mean Soup* provides a great opportunity to discuss other anger management options (see chapter 6).

Mrs. Katz and Tush

● ●

Ages   5 and Up

Summary   *Mrs. Katz and Tush* shows how friendship and caring can
develop over time. Larnel's mother visits with Mrs. Katz each
day after work. Soon Larnel convinces Mrs. Katz to take a
kitten with no tail, called Tush. The two care for the kitten and
share meals, stories, and a caring friendship.

Themes
❖   Expression of feelings
❖   Appreciation of diversity

Materials *Mrs. Katz and Tush*, by Patricia Polacco

Procedure
1. Have the children sit in a circle.

2. Ask whether they have ever had an older friend? Have a
   couple of them share their stories.

3. Ask how many have ever had a kitten. Have them give the
   thumbs-up sign if they have.

4. Tell them that one of the character's favorite expressions is
   "She was such a person." Have them repeat the phrase
   and tell them you will signal them to repeat the saying by
   giving the thumbs-up sign.

5. Read the story and pause to signal them to repeat the
   phrase.

6. Lead a discussion using the following questions:

   ❖   What were some new words you heard in this story?

   ❖   What did Larnel and Mrs. Katz do during their visits?

   ❖   Why was Mrs. Katz worried about Tush?

   ❖   Who found Tush?

   ❖   What holiday did Mrs. Katz and Larnel celebrate?

   ❖   What feelings did Mrs. Katz and Larnel share?

Dancing, Laughing, and Sharing

A follow-up activity to *Mrs. Katz and Tush*

● ●

Materials

❖ Cassette player

❖ Cassette recording of Polish music or any lively music for dancing

Procedure

1. Have the children look at the picture of Larnel and Mrs. Katz dancing.

2. Have a discussion about how music and dancing can bring us together with friends and neighbors.

3. Play the music and let the children move to the music.

4. Talk about the different feelings the music inspired in them.

Bookmaking

Bookmaking looks simple. Children take a few sheets of paper, staple them together, and they have a book. However, ask any child and they'll tell you this homemade book is as important and valuable as one from a bookstore or library. Why are these books so special? When children make and share their own books with the group, they feel a safety that allows them to communicate at a deeper level than if they addressed the group directly. Also, making and sharing a book allows children to expand their circle and get to know peers outside their usual play group. Working together on a book gives children the chance to relate cooperatively. And, depending on the content, you'll see children exploring feelings, solving problems, building their self-esteem, and developing a sense of community. They're learning strategies for creating the Peaceable Program on their own.

This section includes:

❖ Tips and teachable moments

❖ Bookmaking activities

Tips and Teachable Moments

❖ Whenever possible, praise children's efforts by commenting on some specific part of their work. A general comment like "That's good" may bounce right off. On the other hand, children feel better about themselves and their work when you make specific comments, such as, "I like the way you're covering the whole page with color," or "I like the combination of blue and orange you are using." Children who feel good about themselves are likely to treat others well.

❖ Working on a group book with restless children can become an ordeal. Don't be afraid to say, "I think we need to take a break and move around. We'll work on this another time." The fact is, the dynamics of a group can vary greatly from day to day. It's better to let children enjoy the project than it is to complete the book quickly and painfully.

❖ While it would be ideal to have everyone participate in bookmaking activities, you may need to provide the option of quiet play apart from the group. Though they're on the side, these children will still be listening and taking in ideas.

Photo Book

Children organize photos, dictate text, and make a cover to create a book about a group activity, project, or field trip

● ●

Ages   5 and up

Objective
- ❖ To work cooperatively
- ❖ To foster a sense of community

Materials
- ❖ Camera 📷
- ❖ Film 📷
- ❖ Stiff 8"x 11" paper
- ❖ Staples
- ❖ Pens
- ❖ Masking tape

Procedure:

1. Take pictures of a group activity, project, or field trip.

2. Have children choose the title for their book. Write the title on the cover and allow children to decorate it. This task only takes one or two children. If you have more children who are interested, you could separate the cover into quilt-like squares and let each child decorate one square.

   > **note** This project works well in a small group with different children participating to the degree they desire. You could also set up small groups to work together on different parts of the book.

3. Show the photos to the group and let them arrange the pictures sequentially.

4. Allot one piece of paper for every two photos and another sheet for the front and back covers. Staple pages along the

left margin, fold this edge in, then tape over the staples to create a binding.

5. Folding masking tape into loops with the sticky side out, tape corners of each photo and place them at the top of a page. Following the proper sequence, have the children fill both sides of each page of their book.

6. Ask the children: "What do you think of when you see each picture?" Write their brief stories and reflections under each photo.

7. Read the book to the whole group and put it on the bookshelf for children to read any time.

Books of Their Own Stories

Children dictate stories, draw pictures, and create a book of their work

● ●

Ages   5 and up

Objective
❖ To build sense of community and respect for others

Materials
❖ Paper
❖ Pen
❖ Staples

Procedure
1. Have the children dictate stories to an adult (for tips, see activities in chapter 13). Encourage children to draw pictures to go with their stories and save them. Write each child's name and the date on his or her stories and pictures.

2. Save the children's stories over a long period—perhaps until halfway through the program or until its end.

3. Once children have amassed a good collection, have them make covers for their books.

4. Assemble cover, stories, and pictures in chronological order and staple along the left edge.

5. Read each child's book to the class. Then give the books to the children to take home and share with their families.

Monster Book

Children draw monsters
and create a book about them

Ages   4 and up

Objective
- ❖ To work cooperatively
- ❖ To build community

Materials
- ❖ Paper and markers
- ❖ Monster Cards (see p. 4-27)

Procedure

1. Prepare several sets of Monster Cards.

> **tip**
>
> If possible, make photocopies of the book and let each child take one home. Staple the pages and have children make covers for their own copies of the book.

2. Explain to the children: "Today we are going to work together to draw monsters and write stories about our monsters. Then we will put all the stories together and make a book."

3. Divide children into groups of four. Distribute a set of Monster Cards to each group. Each child in each group will pick a card and will draw the part of the monster written on the card.

4. Have each group dictate a story about its monster. Give everyone the chance to add to the story, but keep it to one page.

5. Assemble the book so that the story and corresponding picture are on facing pages. Put all the stories and pictures in one book.

6. Read the finished book to the class and place it where children can look at it.

Our Community Book

Children generate a book that describes the positive qualities of each person in the group

● ●

Ages 6 and up

Objective
❖ To build self-esteem
❖ To build community

Materials
❖ Camera 💼
❖ Film 💼
❖ Staples
❖ 8" x 11" paper
❖ Masking tape

Procedure:

1. Take individual photos of the children and tape each photo on a piece of paper.

2. Have the group contribute comments on each classmates' positive attributes. Ask the children: "What is she good at doing? What do you like about her?" Give a sample response like, "She's friendly and she can ride a two-wheeler," or "He's nice and he shares."

> **tip**
>
> After the book has been available for children to read for several weeks, you may dismantle it and allow children to take their own pages home. You could also copy the pages and help children make their own books about their peers. Also, to extend the community, add pages about other people connected with the program, such as a secretary or a janitor.

3. Be ready to work with realistic descriptions of the child that could seem neutral or even negative if worded incorrectly. If one child says, "She doesn't talk much," you could re-interpret that comment: "Yes, she's quiet and a

good observer." It is crucial that you be able to put each aspect of a child's personality in a positive light.

4. When everyone has been profiled, put pages together and staple them with a front cover. Use masking tape to make a binding along stapled edge.

Feelings Book

Children complete sentences to create a book about their feelings

● ●

Ages   5 and up

Objective   ❖ Help children explore feelings

Materials   ❖ Paper
   ❖ Pens
   ❖ Staples
   ❖ Masking tape

Procedure   1. Prepare pages by writing the beginning of a sentence at the top of several sheets of paper.

   Here are some suggestions:

   I love . . .
   I wish . . .
   I get mad . . .
   I'm happy . . .
   I don't like . . .
   I laugh . . .

> **tip**
> This works best as a small group activity.

> **note**
> Try to make time to read each child's book to the whole group. Children may enjoy discussing similarities and differences.

   2. Younger children need only two or three pages with one part of a sentence written across the top of each. For older children, distribute five to seven pages with incomplete sentences. For both, include a cover page.

   3. Children can collate and staple their pages and then tape over the staples. Be ready to offer younger children help with this step.

4. While the children color and decorate a page, you can walk around the room reading the sentence to each child and writing his or her responses on their page. Repeat this process for each page.

5. If a child doesn't know what he or she wants to say, come back after working with the rest of the group. It's all right if the child has nothing to say about a page.

What Can I Do When . . . ?

Children create a book
that describes solutions to common problems

● ●

Ages 5 and up

Objective ❖ To develop problem-solving skills

Materials ❖ Blank book
❖ Pens

Procedure
1. Tell the children: "You are going to help me write a book called *What Can I Do When . . . ?* This book is about what to do when there is a problem. The more ideas we have, the better the book will be. Can you help me?"

2. Prop up the book facing the children. Turn to the first page and write, "What can I do when I want something someone else has . . . ?" Read the sentence as you write.

   ▼ tip

   This is a great tool for helping children learn to handle situations on their own. Use it as real problems crop up in your program. When someone has a problem you've dealt with in the book, you can say, "Let's look in our book for some ideas."

3. Ask if anyone has an idea of what you could do. If someone offers an idea, ask the children, "Would this work? If not, how could we change it to work better?" If no one volunteers, get things rolling with an obviously bad idea like, "Can I walk up and take it?"

4. When children agree on a good idea, write it in simple words and draw a quick sketch.

5. Keep adding to your book, but stick to one topic per session.

Mike, The Lonely Dog

Children create a story about the adventures of Mike the dog

● ●

Ages 5 and up

Objective
- ❖ To improve problem-solving skills
- ❖ To explore feelings

Materials
- ❖ Blank book with stapled pages
- ❖ Pens

Procedure

1. Prop the blank book in front of the children and explain to them: "I want you to help me finish writing a story about Mike the dog." Describe Mike and tell them he is lonely or unhappy because he wants the ball the cat is playing with—or whatever problem you think the children need to address.

   note This activity is a lot like "What Can I Do . . .?" (p. 12-11) but its storybook format is better suited for younger children.

2. Ask children what Mike should do and write it down, making a quick sketch to accompany the text.

   tip Even if you get a good idea and write it down, try telling children: "That's a good idea. Mike tried it, but this time it didn't work." Children need to know good solutions may not always work and that they need to bounce back.

3. Explore this solution on the next page. If the idea wasn't such a good one—like "Mike should grab the ball from the cat"— you can ask the children, "What do you think the cat would do then? How would she feel?" Write down these responses as well.

4. End with an idea or solution that works.

Here is a sample of how your story may go.

Mike, the Dog Who Wanted to Play Ball

Mike was a small, brown dog with perky ears and a tail that was almost always wagging. One day he was watching the cat play with a yarn ball, and he was wagging his tail to show he wanted to play. "Can I play too?" he asked.

"No," said the cat, "I just want to balance this ball on my feet," and rolled over.

"Can I have a turn when you're done?" asked Mike. This time the cat didn't even answer. Mike decided to run by and snatch the ball. The cat rolled over, arched his back, and hissed at Mike. Mike sat down. "I wish I had a ball," he said.

"Look in the sack next to the couch," the cat told him. Mike found a whole bag of balls. He took the biggest one and played, throwing it up and catching it before it touched the ground.

Cooperative Journal

Children create a journal of cooperative moments

● ●

Ages   5 and up

Objective
- ❖ To promote cooperation
- ❖ To reflect on past experiences
- ❖ To create a record of the group's positive moments

Materials
- ❖ Chart paper and markers
- ❖ Easel or tape

Procedure

1. Ask the group to tell you what it means when two children cooperate. While young children may have difficulty with this term, they are certainly capable of learning it. If necessary, you can say, "Cooperation is when people work together to try to get something done." Then say, "Let's get all settled and quiet and think about today. As we think, we won't talk out loud. Think to yourself. When you came here this morning, who did you play with? What did you do? Where did you go? Did you cooperate with anyone? Did anyone cooperate with you?"

> **tip**
>
> This activity works best with older children (ages six and seven).

2. Ask children to tell about one time they cooperated or someone cooperated with them that day. Encourage them to include their feelings.

3. Write down the children's comments, using their own words and leaving room for an illustration above each comment. Stop when the responses get repetitious or you've run out of time.

4. Ask children to draw illustrations for each comment after you are done.

5. Add this chart paper to a collection of cooperative moments from other days, create a cover, and make a book.

6. On a difficult day, read the book to the group, reminding them of all the positive moments they recently had together. This helps change the tone of the group and returns them to a positive way of being together.

7. On a positive day, read the book to the group, celebrating their ability to get along together, and add another page to the book.

Storytelling in the Peaceable Classroom

by Carol Wintle

Storytelling can be magical and fun. It is a powerful way to capture children's attention. When you tell children stories you can be creative and experimental. You don't have to be encumbered with reading, showing pictures, and turning pages. You can see exactly how the children are reacting to what you are saying.

Through stories, children get to stand in someone else's shoes and try on a variety of new experiences. They learn about the difficult challenges and wonderful adventures of other people and, in so doing, develop a better understanding of themselves.

Stories can:

❖ Speak directly to young children's emotions in a language they understand

❖ Help children know their feelings and concerns are valid and shared by others

❖ Stimulate children's imaginations and inventive thinking

❖ Familiarize children with a wealth of positive codes of conduct

❖ Help children feel more powerful, safe, and hopeful

In *Stories in the Classroom*, Bob Barton and David Booth write, "The oral tradition—stories told aloud—goes right back to the tribe and its communal life. When children become a community of listeners, they lay aside their own egocentricity, and become a tribe."

This section includes tips and ideas about:

❖ Telling stories

❖ Making up stories for children

❖ Facilitating children as storytellers and actors/actresses

❖ Activities and stories to try out with children

❖ Resources for learning more about storytelling

Tips for Telling Stories

If this is your first time telling stories, there are many things you can do to hone your skills. Try any of the following:

❖ Read the story several times to yourself (both silently and out loud).

❖ Visualize the story as if you were watching a movie of it.

❖ Write an outline of the story to help you clarify the most important points and the sequence of events.

❖ Think about how you want to represent each character and what kind of voices, facial expressions, and body movements you will use.

❖ Decide on the other variations you want to incorporate, such as speaking fast or slow, loud or soft, or using pauses.

❖ Decide how to begin and end the story.

❖ Choose which parts of the story you want to repeat verbatim. (Try to memorize only repetitive rhymes and the beginning and end of the story.)

- If you think you'll need it, write the parts you want to memorize on cards so you can jog your memory right before you tell the story.

- Tell the story out loud without an audience (if you get stuck refer to your outline).

- Tell the story into a tape recorder or in front of a mirror.

- Tell the story to one person.

Making Up Stories for Children

Made-up stories can help a child deal with difficulties he or she may be having. Experiment with making up your own stories by creating simple tales about:

- Everyday events and things the children in your program do and say

- Your own childhood

- Animals

- Children with different names than the ones in your program who are from a different time or place

Here are some general guidelines for making up your own stories for children:

- Have the character(s) in the story encounter a problem, learn new ways of behaving, and succeed in solving the problem they have encountered. Always give your tale a positive ending.

- If you get stuck in the middle of the story and aren't sure where to go next, invite the children to help you by asking them: "And what do you think happened next?" Their ideas should give you a sense of how you could proceed.

- If they suggest something you don't like such as saying, "And then he bombed him," accept their idea and then immediately transform it by saying something like, "And then, yes, he thought about bombing him but he decided to go talk to the wizard first. When he got to the wizard's cave, something amazing happened . . ."

Children As Tellers and Actors

"It is my experience that a classroom in which young children dictate and dramatize their own stories is a classroom of mythmakers who become, in the process, problem solvers."

—Patsy Cooper, *When Stories Come to School*

Making up and dramatizing stories is good for children because it helps them to understand what stories mean. It also provides them with a fun way to communicate with others about things that are on their minds. The process also helps children improve their expressive language skills and develop their self-confidence in speaking before a group.

In making up stories, children frequently repeat lines or themes from the stories their peers have told. This is fine. It shows they are listening to each other and that the material being explored reflects their collective reality.

Sometimes superhero characters and story lines appear in the tales children make up. Allowing this material to be expressed through the creative processes of storytelling and drama is helpful to children because it gives them a constructive way to process the information they are exposed to and allows them to gain control over their feelings and ideas about superheroes.

Telling superhero stories serves another purpose for children. In *When Stories Come to School*, Patsy Cooper argues that children "tell superhero stories for the same reason they are drawn to them: because they are well aware of their own inability to protect themselves from real danger, and superhero stories play out their triumph over the aggression they perceive in our culture." But as any teacher or caregiver knows, superhero stories often contain violent themes. (For a more complete discussion of children's fascination with superheroes and violent play, see "Confronting Violent Play" on page 2-45.)

The Mutual Storytelling Technique

The Mutual Storytelling Game (page 13-15) is based on a technique developed by psychologist Richard Gardner. It provides a safe, fun way for a child to communicate what is on his or her mind, as well as an inviting way for an adult to communicate positive solutions to problems.

In *Windows To Our Children*, psychotherapist Violet Oaklander shows how she uses the Mutual Storytelling Technique with a tape recorder and a pretend radio show.* Here she interviews a six-year-old named Bobby who had been losing many friends because of his tendency to hit, scream, and throw eggs at his peers.

Oaklander: Hello, ladies and gentleman, boys and girls. This is station KOAK and welcome to Story Hour. We have as our guest Bobby. [Oaklander turns to Bobby.] We're glad to have you on the program. Will you tell us how old you are?

Bobby: Six years old.

Oaklander: Let's get right down to our program. Here are the rules, radio audience. Bobby will tell us a story. It must have a beginning, middle, and end. When he is through I will tell a story using the same characters in my story as in his. Each story will have some kind of lesson or moral to it. Go ahead, Bobby.

Bobby: [Long pause, then whispers] I don't know what to say.

Oaklander: I'll help you. Once upon a time there was a . . .

Bobby: A shark.

Oaklander: And this shark . . .

Bobby: Liked to eat people.

Oaklander: What happened?

Bobby: He went around the ocean eating people. That's all.

Oaklander: That's only the beginning. We need the middle and the end.

Bobby: Well, he saw some fishermen and scared them. They fell out of their boat and the shark swam up and ate them up. Then he swam out to sea, far out where it was very deep. That's where he lived. The end.

---

* From Violet Oaklander, *Windows to Our Children* (Gestalt Journal Press, 1978). Used with permission.

Oaklander: Thank you very much for your fine story. What is the lesson?

Bobby: I don't know.

Oaklander: Okay. Now it's my turn. Once upon a time there was a shark who went around eating people. He ate everyone in sight. Some fishermen came along and got so scared they rowed away as fast as they could to get away from the shark. Everyone was afraid of him. Even the other fish and even the other sharks were afraid because sometimes he tried to eat them, too. Pretty soon he got bored with all of it. He wanted to play but no one would play with him. Everyone ran away from him.

Bobby: So what happened?

Oaklander: Well, he didn't know what to do. Finally he went to the king of the sharks in a big, deep cave way out in the ocean, and asked him what he should do. The king of the sharks said, "You have to find someone who will not be afraid of you, who will trust you, so everyone will see that you really want to be friendly. Someone who's not afraid of you might play with you—someone who doesn't know how you've been eating people and scaring people." And the shark said, "Where will I find such a person?" The king of sharks said he'd have to figure that out himself.

Bobby: [In a loud whisper to Oaklander, avoiding the microphone] I know! A newborn baby!

Oaklander: So the shark swam off to find someone who would trust him. Soon he came to a big boat and there was a family with a newborn baby. When the people saw the shark they all ran to hide in the cabin, forgetting the baby in their rush. The shark began to do tricks for the baby. The baby laughed and cooed. When his parents saw this they came back up and made friends with the shark, realizing he wanted to be friendly and wouldn't hurt them. So they became friends and the shark was very happy. The end.

The lesson of my story is if you want to be friends with people you have to act friendly.

Bobby: Can we listen to that again?

Oaklander rewinds the tape and listens to both stories with Bobby. Her story is pretty long compared to his, but Bobby listens with great absorption. When it's through, they begin to talk about his own problems with friends these days, and some things he could do when he's angry that wouldn't drive them away. Bobby asked to hear Oaklander's story four or five times following that session, asking his mother to come in and listen as well.

Storytelling Activities

When telling stories to children (or with them), establish a regular routine. First tell the story, then engage them in a follow-up activity. You may want to use the following activities with the Peaceable Stories provided later in this chapter. Choose from the following activities those you can comfortably integrate into your regular schedule.

Story Pictures

Children draw pictures to tell a story

● ●

Ages   4 and up

Objectives
- ❖ To help children process the concepts presented in the Peaceable Stories (pp. 13-16 to 13-40)
- ❖ To help children communicate what the stories mean to them
- ❖ To help children develop creative thinking

Materials
- ❖ Paper and crayons

Procedure
1. After you have read or told children stories, invite the children to draw a picture of a story. This picture can represent the story the children just heard, a variation of that story, or an original story.

2. The children can use their picture to help them tell a story during Story Circle (page 13-12), place their picture in their Story Journal (page 13-10), or post their picture on the Thumbs-Up and Thumbs-Down Displays (see page 9-7).

Story Journals

Children create folders
to store their Story Pictures

● ●

Ages   4 and up

Objective
- ❖ To help children explore the concepts presented in the Peaceable Stories (pp. 13-16 to 13-40)

Materials
- ❖ A folder for each child
- ❖ Crayons

Procedure
1. Explain to the children that Story Journals are folders where children can privately keep their Story Pictures (page 13-9). It is up to each child to decide if they want to show anyone the pictures they have placed in their Story Journal.

2. Distribute one folder to each child.

3. Invite the children to create covers for their journals. Make sure that each child's name appears on his or her folder.

Story Tapes

Children record their
own stories on a cassette tape

● ●

Ages   3 and up

Objectives
- ❖ To help children explore the concepts presented in the Peaceable Stories (pp. 13-16 to 13-40)
- ❖ To help children communicate what the stories mean to them
- ❖ To enhance creative thinking

Materials
- ❖ Cassette recorder
- ❖ Blank cassette tape for each child

Procedure
1. Ask parents/guardians to supply a cassette tape for their child to use to record their own stories.

2. Designate times when you are available to help a few children use the tape recorder to record their stories. Make a sign-up sheet that gives each child a turn.

3. When the time for a story-recording session arrives, find a quiet place to sit down with the child. Start the tape recorder and begin by asking the child for the title of the story, then have the child tell his or her story. Set a time limit of three to five minutes. At the end of that time period, if the child has not finished the story, end the recording with the words, "To be continued."

4. Allow children to bring their story tapes home to play for their families. They can make up stories at home with their families and sign up to play these stories at Story Circle (page 13-12).

Story Circle

Children tell stories to each other

● ●

Ages   5 and up

Objectives

❖ To help children communicate what the Peaceable Stories mean to them

❖ To improve listening skills

Materials   None

Procedure

1. Designate a time (or times) each week when Story Circle will happen. During Story Circle the group sits in a circle and tells stories. During this time, an adult might tell a story, the children might tell stories they have made up, retell stories they have heard, or play a Story Tape (page 13-11).

2. You can also try some round-robin storytelling. This is when the group together retells a story that has just been told to them. Explain to the children that everyone gets to help with the retelling. Each child uses his own words to tell a different part of the story. Start with one person and go around the circle with the next child adding as much or as little as he likes. Explain to the children that it is fine to say "pass" if they don't want to help retell the story. You could also tape the group's retelling and listen to it again.

Story Dramas

Children make up a story and then act it out

· ·

Ages 6 and up

Objectives
- ❖ To help children explore the Peaceable Classroom concepts
- ❖ To enhance creative problem-solving

Materials
- ❖ Paper and pen
- ❖ Carbon paper

Procedure
1. Announce to the children you will be inviting them to make up a story that can be acted out at Story Circle. Establish a regular time every day or every few days (about ten to twenty minutes) to meet with one or two children to transcribe their stories. It is helpful to make a list of times and the names of the children assigned to those times.

2. During meeting time, have the child dictate a story to you while you write it down. Use carbon paper so that you and the child will each have a copy of the story. Children generally need from two to ten minutes to tell a story. To make sure you get to each child on your list, you may want to impose a one-page limit on the length of a dictated story. Any story that is longer than one page can end with "to be continued."

3. Establish a schedule for dramatizing children's stories. Ideally, dramatization of a child's story occurs the same day the story is dictated.

4. To dramatize a story, the author chooses which part he or she wants to play. You can decide which children will play the other parts or let the author of the story make this

decision. Since it is important that no children be excluded from this process, you might want to limit how many times each child can be chosen or state that everyone in the group has to have a chance before anyone gets to go twice.

5. No rehearsal is needed. As you read the story aloud, children perform the parts they have been assigned. Not using props in the dramatizations helps to keep the process simple and uncomplicated. Dramatizations are usually pantomimed. However, if a child's story includes dialogue, the actors can repeat the lines after you have read them.

6. Establish a "no-touching rule." This will help keep dramatizations safe. Remind children of this rule as often as needed.

7. After a tale has been enacted, place your copy of the story in a three-ring binder marked "Story Dramas."

The Mutual Storytelling Game

A child and the caregiver take turns inventing
and telling a story to each other

● ●

Ages   5 and up

Objective
❖ To reinforce Peaceable Classroom concepts with a child
   who needs extra attention

Materials
❖ Cassette recorder
❖ Blank cassette tape

Procedure
1. Explain the rules of The Mutual Storytelling Game.

   ❖ The child tells a story.

   ❖ The child tries to explain what the lesson of the story is.

   ❖ You tell a story.

   ❖ You tell what the lesson of your story is.

2. Turn on the tape recorder. Introduce the radio station.
   Introduce the child. Help the child get started telling a
   story by saying, "Once upon a time . . ."

3. If the child gets stuck ask questions like, "And then . . ." or
   "What happened next?"

4. When the child finishes telling her story, ask what the
   lesson is. If the child can't think of one, let it pass.

5. Tell a story that has the same characters and starts the
   same way as the child's story does. Finish the story with a
   positive solution. Have the lesson of your story build on
   one of the Peaceable Classroom themes.

Peaceable Stories

Several Peaceable Stories and accompanying activities are contained in this section. They include:

- ❖ The Sun and the Wind
- ❖ Two Wolves Lose
- ❖ Two Wolves Win
- ❖ Two Donkeys
- ❖ Two Kids Lose
- ❖ Two Kids Win

Descriptions of other Peaceable Stories and activities are also listed, including:

- ❖ The Great Big Enormous Turnip
- ❖ The Mouse and the Lion
- ❖ The Rabbit and the Elephant
- ❖ The Ox and His Master

Telling any of these tales to youngsters will help them develop the skills they need to express feelings, communicate effectively, cooperate, and solve problems. The stories can be used with or without the storytelling activities described on ppage 13-11 to 13-13.

The Sun and the Wind

Children listen to a story, then act it out

● ●

Ages   5 and up

Objective   ❖ To reinforce the idea that it is better to be nice to people than to bully them

Materials   ❖ "The Sun and the Wind" on page 13-19

Procedure   1. Prepare for this activity by learning the story "The Sun and the Wind."

2. Gather the children in a circle. Explain that you are going to tell them a story called "The Sun and the Wind." Tell the children, "There are two parts in this story. When the Wind speaks we will wave our arms in the air and make whooshing sounds. When the Sun speaks we will spread our fingers wide and hold our hands with our thumbs pointing towards our ears."

3. Teach the children the song the Sun sings. Use the tune of the song "You Are My Sunshine."

   I am the sunshine. I am the sunshine.

   I spread happiness. Oh yes I do.

   I shine with kindness. I shine with caring.

   You can be like sunshine too.

4. Tell the story, giving the Wind a harsh voice and the Sun a gentle one. Enjoy yourself!

5. After telling this story, invite the children to draw Story Pictures (page 13-9). They can put their pictures into their Story Journals (page 13-10), or post them on the "Thumbs-Up and Thumbs-Down Displays" on page 9-7, depending

on whether their pictures depict the Sun's gentle action or the Wind's harsh approach.

6. Invite the children to retell this story on their Story Tapes (page 13-11) or at Story Circle (page 13-12).

7. Involve the children in dramatizing "The Sun and the Wind." There are many ways you can do this: by having three characters (Sun, Wind, and child); a Sun, a Wind, and a group of children; or several children can play the Sun, several children play the Wind, and the rest play the group of children. Remember to enforce the "no-touching" rule.

The Sun and the Wind*

The Wind had been blowing its cold, prickly breath all morning long and was feeling very, very strong.

[Make a whooshing sound. Wave arms around.]

The Sun had been shining its bright light all morning long and was also feeling strong.

[Spread hands wide, thumbs pointed at your ears.]

The Sun sang to itself as it shone.

I am the sunshine. I am the sunshine.

I spread happiness. Oh yes I do.

I shine with kindness. I shine with caring.

You can be like sunshine too.

The Wind thought it was better than the Sun. "When I blow my cold, prickly breath I am more powerful than you," hissed the Wind to the Sun.

[Make a whooshing sound. Wave arms around.]

"No, you're not," smiled the Sun and shaking her head with glee.

[Spread hands wide, thumbs pointed at your ears.]

"You are not stronger than I, for . . ." and the Sun began to sing its song . . .

I am the sunshine. I am the sunshine.

I spread happiness. Oh yes I do.

I shine with kindness. I shine with caring.

You can be like sunshine too.

The Wind did not like the Sun's song. Scowling and wagging its finger at the Sun, the Wind argued back, "No. No. I am more powerful than you!"

"No, you're not," smiled the Sun.

[Spread hands wide, thumbs pointed at your ears.]

_____

* © 1996 Carol Wintle. Adapted from a Jean de la Fontaine fable.

"Yes, I am."

"No, you're not."

"Yes, I am."

"Okay. Let's see who is the strongest," challenged the Sun. "Do you see those children waiting for the bus to take them to school? They all have on their winter coats, hats, mittens, and scarves. Let's see which one of us is powerful enough to get the children to take off their winter clothes."

"Okay," said the Wind. "I accept your challenge."

So the Wind began to blow its cold, icy breath at the children.

[Make whooshing sound. Wave arms around.]

It blew and blew for all it was worth. It pushed and pushed at the children. It pulled and pulled at them. But the more the Wind blew and pushed and pulled, the more the children held their coats, mittens, hats and scarves closer and closer to their bodies. The Wind tried and tried and tried, but it could not get the children to take off their winter clothes.

"Now it's my turn," smiled the Sun.

[Spread hands wide, thumbs pointed at your ears.]

The Sun shone sunny beams all over the children's faces and bodies. The children began to feel warm. The Sun shone brighter and brighter. The children felt warmer and warmer and warmer. They began to unbutton their coats. The took off their scarves. They took off their mittens. They took off their hats. They took off their coats.

"You are not more powerful than me," said the Sun.

"I see that you are right," replied the Wind.

The Sun sang its song. As the children waited for the bus, holding all their winter clothes in their arms, they sang the Sun's song, too. And the Wind decided to join in by dancing gently around the children as they sang . . .

We are the sunshine. We are the sunshine.

We spread happiness. Oh yes we do.

We shine with kindness. We shine with caring.

You can be like sunshine too.

Two Wolves

Children listen to two stories and discuss them

● ●

Ages
5 and up

Objective
- ❖ To reinforce the concepts of thumbs-down and thumbs-up conflict resolution

Materials
- ❖ Two wolf puppets. (to use these puppets, slide your index and middle fingers into the pockets on the back of each wolf)
- ❖ The stories, "Two Wolves Lose" (page 13-23) and "Two Wolves Win" (page 13-25)

Procedure
1. Introduce or review the concepts of thumbs-up and thumbs-down solutions (see "Thumbs Up, Thumbs Down" on page 8-13).

2. Tell the story "Two Wolves Lose" (page 13-23). Use the wolf puppets to enact this story as you tell it. Feel free to change the characters in this story into any two animals or characters for which you have two puppets or figurines.

3. Lead a discussion of the story using the following questions:

   - ❖ What is the problem the wolves are having?
   - ❖ How do you think the wolves are feeling?
   - ❖ Did each wolf get what he wanted?
   - ❖ Did they cooperate?
   - ❖ Did they find a thumbs-up solution?
   - ❖ What could the wolves have done differently?

4. Tell the story "Two Wolves Win" (page 13-25).

5. Lead a discussion of the story using the following questions:

❖ Did the two wolves cooperate with each other?

❖ How did they cooperate?

❖ How do you think they are feeling?

❖ Did the wolves find a thumbs-up solution?

6. Invite the children to draw Story Pictures (page 13-9), make Story Tapes (page 13-11), or retell these stories at Story Circle (page 13-12). They can use the wolf finger puppets or other figurines when they tell their stories.

Two Wolves Lose*

Once upon a time there were two wolves. One wolf lived high up on a mountain close to the clouds. The other wolf lived way down in a valley next to a lake. Between the mountain and the valley was a narrow bridge with a river flowing underneath.

The mountain wolf loved living on the mountain, but sometimes he liked to visit the valley and sit next to the lake. The valley wolf loved living in the valley, but sometimes he liked to go for a walk up the mountain to see the view from above.

One time, when the mountain wolf was crossing the bridge to go to the lake, the valley wolf was crossing the bridge to go for a walk on the mountain. The wolves met in the middle of the bridge.

"I'm crossing this bridge, so let me go on," said the mountain wolf.

"Well, I'm crossing this bridge too," said the valley wolf, "So you should move."

"Out of my way!" snapped the mountain wolf.

"No," said the valley wolf, scrunching up his face.

"Move off!" growled the mountain wolf, raising his voice.

"I was here first!" snarled the valley wolf.

Neither wolf would move.

They stood there glaring at each other.

Then they began to push.

They growled and snorted and pushed and pushed.

Until . . .

They pushed each other right off of the bridge into the river below.

Wet and furious, the mountain wolf climbed from the river and stomped off to the mountain. Wet and furious, the valley wolf climbed from the river and stomped off to the valley.

---

* © 1992 by Margaret Read MacDonald. Reprinted by permission from "Two Goats on a Bridge," from *Peace Tales: World Folktales to Talk About.*(North Haven, Conn.:Linnet Books, 1992)

The mountain wolf muttered to himself, "That valley wolf is mean. He's selfish. He's a brute."

The valley wolf went home muttering too, "That mountain wolf ruined my day. What a disagreeable fellow is he."

Two Wolves Win*

Once upon a time there were two wolves. One wolf lived high up on a mountain close to the clouds. The other wolf lived way down in a valley next to a lake. Between the mountain and the valley was a narrow bridge with a river flowing underneath.

The mountain wolf loved living on the mountain, but sometimes he liked to visit the valley and sit next to the lake. The valley wolf loved living in the valley, but sometimes he liked to go for a walk up the mountain to see the view from above.

One time when the mountain wolf was crossing the bridge to go to the lake, the valley wolf was crossing the bridge to go for a walk on the mountain. The wolves met in the middle of the bridge.

"I'm crossing this bridge, "said the mountain wolf.

"Well, I'm crossing this bridge too," said the valley wolf.

"I was here first," insisted the mountain wolf.

"No. No. You are mistaken," said the valley wolf.

"Well, this is quite a problem we have," said the mountain wolf.

"Yes, we do," said the valley wolf.

"I don't want to have to go back the way I came," said the mountain wolf.

"Well I don't want to either," said the valley wolf. "Maybe we could be very careful . . ."

"And manage to squeeze past each other . . . ," added the mountain wolf.

"… without falling off this narrow bridge," concluded the valley wolf.

"Let's try," they both agreed.

Very carefully the two wolves squeezed by each other. They were both successfully able to continue on to the other side.

"What a cooperative, kind wolf," remarked the mountain wolf as he went on his way.

---

* © Carol Wintle. Inspired by the story "Two Goats on a Bridge" in Margaret Read MacDonald, *Peace Tales: World Folktales to Talk About* (North Haven, Conn: Linnet Books, 1992).

"What a cooperative, caring wolf," said the valley wolf to himself as he looked around enjoying the view.

"I like that fellow," they both thought to themselves. "I wouldn't mind meeting that wolf on the bridge again."

Two Donkeys

Children listen to a story
about conflict resolution and discuss it

● ●

Ages   4 and up

Objective

* ❖ To reinforce the concepts of thumbs-up and thumbs-down conflict resolution

Materials

* ❖ The story "Two Donkeys" (page 13-27)
* ❖ Two Donkeys pictures (page 13-31)

Procedure

1. Introduce or review the concepts of thumbs-down and thumbs-up solutions (see "Thumbs Up, Thumbs Down" on page 8-13).

2. Use picture 1 and picture 2 to tell the story "Two Donkeys" up to the point where it says, "They he-ha'd and he-ha'd and he-ha'd until they were tired. And also very hungry."

3. Lead a discussion using the following questions:

    * ❖ How do you think the donkeys are feeling?
    * ❖ What is their problem?
    * ❖ What can they do about their problem?
    * ❖ What do you think they will do?

4. Tell the rest of the story using pictures 3 and 4.

5. Lead a discussion using the following questions:

    * ❖ How do you think the donkeys are feeling now?
    * ❖ Did the donkeys cooperate with each other?
    * ❖ How did they cooperate?
    * ❖ Did they find a thumbs-up solution?

6. Invite the children to draw Story Pictures (page 13-9), make Story Tapes (page 13-11), or retell this story at Story Circle (page 13-12).

Two Donkeys*

Once upon a time, there were two donkeys tied together in a barn. Each of the donkeys had their own pile of hay, one pile on the left and one on the right. The donkey on the left wanted to eat from the hay pile on the left. The donkey on the right wanted to eat from the hay pile on the right.

At the same time, both donkeys went to eat at the pile of hay that they wanted, but the rope tying them together was too short. Neither donkey could reach their pile of hay.

"Ow," they both said at once.

"Let me get at my hay," they both cried.

"You aren't letting me eat," said one.

"You aren't letting me eat," said the other.

"Be nice."

"No you be nice."

They argued. They pulled to get their way. They whined. They bawled. They he-ha'd and he-ha'd and he-ha'd until they were tired. And also very hungry.

STOP FOR DISCUSSION!

Well, let's see what happens. The donkeys were bawling. They were tired and hungry. Suddenly one of the donkeys said, "This is stupid. If we keep this up, neither of us will eat."

"You're right. Let's not fight."

"Let's cooperate!"

"If we put our heads together, we might know what to do."

So that is what they did. They sat down and rested. They put their heads together. They thought and thought.

"I know," said one.

---

* © 1996 Carol Wintle

"What?" said the other.

"Let's share! You can help me eat my pile. Then we can both eat yours."

"What a brilliant idea. I love it."

So the donkeys ate the hay together until their stomachs were full. They were happy for the rest of the day.

Two Donkeys (1 & 2)

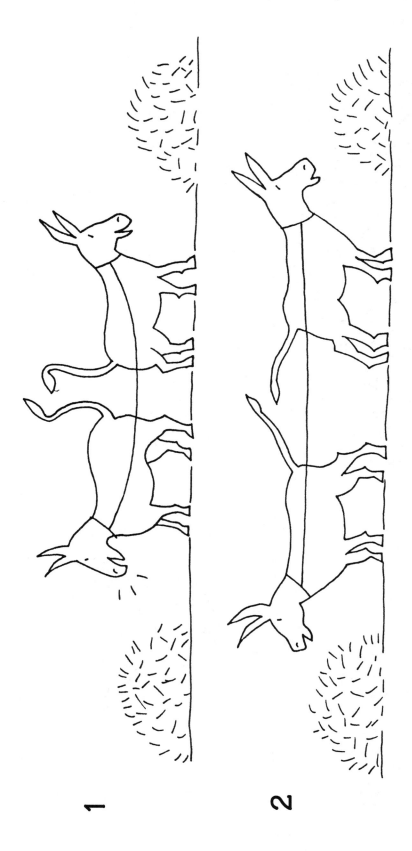

1

2

Two Donkeys (3 & 4)

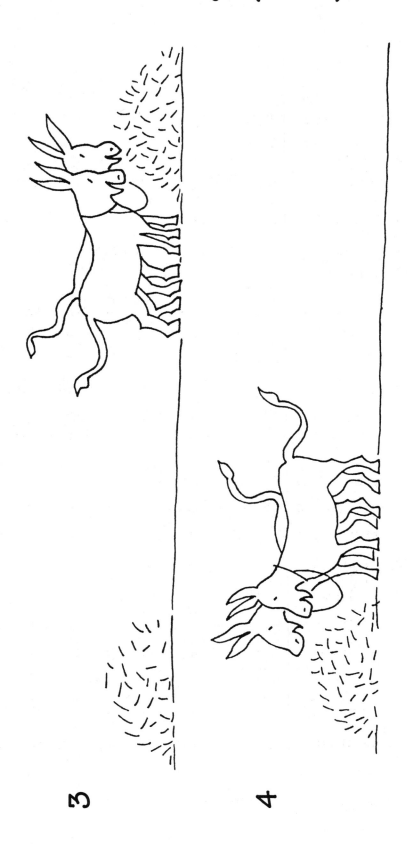

3

4

Two Kids

Children listen to a story, then discuss it

● ●

Ages   4 and up

Objective

❖ To reinforce the concepts of thumbs-up and thumbs-down conflict resolution

Materials

❖ Two dolls or people puppets

❖ The stories "Two Kids Lose" (page 13-35) and "Two Kids Win" (page 13-36)

Procedure

1. Introduce or review the concepts of thumbs-up and thumbs-down solutions (see "Thumbs Up, Thumbs Down" on page 8-13).

2. Use two dolls or puppets to enact the "Two Kids Lose" (page 13-35) story as you tell it. Feel free to change this story to be about two animals or children having a conflict over a ball, or wanting to be the first in line, or any problems children in your program may be having.

3. Tell the "Two Kids Lose" story up to the point where they begin to push at each other.

4. Lead a discussion using the following questions:

   ❖ How do you think the children are feeling?

   ❖ What is their problem?

   ❖ What could they do to solve their problem?

   ❖ What do you think they will do?

5. Continue telling the story.

6. Lead a discussion using the following questions:

   ❖ How do you think the children are feeling now?

   ❖ Did they solve their problem?

❖ Did they make a thumbs-up or thumbs-down choice?

❖ Did they cooperate with each other?

❖ Do you like the choices they made?

❖ Would you like to hear a story where the children tried one of your ideas?

7. Tell the "Two Kids Win" story (page 13-36), changing it to include the children's thumbs-up suggestions.

8. Lead a discussion using the following questions:

❖ How do you think the children are feeling now?

❖ Did they solve their problem?

❖ Did they make a thumbs-up or thumbs-down choice?

❖ Did they cooperate?

❖ Do you like the choices they made?

9. Invite the children to draw Story Pictures (page 13-9), make Story Tapes (page 13-11), or retell these stories at Story Circle (page 13-12).

Two Kids Lose*

One day there were two children who both wanted to play with a doll house at the same time. Each of them wanted to have the doll house all to themselves.

They both said, "I got here first."

They both said, "You had it yesterday."

They both said, "It's my turn."

They argued. They raised their voices. They whined. They made angry faces at each other. They stamped their feet. They began to push at each other.

STOP FOR DISCUSSION!

Their teacher came along and said, "Neither one of you will be able to play with the doll house today unless you find a way to cooperate." She gave them several suggestions, but they refused to cooperate. So neither one of them was allowed to play with the doll house that day.

---

* © 1996 Carol Wintle

Two Kids Win*

One day there were two children who went to play with the doll house at the same time. Both of them wanted to have the doll house all to themselves.

"I want to play here by myself," they both said at once.

"I got here first," they both said.

"You had it yesterday," they both said.

They looked puzzled. They scratched their heads. They smiled at each other. They spoke quietly.

"Let's take turns," one said.

"No, I want it the whole time," said the other.

"But that's not fair."

"What can we do?"

"Ask the teacher?"

"Let's try a thumbs-up idea."

"Okay. But what?"

"I know, let's set the timer. You have it for ten minutes. Then it's my turn."

"Or I can have it today and you have it tomorrow."

"We could flip a penny to see who goes first."

"You can go first. Come get me when you are done."

"Okay."

They shook hands and then took their turns. Both of them got to play with the doll house that day.

_____

* © 1996 Carol Wintle

The Big, Big Carrot

Children listen to a story, then act it out

● ●

Ages   4 and up

Objective   ❖ To reinforce the importance of cooperation

Materials   ❖ "The Big, Big Carrot" ▪

❖ Or, tell your own version of "The Big, Big Turnip," by Leo Tolstoy

Procedure: 1. Read or tell the story "The Big, Big Carrot."

2. Involve the children in a dramatization of this story. Or, try the follow-up activities described in "The Big, Big Carrot" such as making stick puppets for the children to use to tell this story or another.

3. Invite the children to draw Story Pictures (page 13-9), make Story Tapes (page 13-11), or retell this story at Story Circle (page 13-12).

The Mouse and the Lion

● ●

Ages   5 and up

Objective   ❖ To promote cooperation

Materials   ❖ A copy of the Aesop fable, "The Mouse and the Lion."
                (A very nice retelling of this fable can be found in *Who's Afraid . . .? Facing Children's Fears with Folktales* by Norma Livo, Teacher Ideas Press, 1994.)

In this story, a lion allows a mouse to go free and is later freed from a trap by the mouse.

Procedure   1. Tell the children the story "The Mouse and the Lion."

   2. Ask children to draw pictures about something they have done to help someone else. Play the "Once Upon a Time Game"(page 9-9) adding the line, "Something Rose does to help is… [e.g., show Larry how to tie his shoes]."

   3. Involve children in a dramatization of this story.

   4. Invite the children to draw Story Pictures (page 13-9), make Story Tapes (page 13-11), or retell this story at Story Circle (page 13-12).

Additional Resources

Barton, Bob and Booth, David. *Stories in the Classroom: Storytelling, Reading Aloud and Roleplaying with Children*. Portsmouth, N.H.: Heinemann, 1990.

Carlsson-Paige, Nancy and Diane Levin. *Before Push Comes to Shove*. St. Paul: Redleaf Press, 1998.

Carlsson-Paige, Nancy. *Best Day of the Week*. St. Paul: Readleaf Press, 1998.

Corrin, Sara & Stephen. *Stories for Five-Year-Olds and Other Young Readers*. Boston: Faber and Faber, 1989.

Baldwin, Rahima. *You Are Your Child's First Teacher*. Berkeley, Calif.: Celestial Arts, 1989.

Discussion Pictures

Illustrations by Liza Donnelly

The twelve discussion pictures included in this guide depict some of the most common conflicts that arise in early childhood programs. They were developed to provide you with another way to work with your children on conflict resolution skills.

Here are some general guidelines you may find helpful when using the discussion pictures:

- ❖ Discuss one picture per session.

- ❖ Keep the discussion as focused on resolving the conflict as possible.

- ❖ Don't ask all of the suggested questions, but rather pick the ones most relevant to your group's needs.

- ❖ If possible, when the children suggest solutions, have them act out their solutions.

- ❖ After you've discussed a picture, follow it up with a movement activity, for variety.

- ❖ After you've discussed a particular picture, try doing a Peace Puppets session the following day that uses the same situation. It's always interesting to see how much the children have retained or internalized from your discussion!

Procedure

1. Gather the children together in a circle. Hold the discussion picture up for the group to see.

2. Ask some of the following questions:

   ❖ What do you see happening in this picture?

   ❖ What do you think might happen next?

   ❖ Is there a problem in this picture? What do you think the problem is?

   ❖ How do you think this child/these children are feeling?

   ❖ What could the children in the picture do to solve this problem?

   ❖ Can someone show me what that would look like?

   ❖ Can someone say what words the children could use?

   ❖ What do you think would happen next if the children used your solution?

   ❖ If you were going to say something to these children, what would you say?

   ❖ If I said something to these children, what do you think I would say?

   ❖ Have you ever had something like this happen to you? Tell about it.

Topics of the Discussion Pictures

1. Three children are cleaning up after cooking, but only one is doing the work.

2. A group of children are lining up for a drink of water, when one child cuts in line.

3. One child hoards all the dolls in a play corner.

tip

There is a dinosaur somewhere in every discussion picture. For added fun, ask the children to try to find the dinosaur!

4. One child won't share the bouncy ball with the other children.

5. One child, who is building a block building, takes up too much room, so the child trying to play with dinosaurs kicks her block building over.

6. Children putting on a puppet show tell a fourth child that they don't need her because they already figured out how it's going to be.

7. One child takes more than her fair share at snack time.

8. Three children on the tire swing won't give it up when other children want to use it.

9. One child falls over another child's foot and wrecks her clay sculpture. She says he did it on purpose.

10. Three children in the doll corner won't let another child join their play.

11. Two boys want the same book at the same time.

12. A girl is trying to help some children with a game, and they accuse her of being bossy.

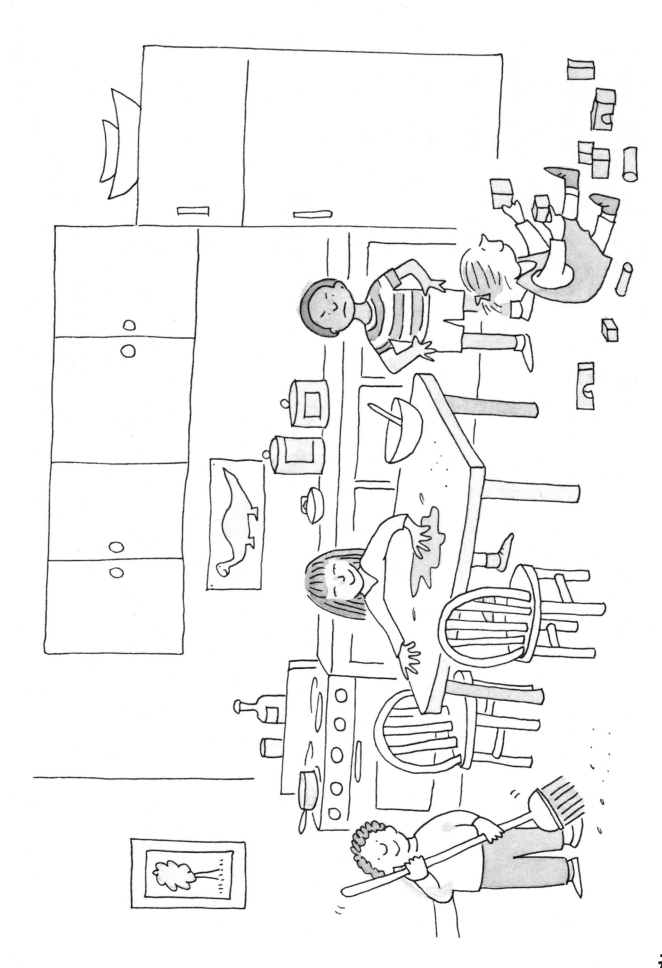

#1

#2

#3

#4

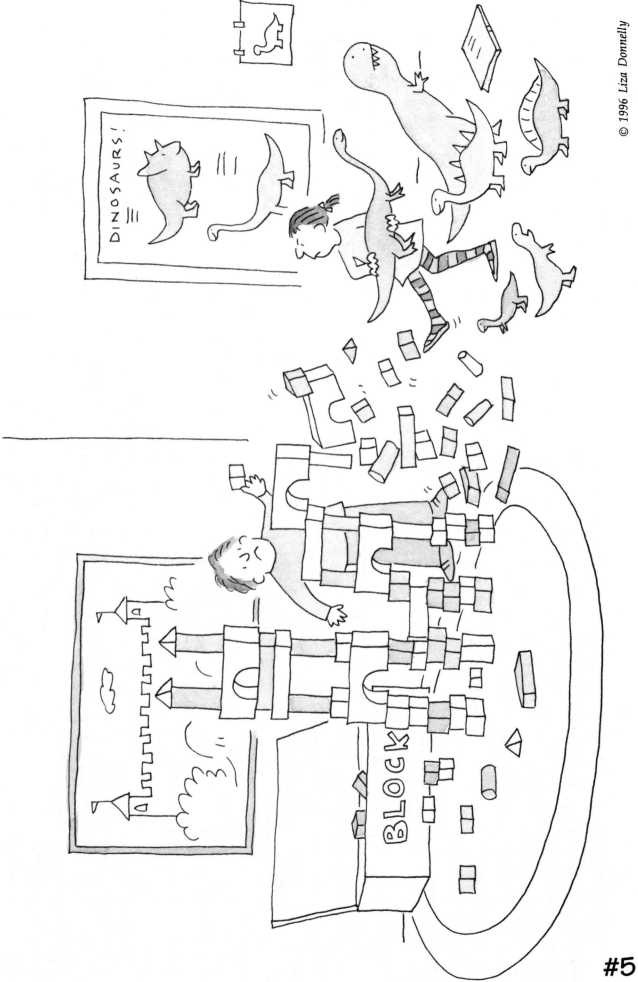

#5

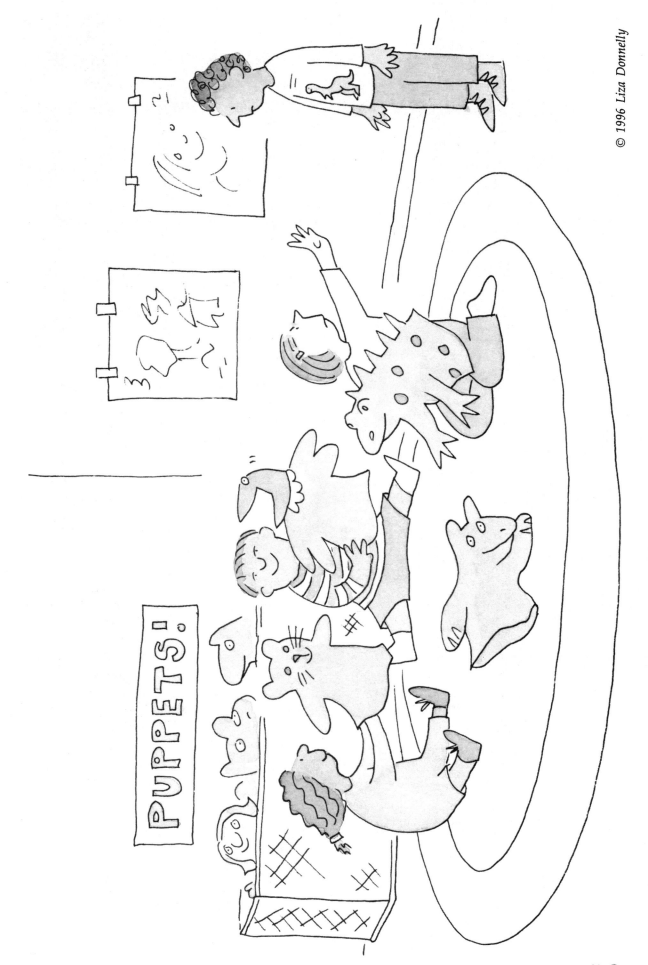

PUPPETS!

#6

#7

#8

#9

#10

#11

#12

Parachute Activities

Parachute play is a delightful component of the Peaceable Program. It's cooperative (you literally can't do it alone!), it builds community, and it's great fun.

Tips and Teachable Moments for Parachute  Activities

❖ Spend time teaching children about the transitions surrounding parachute activities. Teach them how to get the parachute suitcase, open it up, and put it away. These are all important components of parachute play. The more orderly routines children have for the parachute, the more fun they—and you—will have. (And the less likely the parachute is to be torn.)

❖ Parachute play is very vigorous, and young children will tire fairly quickly. The first times you use the parachute, just do two or three positions until you see that the children have the stamina for more.

❖ Young children will have a hard time maintaining the hand grips, because their hand muscles will get tired. Try making it a habit to stop between each parachute position and have children shake their hands.

❖ Parachute play can accommodate fairly large groups, but can also be done with small groups of four or five.

❖ Once children have mastered the various positions for the parachute, add to the fun by having them move to music. Experiment with different rhythms and tempos. Some groups enjoy singing as part of their parachute play.

Parachute Positions and Activities

Folding and Unfolding

Always have the children unfold and refold the parachute in an orderly fashion. This will make the parachute easier to handle and will lengthen its life. Unfold it by laying it on the ground and having one or two children unfold it. Refold by laying it out flat like a pancake, then folding that in half. Next, fold it over to form quarters. Fold two more times to make a pie slice shape, and then bring the point (where the mesh hole is) over to the edge of the chute. Three equal folds and you'll be ready to put it back in the sack.

Pancake

To make a pancake, lay the parachute flat on the ground with the children holding the edges or handles.

Soup Bowl

Children stand holding the handles of the parachute to produce a bowl shape.

Shake, Rattle, and Roll

From a soup bowl, have the children begin shaking the parachute. Put some soft balls■ in the center and you have a popcorn machine.

Ballooning

From the pancake position, count to three and have all the children lift the parachute as high as they can. The parachute should balloon as the children hold it.

Cats, Dogs, and Ducks

Have children "number off" as a cat, dog, or duck. Have the group form a balloon with the parachute, then call out "Duck!" and all the ducks run to stand in a new spot around the circle. Repeat with cats and dogs until everyone has had a chance to change their spot several times.

Bubble

Have the children balloon the parachute, then have them squat down, pinning the edges of the parachute to the ground in front of them. This forms a bubble, which, once the air leaks out, will become a pancake. To speed this process, you can have children lie on the parachute to squeeze the air out.

Tent

This is probably children's favorite parachute position. Have the children balloon the parachute, then have them move quickly inside the parachute and sit down along its edge.

Merry-Go-Round

Have children make a soup bowl, then hold on with their left hands only. Have them turn so they all face the same direction. Have them walk slowly to the left, pulling the parachute tight as they do. Eventually they can walk more and more quickly, and even run while doing the merry-go-round. If they are running they will need to be careful. It helps if you have a stop signal, such as raising your arm above your head. After the children have mastered the merry-go-round in one direction, they can learn to go in the other direction.

Wave

Divide the group in half. (An easy way to do this is to think of the circle as a clock. Decide where twelve o'clock is, then divide the group at the line between nine o'clock and three o'clock. Everyone above that line is one group, everyone below is another.) Assign a name to each group such as the Kangaroos and the Rabbits. Have the children kneel down and hold the parachute in the pancake position. Call "Kangaroo," and those children should jump up while holding on to the parachute. Then call "Rabbit," and when these children jump up there will be a ripple motion in the parachute.

Colored Bubbles

Divide the children into fourths (using the clock approach, divide along the nine o'clock and three o'clock line, then along the twelve o'clock to six o'clock line.) Assign the name of a color to each group. Have the children begin in the pancake position and have them all balloon the parachute, lifting it as high as they can. Call out the names of the groups, one by one, and have those children squat down, holding the edge of the parachute to the ground in front of them.

Birdy

Start standing with everyone holding the parachute with their right hands. Demonstrate two motions to the children: "bird up," which means lifting your right arm up while holding the parachute, and "bird down," which means lowering your right arm while holding the parachute. Have the children move in a circle and call out "bird up" and "bird down" as you move.

Involving Parents/ Guardians

Enlisting the support of parents or guardians is a critical element in the Peaceable Program. Children often have very different experiences at home and in the early childhood classroom. The parent-caregiver connection is vital in helping the child feel secure in making this transition. Children will also learn to manage conflict more easily if the adults in their lives share similar expectations about the ways we solve problems.

Involving parents can be challenging. Many parents have time only to drop children off in the morning and pick them up at the end of the day. In some cases, caregivers and parents may not share the same first language, making communication difficult. Parents and caregivers may also have different values or different approaches to handling conflicts. To communicate effectively with the parents in your program, you need to understand the issues and concerns they are dealing with.

In this section you will find:

❖ A questionnaire about the parents in your program

❖ Ways to communicate with parents

❖ Activities and ideas for involving parents

❖ Suggestions and strategies for parent visits and parent conferences

❖ Sample letters to send home describing ways families can reinforce lessons of the Peaceable Program

Who are the Parents of the Children in Your Program?

This questionnaire is intended to help you think about the specific issues and challenges confronting parents of the children in your program. This information may be useful in helping you decide how best to communicate with them. You can also use it to determine which ideas and activities are most likely to be successful for involving parents. Feel free to adapt the questionnaire to include questions that are relevant to your program.

❖ How many parents have partners?

❖ How many parents are employed?

❖ How many parents are able to visit the program during the day?

❖ How many are able to attend meetings or conferences after hours?

❖ What are the cultural backgrounds of the children in the group?

❖ What languages do the children's families speak at home?

❖ What seem to be the primary concerns of the parents in your group?

After gathering information to answer these questions, ask yourself the following questions:

❖ What are my expectations of the parents in my program?

❖ What can I do to help them meet these expectations?

❖ What do I need to learn about their language or cultural traditions?

❖ What issues may affect their participation in the program?

❖ How can I encourage them to participate?

Communicating with Parents

Parents can be your strongest allies in supporting the goals of your program. By reinforcing at home the lessons you are teaching in the Peaceable Program, they can help their children develop important social and emotional skills.

Written Communication

Parent support begins with parent communication. If parents don't hear from you about what's going on in the program, the only sources of information they have are their children. Though the simplest solution is to write a regular letter to parents describing program activities and goals, parents do not always read them. Some ways to cut back on this problem are the following:

- ❖ When parents enroll in your program, let them know that you will send regular bulletins home and that you depend on parents to remain informed.

- ❖ If the majority of parents in your group use a first language that is not English, find someone to help translate written communications.

Written bulletins should include children's drawings or dictated writing so that you can share this work with parents. If children in your group are working on a particular goal, such as listening or problem solving, include a brief sentence about what each child has contributed. Children may be able to draw or dictate this part themselves depending on their abilities. You can also send home Parent Connections when appropriate. (See page 16-7 for a sample letter to accompany the Parent Connections.) The Parent Connections accompany the following chapters:

- ❖ Parent Connections #1 and #2: Cooperation (chapter 4)

- ❖ Parent Connections #3 and #4: Communication (chapter 3)

- ❖ Parent Connection #5: Emotional Expression (chapter 5)

- ❖ Parent Connection #6: Understanding Anger (chapter 6)

- ❖ Parent Connections #7 and #8: Appreciating Diversity (chapter 7)

- ❖ Parent Connections #9 and #10: Conflict Resolution (chapter 8)

- ❖ Parent Connections #11 and #12 focus on media literacy and dealing with television violence and can be sent home any time these issues are addressed in your program.

You will also find sample letters to parents at the end of this chapter to inform parents and guardians about the routines and activities you are using in the Peaceable Program (see pp. 16-7 through 16-12). Each letter describes things parents can do at home to reinforce the skills and concepts their children are learning in your program.

Meetings and Conferences

Conferences are one of the traditional ways parents and caregivers communicate about a child. Sometimes parent conferences can be challenging. Many parents find it difficult to visit the program during the day or to meet with you after hours. They may not be comfortable with what you are teaching or may even contradict you. It can be easy to blame parents when you see children in your program acting out repeatedly. In these situations, it's important to consider the pressures parents may be under and to explore the factors underlying their behavior.

When you're discussing a problem with parents, try to find some common ground. For instance, suppose you are working with a child who hits. Some parents may say, "We taught him to do that." It may seem like you are at cross-purposes with one another. But if you listen carefully, you may find that they are concerned about teaching the child to stand up for himself. This is your common ground—you want the child to stand up for himself, too! You just don't want him to do it by hurting others. Now that you've found common ground, you can enlist the parents' help by asking, "How can we teach Matthew to stand up for himself without hitting?"

Another example might be a Haitian girl who comes to your program in fancy dresses that make it uncomfortable for her to play with sand or paint. Her parents are upset when she comes home in stained or dirty clothing. When they come to a conference to talk about it, you discover that in the Haitian culture, dressing for school is a sign of respect. The child's parents go to a great deal of effort to make sure that her hair is neatly braided every morning and that she has a clean, pretty dress to wear.

You might explain to the parents that children in the program need to use materials like sand and paints because that's the way they learn here. It's important to show that you appreciate their efforts in getting their daughter ready for school, and that you recognize that returning her in dirty clothes distresses them. Perhaps you can come up with a compromise, such as keeping an extra set of casual clothing at school that she can change into when she arrives, keeping her nice clothes clean so that she can change back into them at the end of the day.

Activities and Ideas for Working with Parents

When planning events or activities that involve parents, try to be realistic about their needs. For instance, if a large number of the parents in your program are single parents, you may need to find someone to provide child care during parent conferences. If many speak languages other than English, you may need to get help to translate the notices you send home. And if parents come from a cultural background in which the conflict resolution techniques you're teaching are unfamiliar, you may need to schedule special time with parents to help them understand and support your techniques.

Pick-Up Time

Though drop-off and pick-up times are usually hectic, they can provide an opportunity for daily contact. Once or twice a week, give a few children a chance to share some of their projects with their parents, tour the room together, or spend a few minutes discussing something the child is proud of. Let children know ahead of time that their turn is coming up so they can prepare what they want to share.

Parent Visitors

Encourage parents to visit the program if they are able to come in during the day. Invite them to share a particular activity such as cooking, teaching children a few words from another language, or storytelling. Parents can also be enlisted to help lead an activity or game.

Parent Classes

It is often hard to get parents to attend events where you can share information about what their children are learning. Some programs have attracted parent involvement by offering classes on topics that directly affect parents' own lives, such as filling out tax forms, learning English, or job hunting. While these subjects may not seem related to your program, supporting parents in practical ways enables them to help their children.

Parenting workshops on specific topics such as sibling fights, courtesy, and positive discipline, may also encourage parents to get involved.

At-Home Charts

Children love to take surveys or keep charts. If the group is working on a particular topic such as sharing, taking turns, or saying please and thank you, ask children to keep track of how they do some of these same things at home. Parents can help by writing, adding stickers, or attaching drawings.

Other Activities for Parents

The Changing Channels Kit includes a booklet of activities parents can do with their children around such themes as conflict resolution, cooperation, feelings, and more. (For more information or to order, call ESR at 1-800-370-2515.) Songs on the audio tape included with the kit express these themes as well. After children in your program listen to the tape, they can teach the songs to their parents.

Sample Introductory Letter

Dear Families,

The Adventures in Peacemaking program at (*name of early childhood center*) is helping us to learn new ways of working together. The children in (*name of group*) have been working on the theme of (*theme*) .

You can help your child (*child's name*) learn about Adventures in Peacemaking at home. Parent Connection # _____ has several ideas for working on the theme of (*communication, cooperation, emotional expression, appreciation of diversity, conflict resolution skills*).

Send us a note or drop by and tell us how the activity worked at home.

Don't forget to check out the assortment of children's books and adult resources in the Adventures in Peacemaking Lending Library.

Sincerely,

(*Your Name*)

Sample Parent Letter
on Conflict Resolution*

Dear Families,

Our early childhood program is participating in a new program called Adventures in Peacemaking. The goal is to create a Peaceable Program in which children learn to work together and resolve conflicts without fighting. Children will learn and practice five basic skills:

- ❖ Communication
- ❖ Cooperation
- ❖ Expression of feelings
- ❖ Appreciating diversity
- ❖ Conflict resolution

As part of the program we are teaching children some new strategies for calming down when they are angry and for working out conflicts together. Included with this letter are two charts. One outlines the steps your child is learning for calming down when he or she is upset or angry. The other outlines the steps we are using in the program to help children "talk problems out together." You can use these step-by-step processes to help your child practice these strategies at home.

You may also want to create a Peace Place in your home—a cozy, quiet corner where children can go when they are upset or angry. You can post the two charts there to help remind children to practice the skills they are learning in school.

Thank you for your support. Please let us know how we can continue working together to help all children in our program feel safe and secure.

Sincerely,

* You may want to send copies of "Calming Down" (see p. 6-13) and the "Talk It Out Together Chart" (see p. 8-18) along with this letter.

Sample Parent Letter on Music

Dear Families,

Our early childhood program has received some wonderful resources to help us teach Adventures in Peacemaking. One of these resources is a Lending Library of audio cassette tapes and CDs with songs and stories that focus on themes related to our Peaceable Program. Several of them include parent guides and/or activity books for children.

Below is a list of the tapes and CDs available through our Lending Library. Please stop by at drop-off or pick-up time and check out a tape or two to bring home. Your child may already be familiar with some of the songs and stories and will enjoy sharing them with you.

Sincerely,

Adventures in Peacemaking Lending Library (Tapes and CDs)

"Changing Channels." This tape by Grammy award-winning songwriters Marcy Marxer and Cathy Fink comes with a parent guide and activity book to help children and parents counter some of the negative effects of television and develop media literacy skills. It's packed with fun-to-sing, educational songs and stories like "50 Things I Can Do Instead of Watch TV," "Turn It Off, Change the Channel, Leave the Room," "Buy Me This and Buy Me That," and "Ballet-Dancing Truck Driver." It also includes a resource list.

"Linking Up!" This CD and activity book by another award-winning songwriter, Sarah Pirtle, features 46 songs that promote caring and cooperation. Twenty of the songs are bilingual in English and Spanish.

"Tales Around the Hearth." This cassette tape by storyteller Heather Forest presents stories from many times and countries, from Aesop's fables to African folktales and Norwegian fairy tales. A perfect companion for your bedtime ritual.

"You'll Sing A Song." Ella Jenkins' classic cassette tape features simple songs from many cultures, including "Shabbat Shalom," "Miss Mary Mack," "Dulce, Dulce," and "This Train." Great for long car rides!

"Teaching Peace." The songs on this tape by Red Grammer are easy to learn and sing together—and they'll make you feel good! Songs include "Say Hi, I Think You're Wonderful" and "Teaching Peace."

Sample Letter on Routines and Rituals

Dear Families,

As part of our early childhood program, we use many routines and rituals to help children feel that they are part of a caring community. Routines help children know what to expect each day when they are away from home. This helps them feel secure and comfortable. Rituals celebrate our joys and accomplishments both as individuals and as part of a group. This helps children gain confidence in their own abilities and take pride in being part of the group.

Here are a few routines and rituals that your child may enjoy using at home!

- ❖ Invent a special handshake for each person in the family. When your child comes home, use your special handshake as you greet him or her by name.

- ❖ Set aside a time, perhaps during meals, when each person in the family takes a turn telling something about their day.

- ❖ Make up songs that include your child's name or celebrate your child's accomplishments. Many of the songs on "Linking Up!" and other audio cassettes available through our Lending Library can be adapted to include your child's name.

- ❖ When you catch your child being good—feeding the family pet, helping with chores, sharing a toy—let him or her know you noticed. Try to be as specific as possible in describing what the child did or said ("I liked the way you hung up your coat when you came in") and in saying what was good about it ("That was very responsible!").

- ❖ Children often have trouble with transitions. To help children manage their daily routines, such as putting away their toys, brushing teeth, and getting ready for bed, you may want to let them know that a transition is coming a few minutes ahead of time. Then, when the time comes, you can engage them with small talk as you help them move into the next activity.

If you have routines and rituals that work well for you at home, please share them with us so that we can incorporate them into our program.

Sincerely,

Sample Parent Letter on Children's Books

Dear Families,

Our early childhood program has created a Lending Library of children's books to help us in Adventures in Peacemaking. The books help to reinforce the themes of the Peaceable Program:

- ❖ Communication
- ❖ Cooperation
- ❖ Emotional expression
- ❖ Appreciating diversity
- ❖ Conflict resolution

Children in our program love these books. You are welcome to check any of the following books out of our Lending Library to read with your child at home:

All the Colors of the Earth, by Sheila Hamanaka. This story helps children understand that differences in skin color are a natural part of being human.

Anansi the Spider, by Gerald McDermott. In this Ashanti folk tale, Anansi the Spider sets out on a journey. Threatened by Fish and Falcon, he is rescued by his sons. But which one of them should he reward?

Chrysanthemum, by Kevin Henkes. A little girl loves her name—until she goes to school and other children make fun of it. Mrs. Twinkle, the music teacher, helps the children see that Chrysanthemum is a terrific name!

I Like Me, by Nancy Carlson. This story helps children realize that each of them is unique and special.

It's Mine, Leo Lionni. Three frogs bicker all day long. But when a storm arrives, they realize that they need to share to survive.

Mama, Do You Love Me?, by Barbara M. Joosse. A child plays with different emotions to test Mama's love.

(continued on next page)

Mean Soup, by Betsy Everitt. A sympathetic mother teachers her son a humorous way to cope with having a bad day.

Now One Foot, Now the Other, by Tomie dePaola. A story that illustrates the unconditional love between a grandfather and his grandson.

The Rainbow Fish, by Marcus Pfister. This story about jealousy helps children understand how sharing can lead to friendship.

Smoky Night, by Eve Bunting. Set during the Los Angeles riots of 1992, this story tells how a lost pet brings people together.

Someone Special, Just Like You, by Tricia Brown. Engaging photos show children with physical disabilities enjoying the everyday pleasures of childhood

You can also borrow the small tote bag, journal, and stuffed frog included in the Adventures in Peacemaking kit. Bring the frog home in the tote bag to "read" along with you and your child. Your child can write or draw in the journal about the frog's visit to your home. Then send the frog, bag, and journal back so your child can share the frog's adventures with the class!

Thanks for your participation.

Sincerely,

Activity Index

By Chapter

Activity Index

Alphabetically

The Early Childhood Adventures in Peacemaking
Kit of Manipulatives

All the materials needed to make this activity guide come to life!

Full Kit Includes:

Toys & Crafts:
- ❑ 1 Polaroid One Step Camera
- ❑ 2 packs of Polaroid 600 instant film
- ❑ 1 parachute (12' with handles)
- ❑ 1 Peace Puppet kit
- ❑ 10 pairs of rhythm sticks
- ❑ 3 pairs of maracas
- ❑ 3 tambourines
- ❑ 2 wolf puppets
- ❑ 6 sponge balls
- ❑ 1 stuffed frog
- ❑ 1 mini tote bag
- ❑ 3 composition books
- ❑ 1 talking stick ("space tube")
- ❑ 12 bean bags
- ❑ 4 sheets of compression sponge paper
- ❑ 4 sets of Crayola multicultural crayons
- ❑ 1 roll of grip liner

Children's Books:
- ❑ *Chyrsanthemum*
- ❑ *It's Mine!*
- ❑ *Anansi the Spider*
- ❑ *All the Colors of the Earth*
- ❑ *Someone Special Just Like You*
- ❑ *Mrs. Katz and Tush*
- ❑ *Smoky Night*
- ❑ *Now One Foot, Now the Other*
- ❑ *I Like Me!*
- ❑ *Momma, Do You Love Me?*
- ❑ *Mean Soup*
- ❑ *The Rainbow Fish*
- ❑ *"The Big, Big Carrot" Cut & Tell Cutout*
- ❑ 1 box of book plates

Music and Story Tapes:
- ❑ "Linking Up"
- ❑ "You'll Sing a Song, I'll Sing a Song"
- ❑ "Tales Around the Hearth"
- ❑ "Teaching Peace"

Books for Parents and Caregivers:
- ❑ *Teaching Young Children in Violent Times*
- ❑ *Who's Calling the Shots? How to Respond Effectively to Children's Fascination with War Play and War Toys*
- ❑ *Battles, Hassles, Tantrums & Tears*
- ❑ *Changing Channels: Preschoolers, TV, and Media Violence, A Guide for Parents (and Other Grownups)*
- ❑ Safety for Children Kit

For more information call 1-800-370-2515 today!

Items are subject to substitution based on availability.

Mini Kit includes:

Toys and crafts:
- ❑ 1 parachute (6' with handles)
- ❑ 1 Peace Puppet kit
- ❑ 1 stuffed frog
- ❑ 1 talking stick ("space tube")
- ❑ Grip Liner for "Lily Pads"
- ❑ "Linking Up" CD

Children's Books:
- ❑ *Smoky Night*
- ❑ *Mean Soup*
- ❑ *Colors of the Earth*
- ❑ *Chrysanthemum*
- ❑ *It's Mine!*
- ❑ *I Like Me!*
- ❑ *Anansi the Spider*

Items are subject to substitution based on availability.

Other Early Childhood Resources From ESR

Linking Up: Building a Peaceable Classroom Using Music and Movement
Sarah Pirtle

Linking Up! is an exciting new teacher's guide and audio recording that helps educators foster positive social skills in three- to nine-year old children through music and movement activities. The audio recording features 46 simple songs that promote caring, cooperation, and communication. Twenty of the songs are bilingual, with lyrics in both English and Spanish.

The teacher's guide contains more than 100 activities to use with the songs. The guide includes sheet music, song lyrics, and a core activity for each song, as well as numerous extensions, tips, and inspirational stories to help you build a Peaceable early childhood classroom.

Sarah Pirtle's songwriting has won numerous awards, including, most recently, the Oppenheim Gold Seal Best Audio Award and the Parents' Choice Classic Award. This recording and guide are the culmination of over 20 years' experience working with young children to build caring classroom communities.

Cassette
Preschool–Grade 3
ESR 1997

Teacher's Guide with CD
Preschool–Grade 3

Teaching Young Children in Violent Times: Building a Peaceable Classroom
Diane E. Levin, Ph.D.

Teaching Young Children in Violent Times helps preschool through grade 3 teachers create a classroom where children learn peaceful alternatives to the violent behaviors modeled for them in society.

Part I of this essential guide explores the developmental roots of young children's thinking and behaviors on issues ranging from conflict to prejudice to violence and provides a cultural context for the violence in children's lives. Highly-effective dialogs between young children and teachers are offered with a framework for teachers to extend children's thinking in developmentally appropriate ways.

Part II includes practical guidelines and activities for creating a Peaceable Classroom. Learn how to use puppetry, games, play, class charts, curriculum webs, and graphs to help young children resolve their conflicts peacefully and respect one another's differences. This highly-acclaimed book is a must for early childhood educators, parents, and policy makers.

Preschool-Grade 3
193 pages, ESR 1994

Changing Channels: Preschoolers, TV, and Media Violence

Are you worried about the messages that children receive from TV? This exciting kit includes everything parents and other adults need to help counter the negative effects of television and other mass media on young children. The kit includes:

♦ An audiotape from Grammy-award winning songwriters Cathy Fink and Marcy Marxer (and friends), packed with fun-to-sing and educational songs and stories, including "Ballet Dancing Truck Driver," and "50 Things That I Can Do Instead of Watch TV."

- Easy, fun activities that accompany the cassette for adults and children to do together to help children become "media smart."
- A guide for parents (and other adults) to help them deal with the "buy me thats," violent play, and other possible results of TV watching, including guidelines for how to effectively limit television and talk with children about what they have seen.
- Recommended videos, books, computer software, and easy-to-do activities and tips for providing alternatives to TV.

Preschool-6
ESR/Work Family Directions 1996

Elementary Perspectives: Teaching Concepts of Peace and Conflict
William J. Kreidler

This outstanding curriculum offers more than 80 activities that help teachers and students define peace, explore justice, and learn the value of conflict and its resolution.

Students read, write, draw, role-play, sing, and discuss their way through a process that helps them acquire the concrete cooperative and conflict resolution skills needed to become caring and socially responsible citizens.

Grades K-6
269 pages, ESR 1990

School-age Adventures in Peacemaking: A Conflict Resolution and Violence Prevention Curriculum
William J. Kreidler and Lisa Furlong
with Libby Cowles and IlaSahai Prouty

How do you create a program that fosters mutual respect and the creative resolution of conflict? *Adventures in Peacemaking* includes hundreds of activities, ideas and tips for creating a Peaceable Program—designed to meet the unique needs of afterschool programs, camps, and recreation centers.

Adventures in Peacemaking blends ESR's innovative conflict resolution curricula with Project Adventure's activity-based programming. The complete program includes an activity guide, kit of manipulatives, lending library, and training.

The **activity guide** can be used alone, or along with the kit of manipulatives. The guide includes hundreds of hands-on, engaging activities that teach basic conflict resolution skills through drama, cooperative challenges, cooking, and art.

The **provider kit** includes a broad range of manipulatives to use in conjunction with the activity guide. Hard-to-find items such as foam "lily pads," spot markers, buddy ropes, Feelings Cards, and much more are at your finger tips. Rather than wasting valuable program time looking for materials, you can bring *Adventures in Peacemaking* "out of the bag" and directly into your children's hands. Two versions of the kit are offered: a full kit and a mini-kit. The full kit includes key materials needed for the activities and optionally also includes three, six-week "clubs" (thematic, sequenced activities). The mini-kit contains the most-difficult-to-find and most-often-used items.

The **lending library** includes valuable resources such as specially selected books, games, videos, and cassettes for helping families create "Peaceable Homes."

Activity Guide
Grades K-6, 330 pages

Teaching Conflict Resolution Through Children's Literature
William J. Kreidler

Children's books are an ideal vehicle to teach conflict resolution and other social skills. This comprehensive guide shows you how. Easily-implemented activities introduce conflict resolution skills including identifying problems, expressing feelings, understanding other points of view, and appreciating diversity. Over 25 children's titles are suggested with discussion questions and activities to help children explore the theme of conflict resolution.

Grades K-2, 112 pages
Scholastic Professional Books 1995

Creative Conflict Resolution: More Than 200 Activities for Keeping Peace in the Classroom, K-6
William J. Kreidler

Creative Conflict Resolution is a definitive manual that provides elementary school teachers with thoughtful, effective ideas for responding to everyday classroom conflicts. Teachers learn to turn conflict into productive opportunity, helping students to deal nonviolently and constructively with anger, fear, aggression, and prejudice.

Creative Conflict Resolution offers over 200 classroom-tested activities and games and over 20 different techniques with examples. This book is widely used and highly recommended.

Grades K-6
216 pages
Scott, Foresman and Company 1984

Roots and Wings: Affirming Culture in Early Childhood Programs
Stacy York

Help young children soar beyond prejudice and discrimination—give them *Roots and Wings*. This highly recommended resource for early childhood educators includes over 60 activities to support young children with an awareness of their cultural roots and the skills to respect differences. Learn how to respond to children's questions about race, culture, and discriminatory behaviors, and take advantage of teachable moments. Ideas are included for integrating cultural awareness and prejudice reduction into all aspects of your program.

Preschool-Grade 3
205 pages, Redleaf Press 1991

On-site Training

Implementing Early Childhood Adventures in Peacemaking

A team of professionals with a wide range of early childhood experience are available for introductory and advanced training for implementing *Early Childhood Adventures in Peacemaking* and developing Peaceable Early Childhood Classrooms.

For more information call 1-800-370-2515.